Every Day With Jesus

Every Day With Jesus

George Duncan

World Wide
PUBLICATIONS
A ministry of the Billy Graham Association

1303 Hennepin Avenue
Minneapolis, Minnesota 55403

ISBN 0-89066-059-X

Every Day With Jesus by George Duncan,
© 1975 George B. Duncan.

First published   1975
Reprinted   1976, 1979, 1982, 1984

Special Edition, World Wide Publications, 1303 Hennepin Avenue,
Minneapolis, Minnesota 55403.

Printed in the United States of America.

FOREWORD

I first became acquainted with George Duncan during our London Crusade at Harringay Arena in 1954. At that time, he was serving as vicar of Christ Church on the northern fringe of London and his congregation was heavily involved in the crusade work. My memories of that thrilling time in London are rich with the warmth of the British people and their enthusiastic response to the Gospel.

In the years since that first encounter with George Duncan, I have been enriched by the friendship and support of this gifted man of God. Along with a widely successful pastoral ministry in Scotland and England, the Rev. Duncan is well-known as an author, radio host and television personality. He is a gifted speaker who has traveled the world speaking at conventions, conferences and retreats.

Our Team has had the privilege of working closely with George Duncan on a number of occasions, as we have ministered together to people from around the world. I have always benefited from his insight into God's Word and been challenged by the practical applications he so clearly draws from his study. He is a man of prayer and a man of action.

Your life will be blessed and your walk with the Lord will be strengthened by the wisdom the Rev. Duncan shares in these daily readings.

Billy Graham

To those whose love
in the Fellowship of the Gospel
has sustained me in my ministry
throughout the years and around the world

Living is Building *Lk 6: 46-49*

Therefore whosoever heareth these sayings of Mine,
and doeth them, I will liken him unto a wise man, which
built his house upon a rock

Matthew 7:24

At the end of Christ's great Sermon on the Mount He puts the alternative between building on the rock and building on the sand. Build we must—our characters, our destinies!

Life as Jesus saw it is *creative*. Behind that view of life lie two thoughts. In the first place there is the nature we share, the nature of God Himself. The Bible tells us that God created man in His own image, and although much of that image has been damaged by man's sin, yet traces remain. Our God is a creator God and we share that creative instinct with Him. Man must create. There is also the future we shape for we are building not just for today but for tomorrow and indeed for eternity.

Life as Jesus saw it is *selective*. As we read through the story of the two builders we see the choices we must make. The choice supremely is whether as a foundation we build on Christ's words or on our thoughts. The epistles tell us that our choices also determine the materials we use in our building. The foundation may be secure or insecure, the materials may be good or bad. We see also the forces we must meet. Christ speaks of the rain, of the wind, of the flood—the rain of sorrow, the wind of temptation, the flood of death. We must all meet these forces. There is no escape!

Life as Jesus saw it is *decisive*. There is here an equality in the opportunity we have. Both builders had the chance of hearing Christ's words, but they chose differently, and that difference and that choice proved decisive. How true that is of so many going to the same church, hearing the same preacher, possessing the same Bible, and yet choosing so differently. There is also a finality in the outcome we see here. The one house fell and "great was the fall of it" while the other house stood. The Bible stresses that of all the choices we make in life, the choice we make about our attitude to Jesus Christ is the most decisive, affecting both this life and the one to come. It would be well if each of us took time to think over our own attitude. We are hearers of His word, but are we doers of it in the obedience to which faith leads?

For it is not the hearers of the law who are righteous before God but the doers of the law who will be justified. Rom 2:13

Be doers of the word, and not hearers only, deceiving yourselves James 1:22

1

The Growth of Love

This I pray, that your love may abound yet more and more in knowledge . . .

Monday

Philippians 1:9

A new love for God comes into our lives with the new life of God. But that love can and must grow. And although love may be there, it may not be strong. This prayer of Paul suggests that the purpose of God and the need of so many of our lives is that our love should grow—"that your love may abound yet more and more."

But if it is to grow it must be "in knowledge." You cannot love a person you do not know but this is just the mistake that so many Christians are making. They are trying hard to love a God they do not really know. And they do not know God because they spend such a very little amount of their time with Him. They so seldom spare time to be with Him with their Bibles open, their knees bent, yes, and their wills bent too.

Paul put right in the very forefront of His spiritual ambition and program "that I may know Him . . ." This should be our ambition too! As we get to know Him through His word and in His service, just because He is so absolutely worthy, we shall come to love Him "more and more." Stop for a moment to ask yourself, "How far do I really love my Lord?" and, "If I know that I do not love Him as I should, have I any idea as to the reason?" *I need to spend more time in His word.*

Gratitude

I thank my God upon every remembrance of you

Tuesday

Philippians 1:3

I paused when I read the words "I thank" and I asked myself, "Is gratitude one of the graces we are losing today?" We are living in days when there is a very real tendency to take everything for granted. The welfare state is contributing to this attitude but it is spreading into the Church. We evangelical Christians are beginning to take the grace of God for granted.

"I thank," wrote Paul. When did we last give thanks to God? I wonder how many churches have ever had a praise meeting? I know some have prayer meetings, and I know a number that don't. I am always sorry for a church that doesn't have a prayer meeting, for a church that doesn't pray won't have much blessing. But how many churches ever stop to give *thanks* to God? Isn't gratitude a lovely thing? Don't we feel hurt if we give a gift to somebody and he never stops to say thank you? I wonder how many times God is hurt by our lack of gratitude? I wonder whether we are grateful enough, not only to God, but also sometimes to members of the church?

"I thank." That is the first thing that Paul mentioned—his gratitude. Our Lord healed ten lepers and only one came back. Our Lord said," Were there not ten cleansed? But where are the nine?" Is there but one that has returned to give thanks? Only one grateful? We need to cultivate the spirit of gratitude in our relationships, remembering to say thank you. We must not forget to express our appreciation for kindnesses done for us. People ought to be able to say about Christians, "These people must have something because they are so nice." Well, let us be nice and let us be grateful, even if everything isn't always just exactly as it ought to be or as we would like. What a difference it makes to a person when he is thanked and feels he is appreciated. *Let me never forget to say Thank you and especially to thank God for His love + His blessing*

Having Convictions

4

I know whom I have believed, and am persuaded that He is able to keep that which I have committed unto Him against that day

Wednesday

2 Timothy 1:12

I would like to think that if I had been in business I would have had very real convictions about two things. First, about the worth of the goods I was trying to market and second, about the need for them. I would not like to be selling things of no real worth or goods for which there was no real demand. To be a good businessman it is essential to have deep convictions about the worth of one's goods or services and the need for them.

That is exactly where we must begin in the Christian realm. You remember how the early Church was so fully convinced of the worth of the goods they offered. Tragically that conviction is lacking today. We lack conviction that the goods we offer are valuable. It is of utmost urgency that we enter into a fuller experience of Christ, not only that we might have life more abundant, but that we are so convicted about its worth that we can then offer it to others. Apart from the forgiveness of our sins, what are we working out in practical daily living that is worth handing on to another person? In the early Church it was personal experience of Jesus that

3

was so completely satisfying and so tremendously worth having that they preached and emphasized Him.

Sharing Everything

I will love him, and will manifest myself

Thursday

John 14:21

How wonderful is the love relationship between husband and wife when they are joined in the Lord! At the center lies the wonder of a great sharing, an unveiling of the deep things of the heart, mind and spirit. Within this relationship we can share fears that we hate to admit exist, failures that we are ashamed even to think about. We can talk of triumphs that we would not share with anybody else because they would think we were boasting. Together we can enjoy the dreams, the hopes, the plans that only love makes possible.

Jesus said, "He that loveth Me, . . . I will love him, and will manifest Myself to him." There is a closer, deeper intimacy of heart with heart and mind with mind into which Jesus is waiting to welcome you when you become truly, fully and wholly His.

May I truly become that person. I will if I am faithful to His commandments and obedient to His word.

The Scale of our Victory

We are more than conquerors *God gives us victory through Jesus.*

Friday

Romans 8:37

Again I am challenged to the depths of my being, for I find that our victory is one in which there need be no delay. Paul does not say "we *shall be*" but "we *are* more than conquerors." Those who remember the early years of the second world war will recall those dreary months and years of waiting before the armed might of a seemingly victorious enemy was challenged. Victory seemed a long way off. It was promised in that calm, strong voice of Sir Winston Churchill that came over the radio in those dark days, but that was all. Britain was left alone, beaten to the wall, defenseless, without weapons and blasted with bombs. Would victory ever come?

How many of us, in our Christian experience, see victory like that? It seems only a remote prospect which is almost impossible ever to achieve. We say to ourselves, "Maybe one day we shall" but that is not what Paul says. He says, not we *shall* be but we *are* conquerors. There need be no doubt that we are super conquerors.

4

Does that mean that the Christian is never defeated? No. But it does mean that he never need be! Does it mean that the Christian is without sin? No! But it does mean that he can be without blame and without conscious and deliberate sin.

In these days when so many of us are aware of money matters, we may transfer the metaphor from the realm of fighting to that of finance. If Paul had been talking in terms of money he would have said, "We are multimillionaires" and what millionaire need ever be in debt? A Christian never lacks what he needs when he possesses in Christ the unsearchable riches of God's grace.

Thanks be to God who always leads us in triumph in Christ 2 Cor. 2:14
whosoever is born of God overcomes the world,
and this is our victory - our faith 1 John 5:4

The Coronation of Solomon

7

And they blew the trumpet; and all the people said, God save King Solomon

Saturday   1 Kings 1:39

What a tremendously dramatic ceremony the crowning of a sovereign is! Some of us may remember the coronation service at which young Queen Elizabeth was crowned. In one of my parishes there was a lady who was a close friend of the royal family, and at the coronation service she sat fairly near the Queen Mother. She told me that when the moment came during the coronation service for that stripling of a girl to be crowned Queen she turned to look at the Queen Mother and saw tears streaming down her cheeks. No one could have watched that moment unmoved. Many saw it on television, and watched as the crown was placed upon the one who had the right to wear it—the only one!

There is of course only one person who has the right to the crown in our lives, and that is Jesus Christ. Have we crowned Him? Or is it still just a matter of using Him and turning to Him when it is convenient? How necessary that there should come the moment when we bring the whole of ourselves, every aspect of our lives, all we are, all we have, all we hope to be, and in our hearts place the crown upon His head, recognizing His claim. Then His reign begins. "A greater than Solomon is here."

Christ is the only true King
To the King eternal, immortal, invisible, who alone
is wise, be honor + glory forever 1 Tim 1:17

5

A Triple Benediction

Grace, mercy, and peace

1 Timothy 1:2

What a wonderful blessing or prayer Paul offered for Timothy. First, he sought that sufficient grace which Timothy would need as he faced the burdens, pressures and problems of the work he now had to do. There would come times when Timothy would sense his own inadequacy and Paul wanted him to know then, not the despair that looks within, but the confidence that looks to Christ, who had said to Paul when he was close to despair, "My grace is sufficient for thee." Paul had known all about those hours when the temptation to give up was almost irresistible. He speaks of it when writing to the Corinthians, "We had this experience of coming to the end of our tether that we might learn to trust, not in ourselves, but in God." Paul coming to the end of his tether? Yes, this had been the case. And if it happened in the experience of Paul it would more than likely happen in the experience of Timothy.

Next, Paul sought the mercy Timothy must have. When moments of failure came, the mercy of God, the forgiving mercy, would be what Timothy needed above everything else. We are not finished with the need of forgiveness when we become Christians. Indeed our heightened sensitivity to our failures might bring us to despair but for the mercy of God.

Then, Paul sought for Timothy the peace he could know. Grace for the pressures, mercy for the failures, and peace; peace because he not only knew Christ as Savior but God as Father; a peace that would keep his heart and mind from both the dangers of pride and the darkness of doubt.

What a revealing prayer this is! It is not a long one but it seems to leave nothing unsought or unasked. It would be a lovely prayer for us to pray for other Christians, when during the busy day their names come to mind. We haven't time to pray at length. We haven't time even to close our eyes. We are walking down the street, or standing behind the counter, or just busy at the sink. Wherever we are why not keep this little prayer of three words tucked away for use at such a moment—Grace, mercy, peace.

Leadership

Be ye followers of me

1 Corinthians 11:1

If we are going to live lives that are spiritually meaningful and useful, we must be prepared to make the first move. It seems that there are far too many Christians waiting for someone to ask them to do something while all the time God has called them to act. The word has already gone forth; "Ye shall be witnesses unto me," and "Go ye into all the world and make disciples." Often in Christian communities we sit within the four walls of our buildings and say, concerning the world outside, "Why don't they come?" God is looking at us and saying, "Why don't they go?"

In his book, *Spiritual Leadership*, Oswald Sanders recalls an incident in the high councils of the China Inland Mission when D. E. Hoste, successor to Hudson Taylor, was presiding. They were discussing tests of leadership and D. E. Hoste had said nothing. Someone asked him what he felt the test of leadership to be, and with a twinkle in his eye he said, "I think the test of leadership is to find out if you are leading anybody." That has a quirk of humor about it, but how searching a truth it is. Are we leading anybody? Paul was able to say, "Be ye followers of me." Is there anyone following us? Are we out in front? Are we taking the initiative?

The Gift of Love

Gal 5:22 the fruit of the Spirit is love

The love of God is shed abroad in our hearts by the Holy Ghost which is given unto us

Romans 5:5

"While faith makes all things possible, love makes all things easy" was said by an early speaker at the Keswick Convention. How true the words are! It would not be an overstatement to say that most of our spiritual troubles can be traced to a lack of love. One thing is certain about love, it cannot be "worked up" and this is a fact that the New Testament acknowledges.

The teaching of the New Testament is encouraging in that it speaks of love as a gift (Romans 5:5). The life of the Holy Spirit cannot be divorced from the love of the Spirit. When we receive the life, we receive the love too. Indeed this new love is one evidence of the new life, the new birth—"We know that we have passed from death unto life, because we love . . ." (1 John 3:14). This is the testimony of all who have been born again of the Spirit. A new love has entered with the new life, a love for the Word of God, the House of God, the will of God and the children of God. If there is no love, the chances are that there is no life!

1 Jn 4:12,13 If we love one another God abide in us — us of the Spirit because He has given

Three Dangers

Come and see

Wednesday

John 1:39

Many years ago I heard the Rev. Alexander Frazer, a well-known Scottish preacher, commenting as he read this chapter on the three dangers from which Christ wanted to save these seeking souls. First, there was the danger of generalities. The question Christ posed, "What seek ye?" dealt with that. How many of us are content with generalities in the sphere of religion? We believe in God but never think out the logical implications of that faith. We say we are Christians but have never taken time to think out the specific marks of a true Christian.

The second danger Christ wanted to save them from was the danger of delay. Their reply to His words was as if to say, "Tell us where you stay so we can come sometime and talk things over." Christ's reply was "Come—and come now." It might well be that God has put this book into your hands so you may face up to the danger of delay. You have always wanted to consider Christ and perhaps make up your mind about Him but have never done it yet. Christ's challenge is to you as you read these words: "Come, and come now."

The third danger Christ wanted to save them from was the danger of disillusionment. He not only said, "Come," but he said, "Come and see." These men had been part of a great popular spiritual movement that had drawn crowds. I think Christ wanted them to know that they were in for something far tougher than that. So He led them up some lonely glen where they could see the loneliness of the way that He trod and realize the costliness of the way they would have to tread if they followed Him.

We cannot expect life to be a bed of roses just because we follow Jesus. He say we will experience trials & temptation

8

2

A Commitment to the Will of God

I beseech you therefore, brethren, by the mercies of God, that ye present your bodies a living sacrifice, holy, acceptable unto God . . . and be not conformed to this world: but be ye transformed by the renewing of your mind, that ye may prove what is that good, and acceptable, and perfect, will of God

Thursday

Romans 12:1, 2

The will of God is not something we are just to understand; it is something we are to undertake. And when in the Lord's prayer we say, "Thy will be done," that is precisely what the will of God is all about. It is something to be done. It is not something to be imposed or to be endured but to be done. That is why Paul lays this obligation upon the Christians at Rome. They are to present their bodies a living sacrifice, holy, acceptable unto God, and not be conformed to this world, but transformed by the renewing of their minds that they may prove what is that good, and acceptable, and perfect will of God.

The transformation of our lives will indeed begin as an inward thing, but it will inevitably be worked out through our bodies, whose members are instruments through which the mind is expressed. How clearly such commitment is brought out in our Lord's own prayer in Gethsemane, "Not My will but Thine be done." Be done by whom? By Christ Himself. There must be a commitment to the will of God. It is a will that is to be done and to be done by us.

He who does the will of God abides forever 1 Jn 2:17
3

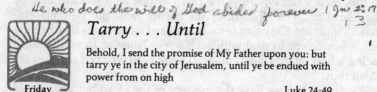

Tarry . . . Until

Behold, I send the promise of My Father upon you: but tarry ye in the city of Jerusalem, until ye be endued with power from on high

Friday

Luke 24:49

Our Lord told the disciples to wait until the Holy Spirit was given and made available, as He was on the Day of Pentecost to them and to all who thereafter should believe. We don't need to tarry in the sense that the disciples needed to wait, but the fact that our Lord told them to tarry underlines the fact that they could not themselves do the work to which He was commissioning them. This teaches us that we cannot by ourselves influence anybody for Jesus Christ.

When I was young I used to think I had to go around trying to convert people. I owe such a debt to Bishop Taylor Smith. He said,

"I don't go about trying to convert people," yet that was what I had been trying to do! I thought, as a Christian, this was my responsibility. The Bishop drove home to me the truth that of course no man can convert anybody. Only the Holy Spirit can do that, but He can and will do it through us if we allow Him to. We have to be available to the Holy Spirit, and He can take and use even the feeblest and most insignificant things we say or do to bring others to newness of life.

What a sermon could not do, perhaps a bouquet of flowers taken to a sickroom will do! The Holy Spirit has an amazing way of working. We can write letters and our letters could achieve what ten thousand sermons would never achieve! It could be just a handshake or a smile, given rather tentatively to somebody who is visiting your church, that could win that person for Christ, just as the hand of Barnabas brought in Saul when the rest of the Church didn't want to have anything to do with him.

The Bishop was right when he said, "I don't go about trying to convert people," but he added, "I go about just bringing God to them."

We can be a witness in so many ways just by our actions & deeds.

The Devil—The Destroyer

Your adversary the Devil, as a roaring lion, walketh about, seeking whom he may devour

1 Peter 5:8

Saturday

In this verse Peter describes the Devil as one who seeks to destroy the Christian. The strength of the enemy must not be underestimated, and that Christian is foolish indeed who thinks that he himself is competent to deal with such a foe. None of us would relish facing a lion unarmed and alone. Thank God we need not face the Devil thus!

We cannot say we have the mastery of the Devil but like the old negro who was taunted by his master after his conversion we *can* say, "We hab de master ob de debil!" In the power of the risen life of our indwelling Lord we have One dwelling within us before whom even the Devil must bow.

We must constantly be in touch with God through His word & by prayer or the devil will get his foot in the door.

The Way People talk about God's Work

And Judah . . . and our adversaries said . . . and I said
. . .

Sunday

Nehemiah 4:10, 11, 14

How constantly people have something to say about God's work, and how differently they comment about it! Nehemiah had undertaken a colossal task and like anybody else trying to do God's will for God's glory, found it tough going. If you read the previous chapters you will see just how difficult things had been. And now everybody was talking about what was happening.

"And Judah said . . ."—this was the voice of doubt. "The strength of the bearers of burdens is decayed, and there is much rubbish; so that we are not able to build." The voice that says, "We can't." Two reasons motivated them; the weariness of men and the massiveness of the task. "There is much rubbish." There will always be this voice, those who are so ready to say, "We cannot do it."

In verse 11 we read, "Our adversaries said . . ." and what they said was, "You won't!" Theirs was the voice of hate. Right from the beginning there were those who opposed what Nehemiah planned to do, and there are always those in whose hearts the natural hostility of man to God shows itself in this way. How vicious was the way in which they talked, "They shall not know, neither see, till we come in the midst among them, and slay them, and cause the work to cease." Let us face it, Jesus was hated by the world and He said we would be hated too. How various were the ways in which these men opposed Nehemiah's plans. In chapter 2 it was ridicule; in chapter 4 it was anger and the threat of violence; in chapter 6 they tried friendliness and then wrote letters.

In verse 20 we hear the voice of trust that says, "God shall." The inspiration of this faith lay in their remembrance of the past (v. 14), what God had promised and what God had performed. He could and would do it again! The vindication of this faith is seen in the fact that God "did." Faith does not mean idleness. These people went on to toil and sweat, but God was working with them. And the enabling, protecting, inspiring grace of God rested upon them as it will rest upon us if we, too, are seeking to do His work in His way and in obedience to His will.

11

Praying within Certain Bounds

Where many were gathered together praying

Acts 12:12

Monday

In corporate prayer there are certain limitations we must be prepared to accept. The number of people, the limited amount of time, and the fact that it is corporate and not private prayer all have a bearing on how we shall pray.

We must not pray too long or for too many things. One kind of prayer inevitably kills the spirit of prayer at a prayer meeting. That is the long prayer that methodically mentions every item suggested by the leader without praying really intelligently or intensely about any one of them. The reaction of the inexperienced is, "Well that's that, there is nothing left to pray for now." It is far better to pray three different times, briefly and intelligently about three separate needs, than to pray at length about all three at the same time.

Remember, this is corporate prayer and we must expect to pray somewhat differently than we pray in the privacy of our own room. One limitation we must seek to overcome, however, is that of our own fears, the fear of praying aloud before others. We are not praying to impress men but to intercede with God.

Remember, too, that God does not judge a prayer by its diction, but by its desire. The feeble, faltering prayer of a novice in the art may do much more than the wordiness of some mature Christian whose prayers, though long, come not from the heart but from the lips.

The Lord

Jesus Christ is Lord

Philippians 2:11

Tuesday

The weekly American paper, *Time*, doesn't usually have much space for religion but some time ago it devoted twelve pages to what it called, "The Jesus Revolution," which was spreading almost like a prairie fire through the United States, mainly outside the churches among young people. Color pictures illustrated aspects of the movement. The first picture, which was most striking, showed a girl wearing a red pullover. On the back of it were just four words—"Jesus is my Lord."

We usually like to say, "Jesus is my Savior," and I question if there are many reading this who cannot say that Jesus is their Savior. But can we honestly say, "Jesus is my Lord"? *If he is my Lord I must honor Him, praise Him and obey Him. His love for me is beyond comprehension.*

A Four-Second Prayer

For their sakes I sanctify myself . . .

Wednesday   John 17:19

During my early days in Christian work it was my privilege to arrange some meetings for Bishop Taylor Smith, at that time quite a legendary figure to me. We met to talk over the arrangements and the Bishop turned suddenly and asked me a question, "Have you sanctified yourself for me?" I was completely baffled and did not know what he meant. He then quoted our text for today. He told me that, as our Lord set Himself apart to be a blessing to His own, so we should follow Christ's example and set ourselves apart to be a blessing to others whom we might meet at any time.

The Bishop went on to say, "I will give you a short prayer that will help you do this." Based on the words of the Master, this was the prayer Bishop Taylor Smith gave me that day—"For Thee, for them, Amen."

I have never forgotten it, and I cannot begin to count the number of times I have prayed it. I reckon that it takes only four seconds to pray! "For Thee, for them, Amen."

"For Thee" says that I sanctify myself for God's glory and the doing of His will. "For them" says that I sanctify myself for others—both Christians and non-Christians whom I will meet that day. The purpose is for their good, bringing some to faith in Christ, or building up others in their faith in Christ. "Amen" indicates that I am the "Amen," the channel through which that prayer will be answered.

What a short prayer to pray, but as God answers it, the results can last throughout a lifetime and beyond, throughout eternity.

Hindering the Unenlightened

Ye entered not in yourselves, and them that were entering . . .

Thursday   Luke 11:52

". . . ye hindered." Our Lord assumes that there were those trying to enter in. I wonder if there are not more of such people than we sometimes think. But the tragedy is that the biggest stumbling block to the unbeliever is the believer—the believer who has refused to enter into the Christian experience in its fullness and stands blocking the way for others who would like to enter in.

Sometimes we ask ourselves wonderingly, "How many have I helped to find the Christian way?" That is God's concern and we shall never know the answer fully until we get to heaven. But there is another question much more searching, "How many people have I put off from the Christian way?" They wanted to find what they thought Christ offered to men and they came to look at my life to see if it was true. What they saw put them off for ever. They went away saying, "If that is the Christian experience, then I am just as well off without it."

The reason for all this is simply our own failure to enter into all that Christ has purposed for us. Are we like the Pharisees in this respect? *Jesus said, "I am the door,—if anyone enters by Me, he will be saved" Jn 10:9 Ps 100:4, 5 The blessings of entering through Him.* *20th*

Fear, Cast Out by Love

. . . Perfect love casteth out fear . . .

Friday   1 John 4:18

How true this is. Is there any authority we obey so readily as the authority of love? Love exercises a dictatorship which is absolute, but how wonderful a dictatorship it is, one that knows no fear.

Sometimes, playing with my children when they were smaller, I would pretend that I was fighting. I might clench my fists and frown, and prance around and push out my fists. But you know what the children would do—they would run straight into my arms! Their love would trust my love and, of course, I would not dream of hitting little ones like that.

"Perfect love casteth out fear." Sometimes our picture of God is the picture of a frowning face, a clenched fist and a dominating presence. But that is not the God we come to know in Christ. While reading the life of Adolf Saphir, I came across the loveliest definition of the life of a Christian which I think I have ever heard. It has no element of tension in it and I believe it has the secret of success. He said something like this: "If you want to live the Christian life as you were meant to live it, get into the presence of God and then do whatever you like!"

Child of God, you should be living in the love of the Father. Get

14

there and you will find that this verse will become true in your experience. The certainty will come that there is no fear in love!

1 Jhn 4: 9,10 God is love and our hope is in Him *21st*

Abundant Living

I am come that they might have life, and that they might have it more abundantly

Saturday

John 10:10

I remember picking up a book one day called *Sleeping through the Revolution* by Dr. Paul Rees. In that book, I came across a quotation from Dr. Stanley Jones's book, *Abundant Living.* This is how the quote ran: "The early Christians did not say in dismay, 'Look what the world has come to' but they said in delight, 'Look what has come to the world!' They saw not merely the ruin but the resources for the reconstruction. They saw not merely that sin did abound but that grace did much more abound."

Dr. Jones added this significant sentence, "The whole secret of abundant living can be summed up in this sentence: 'Not your responsibility but your response to His ability.'" I like that, don't you? "Not your responsibility but your response to His ability."

Those who truly trust in Him will lack nothing.

Does Death Trouble You?

22nd

Let not your heart be troubled: ye believe in God, believe also in Me

Sunday

John 14:1

The thought of death troubles most of us. Yet Jesus Christ said to His disciples, troubled as they were at the thought of His approaching death, "Let not your heart be troubled."

We are, of course, troubled at this by the thought of our own sinfulness. The strange paradox is that the greater the saint, the greater the sense of sinfulness. We don't need the Bible to tell us that "all have sinned, and come short of the glory of God." We know that already, although usually we don't like anybody to tell us. But what is there in our Savior that enables Him to say so convincingly, "Let not your heart be troubled"? Surely in Him and in His death we find the complete answer to our sinfulness. "The blood of Jesus Christ His Son cleanseth us from all sin."

We are often troubled by the thought of our own loneliness, by the simple fact that when we die, as die we must, we must die alone. How sad this seems! When we face the biggest experience

15

that life holds for us, we must go to meet it alone. But the Christian does not really travel alone "through the valley of the shadow of death." The Christian affirms, "I will fear no evil, for Thou art with me." The living Presence we have known all through the journey of life will not forsake us as we enter that valley.

We are troubled, so often, by the thought of our own helplessness. We are quite helpless as far as stopping the advance of death. We may delay the moment when it will lay its hands upon us but we cannot stop it. We are just as helpless as far as knowing anything about it is concerned. We may guess, but we don't know. But Jesus Christ does know! He has been through it and He tells us that death means being with Him, and that everything on the other side has been prepared by Him in His love. What more do we need to know? *Nothing. There is a great peace if we only let it. Jesus is our hope.*

Convincing Evidence

23rd

The Word was made flesh, and dwelt among us and we beheld His glory

Monday   John 1:14

For three years John had rubbed shoulders with his Master. They had worked together, they had lived together. He had seen Him in the crowds and also alone. He had seen Him tired out at night and fresh in the morning. In almost every circumstance of life John had been with Christ, His beloved Master; as close to Him as any earthly relationship could bring him. And it was after this that John wrote, ". . . and we beheld His glory, the glory as of the only begotten of the Father, full of grace and truth."

Under every conceivable kind of pressure the Master never faltered, the glory was never dimmed. Alas! With us it is otherwise. For of so many Christians, both ministers and laymen, we must say that distance lends enchantment to the view. At a distance, in the life of the church and its services and organization, we may appear convincing Christians. But to those who know us intimately—our family or our colleagues at work—that impression is found to be false and fleeting. Yet it need not, it should not be so. For the same Word has been made flesh anew in us and, therefore, the same glory should shine through yet again. Is it shining through our lives?

16

The Disturbance Love Creates

Open to me

Tuesday

Song of Solomon 5:2

"It is the voice of my beloved that knocketh, saying, 'Open to me, . . . my love . . .: for my head is filled with dew, and my locks with the drops of the night'."

Christians believe in the love of God and then promptly make that love a cushion upon which their thinking goes to sleep, forgetting that there is nothing so disrupting, so disturbing, so demanding, so upsetting as love. This, of course, knocks the bottom out of the argument which says that Christians have invented a God of love because they want the comfort that love can bring. Love brings much more than comfort; it brings a challenge. No Christian has ever led a more comfortable life because he has been a Christian, but rather a more uncomfortable life because of the disturbance that love creates.

What contributes to this disturbance? The nature of the bridegroom does. Look inside that closed door and sense the warmth, the comfort, the ease. But now look at the one who stands without, who says, "My head is filled with dew, and my locks with the drops of the night." Her shepherd king, her bridegroom lover, was a man of the fields and of the flocks. He was a man whose life was a life of toil, toil that took him out in all weathers and at all hours. This shepherd king did not fit the pattern of things inside. Inside we have a picture of warmth and outside a picture of toil and work. How utterly incongruous this figure is, drenched with the rain and dew—how challenging the summons!

But what is the nature of our heavenly Bridegroom with His Redeemer's heart? Is He not, too, a man of toil at all hours? Yes, in all weathers! His brow is not wet with dew, but with blood. His locks are not wet with the drops of the night, but with the spittle of His foes who mocked Him on His cross. And so, the nature of the bridegroom contributes to the disturbance that love creates.

We see here, too, the need of the bridegroom. "Open to me," is his cry. His longing is for fellowship. He yearns for someone to commune with, to company with. He longs to come in to her so that she may go out with him—to share his task and his thoughts. "Open to me," is his cry.

How true all this is of Christ! He asks us to open our hearts, our whole lives, to His incoming Spirit so He may fill us with Himself and we may identify ourselves totally with Him. Christ's need is for fellowship and that is why He chose twelve so that they should be with Him, to accompany Him in His redemptive work in the world. He wants our company. He comes in to us so that we may go out with Him.

How disturbing all this is! How demanding! How uncomfortable! But, "Open to Me" is still His cry today!

25th

Wednesday

The Reluctance Love Confronts

I have put off my coat; how shall I put it on? I have washed my feet; how shall I defile them?

Song of Solomon 5:3

There is lethargy here. The bride protests in the words of our verse, "I have put off my coat; how shall I defile them?" "No, No!" she says, "Don't disturb me. I am having such a lovely time. Don't spoil everything; don't upset everything." How like a Christian on a Sunday night, lounging in a chair watching a play on the TV. The rain is lashing against the windows and a glance at the clock shows it is time for church. But who wants to go out on a night like this?

Oh, the lethargy, the laziness that marks the Church today! The need for fellowship with Christ may sound clear but oh, the protests we make! There are members needed in the choir; there are teachers needed in the Sunday School; there are donations wanted for this work or that work; and all that the call to sacrifice produces is protest. The service is too demanding, too upsetting, too inconvenient, and we protest, "Leave me alone. Let me enjoy my religion; let me enjoy my Christian faith; let me enjoy my church; but don't disturb me. Don't make things inconvenient."

But there is more than lethargy here; there is tragedy. At last she moves (verse 5). "I rose to open to my beloved; and my hands dropped with myrrh, and my fingers with sweet smelling myrrh, upon the handles of the lock. I opened to my beloved; but my beloved had withdrawn himself and was gone: . . . I sought him, but I could not find him." She responded, but it was too late. The shepherd king was gone. The relationship was still there, the relationship of bridegroom and bride, but the fellowship was not.

It is possible to be a Christian and yet be out of touch with the Lord. "I sought him, but I could not find him!" Many years ago God gave me a tremendous phrase that has lingered in my mind ever since. The phrase is, "delayed obedience is disobedience."

I was once given a copy of the commentary on the Song of Solomon by Rev. William Still of Aberdeen. In it, he recalls a choice memory of his childhood concerning obedience—something his mother used to say to him—"Obedience means at once."

That reminds me of the little incident that Archdeacon Herbert Cragg recalled in an address at Keswick. A mother was calling her little girl to come down for tea, and back came the reply, "I am coming, Mummy." Five minutes later there was still no sign of her daughter, so once again she called and back came the reply, "I am coming, Mummy." After five more minutes there was still no sign of the little girl, so Mummy called again, "Come down, tea is ready." Back came the reply, "I am coming, Mummy," to which Mummy replied, "Stop coming, and come."

So often it is because of our delayed obedience, which amounts to disobedience, that we lose fellowship with Christ.

The Experience Love Permits

The watchmen that went about the city found me, they smote me, they wounded me

Song of Solomon 5:7

Thursday

The Bible says that "the way of transgressors is hard" and it was C. S. Lewis who said that "pain plants the flag of truth in the mind." The experience that love permits is the experience of suffering. Mercifully it is so because to continue in our disobedience would be to lead to more suffering. God makes it difficult to disobey. We see this in the way the bride was treated. Verse 7 says, "The watchmen that went about the city found me, they smote me, they wounded me; the keepers of the walls took away my veil from me." She found the going rough, and she was treated this way because those who saw her realized her situation.

We face the fact that the world has no time or respect for a disobedient Christian. Sometimes we are tempted to disobey because we feel we will gain favor from the world, but we don't. We lose it! The world knows perfectly well when things are wrong. We see here, too, the way she was troubled. In verse 6 we read, "My soul failed," and in verse 8 we read, "I am sick of love." "The whole thing is making me ill," she says. You will recall the words in the hymn,

> Where is the blessedness I knew
> When first I saw the Lord?
> Where is the soul-refreshing view
> Of Jesus and His word?

I believe that there is a discipline of withdrawal. It is referred to in the book of the prophet Hosea where God says, "Ephraim is joined to idols: let him alone." There are two ways to understand that. Either Judah was to leave Ephraim alone or God intended to leave him alone. And I think in all probability it is the second, but the other could equally apply. Ephraim had to learn in the bitterness of a withdrawal by God and maybe by others that the path of disobedience just didn't pay. So what we do not learn by precept we have to learn by experience.

The Acceptance Love Receives

Thou art beautiful, O my love, . . . comely as Jerusalem
Song of Solomon 6:4

Friday

There are two things that contribute to this happy ending, and first was the conviction the bride had reached. To lose the bridegroom was to find him. Only when she discovered what it was like without him did she know she must have him. When she was challenged by the daughters of Jerusalem (5:9), "What is thy beloved more than another beloved?" she replied with that amazing and wonderful testimony (5:10), "He is the chiefest among ten thousand," and ending, "He is altogether lovely" (5:16). Such a conviction of her lover's beauty brought a testimony to her lips that aroused a longing in others, so that the daughters of Jerusalem cry out enviously (6:1), "Whither is thy beloved gone, . . . that we may seek him with thee."

"Whither is he gone?" was the question, and the answer to this she knew; to his garden, to pasture his flocks. He would not come to her, but if she would find him—and she knew she would—it would be in the place of toil, in the place of obedience. What a welcome she got! "Thou art beautiful, O my love, as Tirzah, comely as Jerusalem," and ending in verse 10, "Who is she that looketh forth as the morning, fair as the moon, clear as the sun, and terrible as an army with banners?"

"Thou art beautiful." How lovely the face of a loved one is when there is no cloud of misunderstanding or reservation to spoil the fellowship. How lovely is the face of a Christian to Christ when there is no cloud of disobedience or reservation to spoil the fellowship between the heavenly Bridegroom and the bride. Can Christ say this of you and me? "Thou art beautiful, O my love."

Defying Christ

Peter saith unto Jesus, Thou shalt never wash my feet
John 13:8

Saturday

Peter was a man with a defiant heart. Christ had moved around that upper room in a silence that could be felt. Men were looking away from each other, not daring to meet each other's eyes. Then the silence was broken. A voice spoke sharp with suppressed emotion, harsh under an almost intolerable strain of intense feeling. It was Simon Peter's voice, and with the hurt of his heart in the sound of his voice, he said incredulously, "Not my feet!" There followed the quiet unhurried tones of the Master's voice, "What I do thou knowest not now; but thou shalt know hereafter." Then a sharp, almost explosive word, "Never! Never!"

Do you know anything of what that refusal of Simon Peter's meant? The motive behind Peter's refusal and the motive behind yours and mine may be totally different, but the issue is the same. "My feet! Thou shalt never wash my feet." Have we been saying the same thing to Christ concerning our lives and His will? "Never!" Like Peter, we have been almost nearer to anger than to any other emotion in our refusal.

How many of us have felt the tide of anger and resentment rising until we could have walked out of the service! Perhaps we felt resentment against a preacher, or even anger against God. We may have felt resentment against the person who persuaded us to come. Like the elder brother in the story of the Prodigal Son, we have heard the sound of music and dancing, we have seen the faces of those enjoying the feast, but we have been angry and would not go in. Are we defiant? Are we defying Christ?

A New Testament Christian Home

The house of Mary

Sunday

Acts 12:12

I think we may have made a mistake by making the special buildings we call churches or halls the bases of operation for Christian service. The early Church had no such buildings and so they used their homes. We ought to use our homes a good deal more than we do. One such home was Mary's. What was it like?

21

It was a home to which people turned in need. "When Peter had considered the thing he came to the house of Mary." I doubt that Peter's feet were the first to make their way to the home of Mary. What would draw people there? The warmth of Christian love would draw people in trouble that way irresistibly and so would the wealth of Christian grace. Somehow people had the feeling that Mary would not only accept them at any time of day or night, but that she would be able to assist them, answer their questions and give them the kind of counsel they needed.

It was a home where people knelt in prayer. We are told that it was a home "where many were gathered together praying." I am pretty sure also that it was not the first time that voices of prayer had been heard in that home. There was obviously a place given to prayer in Mary's home. Is a similar place given to it in our homes? As a result, there would be a peace in those hearts gotten through prayer. A well-loved hymn speaks of "taking everything to God in prayer," and suggests that when we fail to do so there is a "peace we often forfeit."

It was also a home from which people went out in service. It was the home of "Mary, the mother of John whose surname was Mark," and at the end of the chapter we are told that Barnabas and Saul "took with them John, whose surname was Mark." I think we can safely say that there was activity centered in that home, a continual going out by one member or another on the work of the Master. But I like to think that there was an ambition cherished in the heart of Mary that one day her son John would go out into full-time service for her Lord. And that is just what he did. What a lovely home this was!

Unfair?

My bonds

Philippians 1:13

When you are in a difficult place it is very easy to become bitter, and I have never met a bitter person who is happy. Bitterness and happiness don't blend. A bitter person is usually rather miserable. Is there a root of bitterness in some part of your life which is spoiling the whole? What, for Paul, might have resulted in bitterness he had wonderfully overcome; he had risen above it and was rejoicing. But potentially the bitterness was there. What was involved that could have made Paul an extremely bitter man?

In Philippians 1:13 Paul speaks of his "bonds in Christ." It is very easy for us to gloss over that phrase—"my bonds." This chain on my wrist! This guard in my room day and night! My bonds! The sheer injustice of them!

Three times Paul had heard the verdict of authority. When he was arrested, the Captain of the Temple Guard said, "This man has nothing laid to his charge worthy of death or of bonds." When he came up for trial before Festus, the new Governor, Festus said, "This man has committed nothing worthy of death." Finally, after Paul appeared before Agrippa and Festus, they consulted together and said, "This man doeth nothing worthy of death or of bonds." Yes, Paul's life was stamped with unfairness and injustice. And he had borne it for so long!

It is not easy to sing when you have been treated unjustly and unfairly. The bitterness of resentment can easily creep into a situation like that. Do you have bitterness in your heart, in your mind, in your soul? Are you resentful? If you are, you are not rejoicing, and the poison will go right through your home, right through your job, into your church. It will be everywhere. Think of Paul and the sheer unfairness of his bonds, and how in spite of everything he continued to rejoice.

The Church—The Body of Christ

The Church, which is His body . . .

Tuesday   Ephesians 1:22, 23

Have you ever stopped to think what light this image of the Church throws upon membership of the Church of Jesus Christ? If I am truly a member of the body of Christ, there are three things that must follow.

First, I must possess the life of Christ. My body is animated by my life; Christ's body is animated by *His* life. We don't belong to the Church until we belong to Christ. As an early father of the Church put it, "Where Christ is, there is the Church." He might have added, "Where Christ is not, the Church is not." To be part of the body of Christ I must, therefore, receive the life of Christ.

As part of Christ's body, I must also submit to the will of Christ. In Ephesians 5:23, Paul speaks of Christ as "the head of the body" (RSV). If I truly belong to the Church of Christ, to the body of Christ, then as the body submits to the dictates of the head and mind, so my life will submit to the will of Christ. One of the distinctive marks of a true Christian is obedience to the will of God.

As part of His body, I must also express the mind of Christ. My desires and intentions find expression through the members of my body—through my hands, my eyes, my feet, my lips. So should it be with the Christian. Your life and mine should express constantly the mind of Christ as if we are truly part of "His body."

The Church—The Building of Christ

Upon this rock I will build My church

Matthew 16:18

In Matthew 16:18 and 1 Peter 2:5, God's Word speaks of the Church as being "the building of Christ." This picture of the Church stirs the imagination. If we think what buildings are like and relate that to the Church of Christ as His building, three implications follow that we must never forget.

First, there will be a design to follow. Those who belong to the Church do not always stop to ask whether what *they* think the Church ought to be or do is in His plan.

There will also be a development to foresee. A building should grow as long as it is under construction. Our churches should be growing structures, either in quantity or quality. There should always be progress and there will always need to be maintenance too.

Finally, there will be a destiny to fulfill. What is the building for? This building may be a school, this a shop, this a hospital, this a home—but the church is a building built for God. We read in God's Word that we are "builded together for an habitation of God through the Spirit." What a destiny! When people come into the fellowship of believers which constitutes the Church universal and local, the one presence they should become immediately aware of is the presence of Christ Himself. When that happens, the destiny of that fellowship has been fulfilled—that church is truly His building. Do we belong to that kind of church?

24

The Church—The Bride of Christ

As a bride adorned for her husband

Revelation 21:2

The Church is called the "bride of Christ" directly in Revelation 21:2 and by implication in John 3:29 and Matthew 25. Such a title suggests three things to me. First, this concept of the Church as the bride of Christ speaks of the revelation that love makes. In John 14:21 our Lord says, "He that loveth Me . . . I will love him, and will manifest Myself to him." Part of the wonder of love lies in the unveiling of the deeper thoughts of their hearts between those who love. So Christ will reveal to His bride the thoughts of His heart.

There are also the resources that love will bring. When a bridegroom says to his bride, "With all my worldly goods I thee endow," he may not be giving his bride very much. But when the heavenly Bridegroom comes into our hearts, all the "unsearchable riches" of His grace become ours. How rich the bride of Christ is.

Thirdly, there is the radiance that love will wear. In Psalm 149 we read that "God will beautify the meek with salvation." How radiant a bride looks on her wedding day as she comes down the aisle! Should not the bride of Christ be even more radiant? There is one verse in the Psalms which speaks of this, where the psalmist says, "Look to Him and be radiant" (RSV). Is there a radiance about us as part of the bride of Christ? What a thrilling thing it is to be related to Christ in this way!

Self-Examination

Examine yourselves . . . live in peace

2 Corinthians 13:5, 11

Paul makes two very practical requests of those who had been his critics and detractors in Corinth and who were causing division in the Church. First, we note where he asks them to look. Paul says it is time your gaze was turned on yourselves, and these words are in the present tense—keep on examining yourselves to see indeed if you are in the faith at all.

The very fact of their being genuine Christians at all was almost suspect in the light of the behavior they had been displaying. And if they were Christians, what kind of Christians were they? Were they really Christians in whom Christ was dwelling? Was this the way the indwelling Christ would have them live and speak? "Criticise me if you like," says Paul, "but why don't you criticise yourselves?"

What kind of Christians are you, you who talk so big, you who say so much about my failures? What about your failure? What a sensible piece of advice! So often those who say most, do least. Paul's counsel is wise. He asks us to look where he asked them to look. Examine *yourselves.*

But we can also see how he asks them to live—live in peace and the God of peace will be with you. Do away with all this divisive thought and talk and God's blessing will be yours. It is possible for critical and quarrelsome Christians to create an atmosphere in which God cannot work. James speaks of this in his epistle, "The harvest of righteousness is sown in peace by those who make peace" (RSV). There is, then, a soil in which the Word of God can work fruitfully, but there is also a soil in which the seed of the Word finds it difficult to grow. Paul realized that if this little group of critics went on with their fault-finding, their squabbling, their whispering, then the work of the Church would suffer and so he says, "Live in peace, and the God of love and peace will be with you."

I Just Can't

Hitherto ye were not able to bear it, neither yet now are ye able

1 Corinthians 3:2

How many Christians there are who are "not able." They are not able to pray aloud at a prayer meeting; they are not able to speak to others about the things of the Spirit.

These may be meriting a word that Paul uses here to describe a certain kind of Christian. The word is "carnal" and has nothing to do with our modern use of the word. It means simply Christians who live lives that just cannot be distinguished from the lives of those who make no profession of being Christians at all. They "walk as men." This kind of Christian is a weakling; he is "not able" to feed himself on the Word of God, but has to be fed like a "babe." Like a baby, he has little, if any, sense of values and is "not able" to distinguish between things that are really important and things that are of no importance at all.

26

A baby is a miracle, but a baby who never grows up and who remains a baby is a tragedy. Part of the Christian Gospel *is* the message of the forgiveness of sins and the re-establishing of a right relationship with God, but it does not stop there! The full message of salvation is the imparting of a new life, the very life of Christ to indwell us. To say "I cannot" does not harmonize with the words of Paul, "I can do all things through Christ who strengtheneth me."

5

Sunday

The Miracle of the Incarnation

The Word was made flesh, and dwelt among us

John 1:14

Here is a simple statement of the miracle that lies at the heart of the Christian faith. I would suggest three thoughts which this claim provokes in our minds.

First, the possibility of the incarnation must be admitted. No man has any right to say that this could not have happened. It is impossible to deny in the light of man's limited knowledge. To say it could not have happened would demand a complete knowledge of both the Creator and the created universe, and no man has that. It is also impossible to deny on the grounds of the basis of man's knowledge. All man's knowledge, even of this material universe, is initially revealed knowledge—revealed through man's perceptive and receptive senses. Christianity affirms that spiritual knowledge is also based upon revelation in which man is initially the recipient.

Then, the necessity of the incarnation can be asserted. Human love demands the making of such a revelation. If people believe in God, they are prepared to believe that love, the highest attribute in the creature man, will be found in the creator God. But love has a distinctive quality—it is never content to remain unknown; it must reveal itself. If God be love, then surely He, too, will want to reveal Himself! Human life itself determines the manner of such a revelation. Humanity is the only level of life that man can truly understand. If God wanted to reveal Himself, it is reasonable to expect that it would be on that level and that He would reveal Himself as a Man.

And finally, the authority of the incarnation must be accepted. This is where the real crunch comes. It is not that man can reasonably reject the idea of God revealing Himself, but that man does not like the revelation that God had made in Christ Jesus. "God . . .

hath . . . spoken . . .," states the writer of Hebrews. And man has to face two facts. The first concerns the ignorance that Christ dispels, and the second, the obedience that Christ demands.

As a child I heard King George V make one of the first royal broadcasts to the Empire at Christmas. He introduced his words to the children of the empire with the words, "Boys and Girls, the King is speaking to you." In Christ, God is speaking—and we have no choice but to obey.

6

Gambling and Covetousness

Take heed, and beware of covetousness

Monday

Luke 12:15

The main condemnation of gambling from the Christian point of view is directed at the motives in the mind and heart of the gambler. The first is that of selfishness. Whenever a person gambles, it is to win. He wants to get—and to get for himself. Such a motive is not worthy of a Christian. The Spirit of God which dwells within the heart of the believer is the Spirit of the love of God—a caring love, a giving love that so loved the world that it gave. How can gambling be consistent with the nature of that God, or contribute to the glory of that God, whose name we bear? Jesus Christ laid down the terms of discipleship in these words, "If any man will come after Me, let him deny himself (say "No" to himself), and take up his cross daily, and follow Me."

Another motive is what we might call carelessness. The Christian is under an obligation, as is every man, to love his neighbor. How can we reconcile that love with an act which takes what belongs to our neighbor without giving him anything in return?

I was brought up in the Scout movement and I always remember a comment made by the Chief Scout, Lord Baden-Powell. I don't know if he was a Christian but he was a religious man with high moral standards. He said, "I don't like to think I am making myself richer by helping myself to the contents of my friend's pocket." If that description of gambling is accurate, it brings gambling so close to stealing as to make the difference between the two scarcely discernible. It involves selfishness, as far as I am concerned and carelessness as far as my neighbor is concerned. Careless, in its original and accurate sense, has been defined as "without regard, without heed, without concern."

In the parable of the Good Samaritan, our condemnation is instinctively directed at the priest and the Levite, who came down the road, saw the man who had lost his wealth at the hands of robbers and "passed by on the other side." What is the essence of our condemnation of these men? Simply that they did not care. Loving our neighbors does not mean taking from them but giving to them. Our Lord says, "Take heed and beware of covetousness."

No Letters

No church communicated with me

Tuesday   Philippians 4:15

The reference here may be about communication that dealt with financial and practical matters, but we can apply it more widely.

I wonder how many people can say this about us—that "nobody wrote!" When did you last write to a missionary? Have you written lately to one who has gone out from your church? A young worker, out on his first term of service wrote, "Before I went out, at my farewell meeting, my church people promised they would write to me, but I haven't had a single letter from either my pastor or the people." Not a single letter!

Missionaries come home and we welcome them back and they stand up in our churches and say, "The first thing I want to do is to thank you for remembering me." I wonder if they say it with almost a sob. They feel they have to say it, but in the desperate loneliness of the mission field they often must have wondered if anybody was remembering them for there was no tangible evidence of it.

I receive prayer letters from a number of missionaries. I know you can't keep in touch with every missionary, but God will give you a selective ministry of responsibility here, as in other spheres of Christian work. I find the best thing to do, the moment a prayer letter comes in, is to send at least a postcard back in return.

Is there someone you know in the field and you haven't written to that person for months? Why not take five minutes now and send a postcard? If you only knew the desperate loneliness of some missionaries and the kind of disastrous situations that can arise born out of that loneliness. If this happens, where does the fault lie? Perhaps more often than not it is our fault through our thoughtlessness. There has been no evidence of interest. There has been no letter!

How Serious is Sin?

The wages of sin is death

Romans 6:23

The Bible does not take a light view of sin. The seriousness of sin lies in two aspects of it. First, in the power of sin. David the king cried out in an agony of soul, "My sins are mightier than I." Jesus Christ added His verdict on the power of sin when He said, "Whosoever committeth sin is the slave of it."

These are days when there is much superficial and shallow talk about freedom. We do well to realize that although we may think we are free to do as we like, we are not free to stop doing it. The power of sin to become habitual is something that every life knows. How many there are who are held by habits they cannot break, bound by fears they dare not admit, or caught by consequences they can never undo.

The seriousness of sin is found not only in its power but also in its penalty. We cannot and must not treat sin purely as a social problem or as a personal inconvenience. The Bible states explicitly that sin involves God, and as a transgression of the law it carries a penalty. We could illustrate this very simply from everyday life. Supposing I was driving my car down the main road and in a moment of inattention was involved in an accident. I might regard this accident as one of personal inconvenience to me. It would mean my car being off the road for repairs for a week or two. I might have with me in the car a companion with a warped sense of humor who thought the whole thing intensely amusing.

But I could not have such an accident on a main road in this country without a further element being added to the situation. In a matter of minutes a car would drive up and out of it would come two men in dark blue uniform. I would suddenly discover to my dismay that what to me was an inconvenience and to my friend a matter of amusement, was to them an offence in the sight of the law. The penalty that sin carries with it is stated quite clearly—"the wages of sin is death." And that means separation from God, in this life and in the life to come.

Like Sheep

All we like sheep . . .

Isaiah 53:6

When the Bible likens men to sheep it comes uncomfortably near the mark. Indeed, in some respects sheep have a good deal more sense than many men, but they are timid beasts and so many people are as timid and as easily frightened as a flock of sheep. It takes courage to be a Christian and most of us are not long in finding this out. To go out into the world and live for the clean things, the decent things, the good things, the things of God—this takes courage in a world which has gone morally soft and flabby.

There is an old Scottish motto that every Christian should know and bear in mind. It runs thus: "They say! What say they? Let them say!" To which I would add the words of Jesus Christ to His disciples, "If the world hate you, ye know that it hated Me before it hated you."

Are People Blocking the Way?

They could not come nigh unto Him for the press

Mark 2:4

People got in the way of this man who needed so desperately what Christ alone could give him. I think that some people still make it difficult for others to come to Christ. Even now, it may be that there is someone standing between you and Christ and all that Christ can do for you and through you. It may be someone whom you have wronged, and you don't want to make apology or restitution. It may be someone whose opinion means so much to you—a friend; or someone very dear to you who does not share your beliefs. It may be someone who is particularly difficult to get on with.

This is a problem that challenges all of us at one time or another. It was not easy to find a way through the crowd, but this man managed it and found the blessing that was to transform his life. It may be that if only we could get past those who come between us and our Master, our lives too would be immeasurably enriched.

A Changed Pattern

Lord, what wilt thou have me to do?

Acts 9:6

Before you and I became Christians our pattern of life—what we did, where we went, how we spent our time and our money—was shaped by one of two principles. Paul tells us about them in Ephesians 2. The first principle was that we did only the things that we wanted to do. That is what the Bible calls, "fulfilling the desires of the flesh and of the mind." The other principle was that we imitated others. Our lives took their standards from the society of the ungodly people among whom we worked and lived. But when we became Christians that pattern of living ended. We no longer walked "according to the course of this world."

The decisive principle in the life of a Christian is not that I do what I want or that I do what others do, but that I do what God wants me to do. The old principles have been pushed to one side to make room for the one principle of Christian living.

Saul stumbled across this principle at the very moment of his conversion on the road to Damascus, although many Christians don't seem to find it for years. You will remember his two questions when that light shone dazzlingly bright around him on the road. He heard a voice, saw the light, and asked his first question, "Who art thou, Lord?" I wonder if it was a question asked in complete ignorance of the answer. I am not certain that it was. I think there was a question but also a recognition. While Saul of Tarsus was asking, "Who art thou?" he suddenly realized who it was. "Who are thou? Lord!" Back came the confirming word, "I am Jesus."

Then came the second question, "Lord, what wilt thou have me to do?" That question expressed the principle behind all Christian living. Saul of Tarsus hit it in the very first minutes after meeting Christ and lived by it all the way through his life till he was able to say towards its end, "I was not disobedient."

The Furnishings of Faith

An altar . . . his tent . . . a well

Genesis 26:25

These three things that we find in the life of Isaac are symbolic of three things that should find their place in the life of any man or woman of faith. What would they suggest to our minds? Here is what they suggest to mine.

"An altar" speaks of *dedication* to the will of God. An altar was a place upon which men offered sacrifice. In Isaac's life an altar had been erected. Bishop Taylor Smith used to say that every morning when he woke up, he lay for a moment in his bed making it an altar and offering himself afresh to God. The altar may well have been erected, but the impression is that in the life of Isaac, it was neglected. The word altar does not appear very frequently in the story of his life. Could that explain the comparative mediocrity which marked his life? Have we an altar?

"A tent" speaks of *detachment* from the ways of men. A tent is very easily moved. A house is solid and built into its environment, but a tent can be moved at a moment's notice. The tent suggests the need to develop a spirit of detachment from the pleasures of this world and all that is purely temporal. In the Book of Common Prayer of the Church of England a petition appears, "That we may so pass through things temporal that we finally lose not the things eternal." In order to "pass through," a tent is needed, not a house. The tent also suggests a detachment from the praise of the world. Christ warned us that the world would hate us. It is a bad sign if the world speaks well of us, and a worse sign if we want it to do just that. Where do we live spiritually—in a tent?

"A well" speaks of *dependence* on the word of life. In Psalm 1, the man who reads the Word of God is described as being like a tree planted by the rivers of water. Think of the difficulty Isaac encountered in digging the well. Look back to verses 18-22 and you will see how he and his servants had to fight for the wells. So it always is. The most difficult book in your home to pick up and read is your Bible. The Devil will see to that. But in spite of the difficulty they found in digging the well, they faced the necessity of digging it. It was a matter of digging or dying. They could not live without water. Neither can we live the life of faith without the word of life. We must dig or die!

Doubts that Hurt

Monday

Lord, if Thou hadst been here, my brother had not died
John 11:32

Sickness had come to this home in Bethany and with it the immediate thought of seeking the Master's help. The messenger was swift-footed, beseeching Him to come, but He didn't come! Instead, He

33

seems to have deliberately delayed. In verse 6 we read, "When He had heard therefore that Lazarus was sick, he abode two days still in the same place where he was." It is almost certain that by the time the message reached Jesus, Lazarus was already dead. But He still waited where He was for two more days.

How long those days must have seemed to the stricken family in Bethany. Why this delay? Did it mean that He did not care? Was the One they loved indifferent to their need? Why this inaction? So doubt beats fiercely in the hearts of Mary and Martha, and when they met Him that doubt showed in their greetings. "If Thou hadst been here, my brother had not died." But there would come to both of them a discovery that brought healing.

There is no place like the feet of Jesus for resolving the problems that perplex our hearts. The discovery Mary made at His feet was first that He cared; for when she looked up at her Master, she saw the tears streaming down His face. "Jesus wept," we are told. But the second discovery was a wonderful one: the delay of Christ, the seeming denial, was not without intent. He had told the disciples already it was "for your sakes." And Mary learned the wonderful lesson that Christ had not done a lesser thing, in order that He might raise a dead man!

Is it not so with us still? We, too, come with our prayers and our petitions, pleading with Christ to do that which to us seems so great. And yet all the time, while seemingly denying us our great desire, He is planning in love to do something greater still.

Are you a Spiritual Snob?

God resisteth the proud

Tuesday

James 4:6

Am I the kind of Christian, or rather that parody of a Christian, who feels so much better than other Christians that I look down my nose like any Pharisee and withdraw just a little from having anything to do with them? To be more particular than the Holy Spirit—as the spiritual snob usually is—is surely the most extraordinary form of conceit known on earth.

On the human level, the snob is often the last person who has any right to be snobbish. If you meet a social snob, you are usually meeting someone whose social background, traced far enough back, gives him no right whatsoever to adopt a superior attitude. The real aristocrat is seldom so petty.

Let us then take our standards from the Holy Spirit, for where He is at home, who are we to stand aloof? The Master Himself was full of grace and truth and we do well to seek to be like Him in this, as in all other things.

A Marriage that went Wrong

And Saul gave David Michal his daughter to wife
1 Samuel 18:27

One of the biggest tragedies in the life of David, "the man after God's own heart," lay in his marriage to Michal, a daughter of king Saul. The story of that marriage had three chapters.

There was a *happy beginning* (1 Sam 18:26, 27). The wedding was what would be called today a social triumph for the shepherd lad. We find out, however, that a social triumph can be a spiritual tragedy. And although we have no cause to doubt the reality of Michal's love for David, we learn the truth that human affection is never a substitute for divine grace.

Before very long we sense a *hidden blemish* (1 Sam. 19:11-13) when we read that "Michal took an image." A strange thing for the wife of David to have! Was it possible that although Micah loved David she did not love David's God? The moment he was out of the way the hidden image came out—to serve a useful purpose on this occasion. The existence of the image damaged the spiritual happiness of David and Michal in their married love and the final note is a sad one.

What had started as a happy beginning began to show a hidden blemish and ended up being a *hated bond* (2 Sam. 6:12-23). There is no more tragic picture in the whole Bible record of marriages than this. That wonderful day for David, when he brought back the Ark of the Covenant, meant absolutely nothing to Michal. And the one nearest to him in human relationships was furthest from him in spiritual understanding. In that great service of thanksgiving David had almost been in heaven, but when he entered the door of his own home he found himself in hell. Men and women do well to heed the divine command, "Be not unequally yoked together with unbelievers."

Are You Blind?

. . . and recovering of sight to the blind

Thursday   Luke 4:18

With this word "blind," Jesus Christ defined at least part of the
need of mankind which He came to meet. To be spiritually blind
carries with it all the tragedy of being physically blind, only at a
much greater depth. Think of the *poverty* that blindness inflicts
upon life. How much poorer is a person who cannot see physically!
How much they miss of what others enjoy! But the same is true in
an infinitely deeper way for those who are spiritually blind. The
greater part of reality, the best part, the only enduring part is
closed to them. The richest things in life have never been seen by
them.

If poverty is one mark of blindness, then *peril* is another. A person who is blind does not find his blindness a danger to only himself, but also to others. Our Lord speaks of the blind leading the
blind and both falling in the ditch. What happens if spiritually
blind parents try to lead spiritually blind children? What happens if
blind teachers lead blind pupils? What is the result if blind pastors
try to lead blind people? Surely the great tragedy of our times is
that this is exactly what is happening. No wonder so many people
today are, spiritually speaking, ending up in the ditch!

Are you blind, or have you prayed the prayer of a blind man
long ago—"Lord that I may receive my sight"? Spiritual sight will
come with spiritual life and that life is a gift anyone can receive.

What the Tongue Reveals

If any man offend not in word, the same is a perfect man

Friday   James 3:2

James is speaking of a maturity that the tongue reveals. One of the
first things the doctor does when he wants to know about our
health is look at our tongue. James wants us to remember that
words are deeds just as much as actions. When we speak we act.
And we must face the fact that sin and failure can be ours in what
we say and sometimes in how we say it. But this is, of course, no
new thought. Psalm 39:1 tells us, "I will take heed to my ways, that
I sin not with my tongue." To say what is untrue, what is unkind,

or to say it unkindly, constitutes failure in Christian living and Christian witness.

Matthew Henry, the great commentator, speaks of "tongue sins." What we say, how we say it and why we say it should be taken into account when we consider our spiritual development and maturity. Just as, physically, a clean tongue indicates good health, so in Christian experience the tongue reveals spiritual condition. Our Lord said, "Out of the abundance of the heart the mouth speaketh" (Matthew 12:34). My speech will reveal the kind of person I am. Have I grown in Christian experience? Is there real spiritual insight? Is there grace and love in my heart? If so, the tongue will reveal all this.

Counting on Them

Jesus said All power is given unto Me in heaven and in earth. Go ye therefore, and teach all nations

Saturday

Matthew 28:18, 19

You may have heard the story which has no basis in truth but which nevertheless speaks of the challenge of Christ's commission to us. The story tells how when our Lord returned to the glory, after the first thrill of rejoicing on His return, He was speaking to the archangel Gabriel. After discussing the ministry of redemption, Gabriel is said to have asked our Lord: "And now that you have done all this for men, what plans have you made to carry the message of man's redemption to the ends of the earth?"

The Lord is said to have replied, "Well, there is John, James, Peter, Andrew, and others. That little group of men that I called and whom I have now commissioned are to take the message to the ends of the earth." "But Master," replied Gabriel, "Suppose that James and John, Peter and Andrew, and the rest of the men whom you called and commissioned to take this message, just don't go? Suppose they stay where they are? What other plans have you made?" To which our Lord replied with these words, "If the men whom I have chosen and commissioned fail, I have made no other plan. I am counting on them."

Is it possible that here we touch the very heart of the problem in the life of the Church today? The fact is that God always reaches men through men, through their prayers, through their testimony, through their friendship, through their personality—in different ways, but always with the same plan of reaching men through men. God has no other plan and it is just because He has no other plan,

37

and because so many of us are failing Him, that the work of redemption is so slow.

Today it may be that God's challenge will come to us afresh. "If these men fail I have made no other plan. I am counting on them." He is counting on you! He is counting on me!

The Search for Happiness

. . . And he arose, and came to his father . . .
Luke 15:11-24

Sunday

This parable is possibly the most famous short story in the world! It is known more familiarly to us as the parable of the Prodigal Son, but I like to think of it as the search for happiness.

As we look at the experience of the younger son we can realize the *desires* which mastered him. His basic conviction was that in order to find happiness he had to get away from the authority of his father. Similarly, men in their search for happiness are convinced that they must reject the will of God. These desires were of course selfish. "Give me" summed up his attitude to life. He was no doubt quite sincere, but sincerely wrong, as things turned out. Sincerity is not truth! He was almost certainly stubborn. I am sure his father reasoned with him constantly but to no avail.

We can see the *disasters* which met him. This young man who set out to get, immediately began to lose! He lost his wealth—we read that he "spent all." And if true wealth consists of the opportunities life holds, how easily that wealth can be lost. Setting out to demonstrate his freedom, he lost it. How many others have done the same, finding themselves in bondage to habits they cannot break, to opinions they dare not admit and to consequences they cannot undo? He lost his self-respect—"I am no more worthy to be called thy son." He ceased to believe in his own worth to his father!

We can see finally the *discoveries* which he made. There were three discoveries. He discovered his *folly*—"He came to himself." He had thought himself wise, but had been proved a fool—had thought he was strong, but had been proved weak. He had sought happiness and had found misery. He discovered his *father*—"He came to his father"—and found in him a love that was waiting to lavish on the son all that such love could give. He discovered his *future*—and that was not to live amid the swine troughs, but at the father's table and in the father's presence. As one worthy Scottish preacher put it, the lad was sick o' hame, then he was hame-sick and then he was hame!

A Guest for Supper

I will sup with him, and he with Me

Monday

Revelation 3:20

In the Middle East to have a meal with someone is a token of friendship. When Jesus spoke of entering our lives He went on to say, "I will sup with him and he with Me." The Christian life is intended to be one in which we enjoy the friendship of Jesus.

All would agree that life without friendship is a poor and shabby affair. But here is a friendship more wonderful than any earthly friendship, for it need never be broken and will never end. It follows that we need never be alone, never without company, for wherever we are and whatever we are doing the Savior is with us. "Lo, I am with you alway," was His parting word to His disciples. "I will never leave thee, nor forsake thee."

This friendship will grow and deepen as any friendship will with the passing of days and the communion of heart with heart. And for the Christian this communion will be achieved through prayer and Bible study. But note just one thing about the meal described. Have you noticed how when Jesus comes, at first He is the guest, and then He becomes the host? So the Christian life is not just a life into which Christ has entered, but one in which He is obeyed.

Obedience

Whatsoever He saith unto you, do it

Tuesday

John 2:5

Among the books on my bookshelf is one by Dr. Andrew Murray entitled *The School of Obedience.* That title suggests the fact that obedience is something to be learned. In the school there are two aspects of our obedience to the will of God. There is of course the negative aspect, which we overlook at our peril. I have no time for those people who are so fond of telling us that the Church must stop saying, "No, thou shalt not."

Where would we be in life today if there were not people telling us what we are not to do. The police will tell us if we attempt something on the roads of our land which the law has forbidden. The referee in a football game, the umpire in a cricket match or a tennis match will very quickly tell a player what he or she is not to do, if the rules of the game have been infringed. In every walk of life, in every area of life, there are certain things we are not allowed to do. And in the will of God there are prohibitions which have sound reasoning behind them, reasons that are just as viable as the prohibitions in other areas of life.

But there is another aspect of obedience which we need to grasp, namely that the will of God is supremely positive. God's will is much more a matter of what we *are* to do, than of what we *are not* to do; of what we *are* to be rather than what we *are not* to be. His will is going to affect every area of life, every part of it—my character, my conduct, my career—positively, not just negatively. When we pray in the Lord's prayer, "Thy will be done," we are not praying that His will may be endured but that it may be accomplished.

A Wonderful Mother

Mary the mother of John, whose surname was Mark
Acts 12:12

Wednesday

I am sure that Mark must have borne testimony to his mother's influence. Here, in a few short phrases we get a glimpse of the home in which John Mark grew up. His mother must have given him a wonderful home and a wonderful start. I wonder how many John Marks there are who, if asked to give their testimony, would speak about the home in which they were reared; of the people that used to visit it, the prayers that had been said in it, the activity centered in it; and maybe of the great desire in the mother's heart that one day her son should become a servant of Jesus Christ.

John McNeill, the great Scottish evangelist, had such a mother who said to him one day, "I gave you to the Lord before ever I saw your face." I wonder if that was true of your mother, and whether her hopes and prayers and dreams have been fulfilled.

Stay Where You Are

Continue thou in the things which thou hast learned
2 Timothy 3:14

Bishop Handley Moule translates the word "continue" as "stay." "Stay in the things you have learned." He adds the comment, "Timothy is to find his home there and always to be at home there." The Christian is to find the environment for his thoughts in the Scriptures. Paul is reminding Timothy of the people from whom he had originally learned the Biblical truths. There is almost certainly a reference to his mother and his grandmother. This learning had not simply come from their lips but also from their lives. Whenever Timothy recalled their names there would come to his heart a warm assurance of the truths of which they had spoken and by which they had lived.

It may well have taken the coming of Paul and his further teaching in those early days to lead Timothy into a life of obedience to these truths and so into the definite experience of conversion. The real foundation work, the real origin, however, was traced back to the love and lives of these two believers in his home. And it is significant to note that their work was done when Timothy was a child. Through Scriptures learned and studied then, enlightenment came which revealed to him his need along with a promise of mercy and grace to come in Christ.

What comfort there is for all parents and teachers who faithfully sow the seed of the Word of God in young hearts! Happy indeed are they if they see that seed grow and ripen into fruit. Sometimes the seed may lie dormant for a long time before it suddenly breaks out into life. So often this final touch comes through another hand, another voice, others' lips. Again and again this is found to be the way. A Sunday School teacher may sow the seed faithfully but perhaps a visiting preacher, a different voice proclaiming the same message brings the seed to fruition. But let it never be forgotten that the spiritual harvest could never have come without the earlier, faithful and diligent sowing of the seed of the Word.

24

The Despondency that Love can Know

Behold, he standeth behind our wall, he looketh forth at the windows, shewing himself through the lattice

Song of Solomon 2:9

Friday

Love comes expectantly and eagerly to be faced—with what? To be faced with a wall, a closed door. He must be satisfied only with glimpses of the bride through the lattice windows. What a shattering blow! After coming so far, after doing so much, after having such expectancy in his heart, he is met with a shut door.

Do you ever think how terribly disappointing we can be to Christ? We hear His voice claiming a response from us, and yet we meet Him with a wall between—we keep the door closed. The bride calls him "her beloved," yet she keeps him at a distance. She calls it "our wall" but surely it is one of her building. He longs for fellowship. The fault is never with him but with her and if disappointing for him, how disappointing, too, for her. If he could only catch a glimpse of the bride through the lattice, she could only get similar glimpses of him. She knew what it meant to be held in his arms (2:6) but now she keeps him at arm's length.

What is the trouble? What is the cause? Most commentators suggest that this is the picture of a believer rejoicing in the position he now has, but refusing to enter into the fuller relationship available to him. It is like a girl who gets the man she wants as her husband but then refuses to be a true wife to him. In verse 16 she speaks of her position and assurance when she says, "My beloved is mine." She has him, but the real question is whether he has her. The picture is of a person who claims to be saved but who will have no personal and continual dealings with the Savior. Christ is in the heart, but He is never at home there.

Dr. Alan Redpath tells of his early days in the ministry on the staff of the National Young Life Campaign. He stayed in two different homes in two successive campaigns. In the first, a big wealthy house, he was welcomed by the butler and taken to a little room up in the attic. He saw his hostess only once during that fortnight and then only by special request. The second house was a cottage. When he arrived, the door was open, his hostess stood before him and welcomed him in with open arms, saying, "Now make yourself at home and do whatever you like." Which kind of home do we offer Christ in our hearts?

42

Man's Desperate Need

Stripped . . . wounded . . . half dead

25

Saturday

Luke 10:30

The fact of human need is one that we cannot ignore, but how often we do just this. We live in a world of the most appalling need, whether viewed from the material, spiritual, moral or physical point of view.

There are powers which would rob and destroy, forces that, like the lurking robbers of that eastern highway, wait to spring out and ruthlessly take from men their true wealth. These powers may be rooted in the religions of heathendom, or covered over with all the polish and supposed culture of the western world. They may even be garbed in the dress of the Christian Church. But there is a ruthless power about them that seems irresistible.

The need stares us in the face; the question is, "What are we doing about it?"

26

Sharing the Splendor of Christ

Jesus said I am the light of the world; he that followeth Me shall not walk in darkness, but shall have the light of life

Sunday

John 8:12

Dr. Paul Rees said that in these words "we see that Christ is what we mean by splendor; that everything in life, no matter how glamorous or how decorative we try to make it, is paltry, cheap, tawdry if Christ's glory is not there." What a telling and true statement! Let us look at the words of Christ and seek to grasp their meaning for us.

We see here the *supremacy that Christ claims.* "I am the light of the world." In Christ there is a splendor that will excel. There are degrees of splendor in light, but Christ claims to excel all other degrees of splendor. A man may be a good man, but he would be an infinitely better man if he were a Christian; a home may be a good home but it would be an infinitely better home if Christ were in it. This splendor is therefore also a splendor that will expose. "Light is come into the world, and men loved darkness rather than light, because their deeds were evil." We like to think that we are all right, but when we come into the presence of this light we see ourselves as we truly are.

43

There is also in these words the *proximity that Christ seeks.* ". . . he that followeth Me." There is an intimacy that Christ wants us to enjoy. "Following" speaks of closeness, of nearness. The One who is light is also love, and love is never content to remain at a distance. Love longs to be near and to share, and that means being close either in mind or in body. There is also, then, an authority that Christ wants us to obey, for "following" means obeying. The Lordship of Christ is a truth that runs right through the New Testament. To put it another way, the Christian life is one that has passed "under new management."

And what about the *security that Christ gives?* First He says, "shall not walk in darkness," which speaks of avoiding the perils that can destroy a life. How many people get lost and hurt in the dark! That statement is capped by the assurance of the Presence that will direct a life, "but shall have the light of life." He will shed light upon the pathway that life should take. There is always a negative and a positive side to the will of God, and the Christian should live creatively, constructively and confidently.

27

The Accuser of the Brethren

The accuser of our brethren

Monday   Revelation 12:10

The Bible reveals implicitly the existence of a Devil, and recognizes that part of his character is to accuse the brethren. The attack may be a direct one upon the conscience. It can overwhelm the Christian with a sense of his own unworthiness, depressing and discouraging him from serving Jesus Christ and from knowing assurance of salvation and acceptance before God. Sometimes the attack may be indirect, through the lips of other Christians, or from the world that criticizes the failure evident in his life. Most of us have known this attack of the enemy of our souls and have felt discouraged almost to the point of admitting defeat.

Is there an answer we can give this accuser? There is! A very old and a very complete one. We are told we can overcome him "by the blood of the Lamb." Never at any time is the Christian accepted before God because of his own righteousness. The Christian, having been saved by grace, continues to stand in grace. To move off that ground is to throw our lives wide open to the attack of the accuser. To remain on that ground is to remain where he cannot come. To his foulest and truest taunts we have one answer—the blood of the Lamb which cleanses from all stain and all sin.

Heavenly Wisdom

The wisdom that is from above is first pure, then peaceable, gentle, and easy to be intreated, full of mercy and good fruits, without partiality, and without hypocrisy

Tuesday

James 3:17

Eight words are used here to describe wisdom that is from above. Dr. James Robertson, in *Hidden Resources of the New Testament*, says that this verse "reads like James's veiled picture of the gentle heart of love that many a time beside the bench refused to be provoked by his own bitter tongue," meaning that here we have James's portrait of his own brother, the Lord Jesus Christ.

The word used to describe this attitude of mind is searching and challenging in the extreme. The wisdom that is from above is first of all "pure," completely devoid of all ulterior motives whether for self or for gain. It is "peaceable." It brings people closer together as it brings them closer to the Lord. It is "gentle," or sweetly reasonable: it knows how to temper justice with mercy and does not insist on its own rights. Canon Guy King comments that this kind of attitude is always inventive in finding excuses, not for itself but for others. It is open to reason, "easy to be entreated." It is flexible rather than stubborn. It always has an open mind.

It is "full of mercy and good fruits," having a heart full of pity towards those who are in need either through their own ignorance or their disobedience. Isobel Cameron tells of the godly minister listening to a tale about someone who had been an evildoer, then shaking his head, saying with his lovely smile, "Tut tut, that wasn't evildoing. It was only stupid blundering." Linking mercy with good fruits, James reminds us here that Christian pity is not just emotion; it means action.

This kind of attitude is also "without partiality." Another translation says, "with no breath of favouritism," it knows its own mind and God's and will courteously and firmly not move from this to suit anybody's convenience. Finally, it is "without insincerity or hypocrisy." What a picture of the true wisdom that comes from above. This insight can be produced only by the work of the Holy Spirit.

Touched with Miracle

And the Lord said unto Moses, 'What is that in thine hand?'

Exodus 4:2

Moses was given more than just verbal assurance that in his life and in the task and challenge facing him, he would have the presence of God. God was going to give him visible evidence of His presence. In order to demonstrate that, He said in effect to Moses, "Take that shepherd's rod you have in your hand and throw it down." When Moses obeyed God, the rod turned into a living serpent. God, in other words, touched the symbol of his life and work with a miracle.

God says to you, "What have you got in your hand?" You are a secretary, you have a typewriter—that's what you have in your hand. Or you are a nurse. What have you got? You have a syringe or a bedpan. You are a mother. What have you got in your hand? A saucepan? A teapot? The children's clothes? A sewing machine? God says, "Let me touch your daily work, let me touch it with a miracle. Let people see in your daily life the reality of My presence and My power, and they will listen to you then."

Moses feared that if he obeyed God and went to release the children of Israel from the bondage of Egypt, nobody would listen to him. But when they saw his life touched with God's miracle, they would listen. Even Pharaoh would have to listen—and he did. So will those to whom God sends you, if and when they see your life touched with His miracle.

The Way to Christian Unity

That they all may be one; as Thou, Father, art in Me, and I in Thee, that they also may be one in us

John 17:21

The unity for which our Lord prayed is based upon a living experience of God in Christ. In Galatians 3:28 we read a similar statement by Paul that Christians are "all one in Christ Jesus." The unity of Christians is that of a living organism rather than an artificial organization, religious or otherwise. It is a spiritual unity between people, not necessarily or essentially an ecclesiastical unity. Indeed, outside of Christ there is no unity at all. Christian unity is based upon the sharing of a common life, expressed in a pattern of behavior, motivated and mastered by a new and common love.

There is something totally different here from what is in the minds of those who today talk so much about Christian unity. Many of them, one is tempted to think, have little if any concept of the new birth. Someone has said truly, "The Holy Spirit unites in indissoluble union all hearts that have received the same Lord in faith." This is the position in the New Testament. Anything outside of this is false.

A Close Examination

That which . . . our hands have handled

Friday

1 John 1:1

All of us are familiar with tangible communication. Advertisements and advertisers lure us to take into our hands, for a trial period, the goods they are trying to sell. People call at our doors with sample packets of detergents, or urge us to take some book or a set of encyclopaedia or records for seven-day free trial. They feel that if their products get into our hands so we can examine them closely, try them out and test them, we shall surely buy. It is this aspect of communication that is possibly the most searching and challenging of all as we think of communicating the Gospel.

As John recalls the ministry of Christ and the closeness of their walk and life together, he speaks of "that which our hands have handled of the Word of life." How close an examination can our Christian testimony stand? Think of the distance we preachers keep between ourselves and our people in the pews. We preach about prayer, but we do not submit our own prayer life for examination. We proclaim the victory that is possible in Christ, yet we do not allow our own lives to be closely checked for evidences of victory.

I have often spoken at the Keswick Convention where year after year the sufficiency of the Grace of God in Christ is proclaimed. Someone once said, with a touch of cynicism, that it might be a good thing if, instead of preachers standing on the platform and preaching, their wives be invited to stand and tell how it all worked out at home. This is the challenge the Christian Church must be prepared to face. We must not keep people at a distance. If we do, we run the danger of making them think, and quite rightly, that we are afraid our lives and testimony cannot stand scrutiny.

Are you a Comfy Christian?

Woe to them that are at ease in Zion

Saturday

Amos 6:1

I don't think God's chief difficulty today has anything to do with the sins of the unbelieving world, but rather with the sins of believing Christians. So many of us Christians are rather like that small girl who, returning from a party, was asked by her mother if she had been a good girl. She replied after due thought, "Mummy, I wasn't good and I wasn't naughty. I was just comfy." We retain enough sin in our lives to enable us to get along comfortably in the world, and yet at the same time we do enough of the will of God to keep our consciences from giving us too much trouble in the Christian way.

Are you a comfy Christian? The problem of God has to do with the people of God and their sins, all so very different and so very much their own. The businessman's sins will differ from the preacher's; the mother's sins may differ from the daughter's; the sins of age may differ from the sins of youth. But whatever they are, they remain our sins—yours and mine—and they constitute the problem of God. It is this factor in the spiritual situation that we must face up to before God.

A great Christian once said that revival consists in a new obedience to the will of God. How often God has to say to us, His children, what our earthly parents so often said to us. "When will you learn to do as you are told?"

Be a Barnabas

But Barnabas took him . . .

Sunday

Acts 9:27

This is one of the most exciting chapters in the New Testament for here is a *conversion that was undeniable.* The opening verses of this chapter tell the conversion experience of Saul of Tarsus who became Paul the great apostle. How impossible this must have seemed! No doubt the Christians had prayed that this bigoted enemy and bitter foe of the church might be converted, but I really wonder if they believed it would ever happen. How incredible this must have sounded, when word finally came through to Jerusalem, that the persecutor had become the preacher. The news was no doubt received with incredulity. It just could not be true! How many of us have met people like Saul—people whose conversion to faith in Christ seemed equally impossible?

Then there is a *reception that was unforgivable.* Think of the expectation that must have sustained Saul as he escaped from his enemies at Damascus and traveled the long road to Jerusalem. How he would anticipate asking for the forgiveness of the Church, entering into their fellowship, joining with them in their witness to Christ. But when he got there, he experienced a confrontation that must have shattered him. He found that he wasn't welcome, he wasn't believed, and he wasn't wanted. He was to be the first in a long line of people who have tried to join the fellowship of a church only to find that they were not wanted. It would not have been a surprise if Saul had turned on his heel and walked out for good.

But in contrast to the general attitude of the church in Jerusalem there was an *exception that proved invaluable.* "But Barnabas took him . . ." We need more of his kind, friendly people who, with a welcoming hand and warm heart, will draw new converts into the fellowship. How deceptive the appearance of Saul was—apparently nothing much to look at! There was no hint at all that this little short-sighted man would be one of the greatest Christians ever to live for Christ. How decisive the influence of Barnabas was to prove. If Barnabas had not done what no one else apparently thought of doing or was willing to do, there might never have been a Paul. Think of the churches that would never have existed, the writings that would never have been penned. Barnabas did a simple thing that day, but his action saved a Paul from being lost to the church. If you can't be a Paul, why not be a Barnabas, and welcome some "Paul" into the fellowship!

Mixing Religion with Business

Behold, the hire of the labourers who have reaped down your fields

James 5:1-4

Monday

We need to make it absolutely clear that nowhere in the Bible has God anything to say against the possession of wealth. There is nothing necessarily sinful about being wealthy. But the Bible has a great deal to say about the perils and dangers associated with wealth and its accumulation, and the illusions attached to it.

Scholars are divided as to whether James is speaking of Christians or those who are not Christians but it seems that what he has to say applies to both. James is not concerned with how much wealth they have but how they got it. This is, of course, the Christian attitude. Paul said to Timothy, "The love of money is the root of all kinds of evil." Evil can creep into how I get my money as well as what I do with it and how I am attracted by it.

There are three tests James applies to this question of wealth in the form of three charges. The first is the charge of *injustice*. In verse 4 he says, "Behold, the wages of the labourers . . . which you kept back . . . cry out" (RSV). Upon the least excuse, upon some false charge, wages could be and were often withheld. The wage in those days was so small that it was supposed to be paid daily, and to withhold payment even for a day could cause terrible hardship.

The second charge that James brings against wealthy people is that of *indulgence*. In verse 5 he says, "Ye have lived in pleasure on the earth, and been wanton." He is concerned that so often wealth is spent selfishly or foolishly, if not sinfully. Perhaps this lies partly behind the thrust of the words in the opening verses of this fifth chapter when he speaks of riches being corrupted and garments motheaten. Money has been given us to be used. It should neither be spent selfishly nor stored away uselessly.

The third charge James brings is the most severe of all. It is the charge of *inhumanity*. "Ye have condemned and killed the just" (v.6). It suggests a ruthlessness on the part of wealthy people who go to any lengths in order to amass wealth. How ruthless big financial interests can be, how totally indifferent to the well-being of those from whom they extract the money. James says in effect, "If this is true what have you to be proud about? However rich you may be, however big your bank balance, however fine a house you live in, however fine the clothes you wear, what room is there for pride if you have to plead guilty to the charges of injustice, indulgence, and inhumanity?"

Watering the Plant

Like a tree planted by the rivers of water

Tuesday

Psalm 1:3

Have you ever received a beautiful plant as a present and then one day found it drooping and wilting? The plant was all right; it was a living plant but it was drooping from lack of water. So it is with the life of the Christian, the new life received in Christ. It needs to be nourished. That's where the daily habits of prayer and Bible study come in.

The Christian experience is not just an emotional flash in the pan. This explains why so often there are those who, having gone forward in some evangelistic campaign, have failed to grow in Christian character. This does not mean that we need necessarily doubt the reality or the validity of their decision—although that may in some cases be questioned—but rather that they received a new life and then neglected to nourish it. Robert Murray McCheyne said, "What plant is there, if it be not watered will not wither." There may be nothing the matter with a plant that is withering—it may just require water!

The Cause of Self-Pity

I . . . me . . . my

Wednesday

Luke 15:29

These words occur no less than five times in six lines in my Bible. "Thou never gavest *me*." What a restricted vision this young man had! He was someone in whose vision the foreground was filled with the importance of his own self. In a life where self-pity and grievances exist, it is always because of something that has happened to ourselves. But I see also his distorted values. He says, "Thou never gavest me *a kid.*"

I remember hearing Dr. S. D. Gordon say that you can shut out the light of the sun with a very small coin if you hold it close enough to your eyes. How tragically true it is of the little things that assume great proportions when we hold them close enough to our eyes. How easy it is for the soul with a grievance to lose all sense of proportion. We wanted some little thing, and we have not received it. We wanted an apology and because we never got it we opted out of fellowship and lost years of service. Are we complaining because we have not been given a *kid?*

The Chief of Sinners

Christ Jesus came into the world to save sinners; of whom I am chief

1 Timothy 1:15

Thursday

It is worth noting that Paul does not say that he had been the chief of sinners but that he was still the chief of sinners. Two things combined to make Paul think thus of himself. Firstly, there was the *guilt* that he no doubt constantly recalled and could not deny. He is not content with the generality of the word "sinner" but spells out in detail his tragic past. "I formerly blasphemed and persecuted and insulted." So translates the RSV, and the last of these three words is the strongest. There had been an almost sadistic hatred in his attitude to the early Church. His only plea was that it was done in that ignorance of spiritual things which marks every unbeliever. Such guilt was never allowed to hinder Paul, but it was allowed to humble him. He could never be a proud man with memories like these.

But matching that guilt was the *grace* he had received that he could not describe. In verse 14, Paul speaks of this grace as "the grace of our Lord overflowed for me." A man who knew himself to be the worst of sinners, who called himself not only the least of the apostles but also less than the least of all saints, knew also the grace—the unmerited favor, kindness, pity, and saving power of His love.

J. B. Phillips translates verse 14, "He poured out His grace upon me." How does the old chorus go?

> Grace there is my ev'ry debt to pay,
>   Blood to wash my ev'ry sin away,
> Pow'r to keep me spotless day by day,
>   In Christ for me.

How Paul reveled in the grace of God. In Romans 5:20 he wrote, "Where sin abounded, grace did much more abound."

And the Women

These all continued with one accord in prayer and supplication

Acts 1:14

Friday

We might do well to pause and consider what the Church would do today without the faithfulness of godly women. I wonder how many would be at Sunday services and mid-week meetings in our churches if only the men were there! I wonder how many mission stations would be staffed if only men were called as missionaries. I sometimes think we men in the church should be ashamed of ourselves for the way we leave so much of the work to women.

I understand that every Rotarian is obligated to find out where the weekly Rotary lunch is being held in whatever town he is in that day, and he must be present. Men accept a rule like that in the realm of social friendliness and benevolence. Can Christian men not accept a similar kind of discipline, making it their rule to be at the services of the church every week? Deacons, elders, church wardens, lay preachers, Bible class leaders, Sunday school teachers, are we present regularly or do we leave it to the women?

One of the wonderful things about the women in any church is that usually when they are asked to do something they do it extremely well! In some churches, the moment there is anything to be tackled, those in authority say, "Oh, we will ask the Women's Guild to do it." Why do they ask the Guild, or the Mothers' Union, or the Women's Meeting? Because they know it will be done!

The Salt of the Earth

Ye are the salt of the earth

Saturday

Matthew 5:13

With these words Jesus Christ describes the essential character of the Christian. Salt does at least three things. There is first of all the *task it fulfills*—to prevent decay and corruption. Just by being what he is, the Christian exercises a restraining influence upon evil. This influence may find expression politically, personally, socially, morally and spiritually, but such an influence there must be!

There is also the *taste it improves*. We have all experienced having a plate of soup and saying to ourselves, "A little more salt would improve this." The fact that a person is a Christian should improve and enrich his own life, and the lives of those he meets, not impoverish them. Every experience, every relationship of life will be finer, richer, better because a man is a Christian.

Lastly, there is the *thirst it creates*. Salt makes a person thirsty, and to meet a Christian should make other people thirsty for Christ. These are three functions that salt performs. If we are Christians in reality, then we would do well to pause and ask ourselves if these three qualities are found in our lives.

To me to live is Christ

Sunday

Philippians 1:19-26

In these six, one-syllable words the greatest Christian who ever lived sums up what it meant to him to be a Christian. They are words which every Christian ought to be able to say. If one cannot say them, then that person is either not a Christian at all or a very poor specimen of what a Christian should be.

Being a Christian is *personal.* Paul says, "To *me* . . ." Christianity is not just something theological, traditional, ecclesiastical or denominational but personal—and that in two ways. My acceptance of Christ must be personal. I must receive Him for myself into my heart as the Son of God, the Savior of the world and my Savior. My allegiance to Christ must be personal too. When Saul of Tarsus became a Christian he asked this basic question, "Lord, what wilt Thou have me to do?" The Christian does not conform to society or pursue his own designs. The Christian obeys Christ.

Being a Christian is *practical.* Paul says, "To me *to live* . . ." and life goes on for twenty-four hours every day, not for just one hour in church on Sunday. If Christ lives in us, it means that every moment will be spent with Him. Here is an end to loneliness, for the Christian is never alone. It means, too, that every matter will be shared with Him. Here is the call to holiness, for if there is something I cannot share with Him then it must go out of my life. If there is something He wants to share with me then it must come into my life.

Being a Christian is *possible.* Paul says, "To me to live *is Christ.*" Christ is living out His life in me. Such living is available in Christ because Christ is available to each and to all. It is attainable through Christ because He has the resources I lack. When a person becomes a Christian, it is as if a pauper had married a millionaire. Can we say what Paul could say, "To me to live is Christ"?

Despised

Despised and rejected . . .

Monday

Isaiah 53:3

I shall never forget my father telling me of a boy at school with him who was teased unmercifully by the other boys and given the nickname, "Granny." The reason was simple. When the weather turned cold, he always appeared at school more warmly wrapped up than any other boy. When the others tried to get him to dress more normally, as they did themselves, he always refused. When they twitted him and asked him, "Why?" his reply was always the same. "My granny told me."

Whatever we may think of the granny or the wisdom of her way of dressing her grandson, she certainly had in him a loyal and brave heart that faced all the jeers and taunts of his merciless school friends for her sake! Obedience to Christ may bring us into a similar predicament when we find ourselves isolated because of loyalty to Him. May we give Him similar loyalty and obedience who Himself knew what it was to be "despised and rejected of men."

The Necessity of Trial

. . . though now for a season, if need be, ye are in
heaviness through manifold temptations

Tuesday

1 Peter 1:6

Peter speaks of trials as being essential at times in the life of the Christian. How significant the little phrase, "if need be," or as translated in the RSV, "You may have to." Trials are sometimes a must for the Christian. He amplifies this fact with two statements. He reminds those to whom he is writing of the *brevity of trials*. They are "for a little while." How short, compared to the span of life and certainly in relationship to the vastness of eternity, our trials so very often are. Though they may be intense and demanding, compared with the total span of life they usually last a very short time.

Peter also notes the *variety of our trials*. He speaks of "manifold temptations" and the word means "many-colored." Some trials are painted in dark colors, others in bright colors, and which is the more searching it is difficult to tell. Adversity is sometimes less testing than prosperity and many Christians who endured adversity have fallen under the test of prosperity. But adversity is the main thought here. Peter speaks of being "in heaviness," meaning that the Christian may expect from time to time to pass through dark, difficult and distressing experiences.

The twenty-third Psalm may be descriptive of God's dealing with His people throughout the whole of life. The "valley of the shadow of death" is not necessarily or solely the experience of death itself but may rather be a dark valley lying between one pasture and another. In this case we realize that there are times when God leads us deliberately through this valley, through dark hours, in order that the lessons from that kind of experience may be learned.

This is how trials come. They have to come. They do not last very long. They will come very differently, and we must be alert and ready to face them.

How Simple it all Is!

As little children

Wednesday

Matthew 18:3

Many people get confused about becoming Christians because they assume that it must be a most complicated process. God in His mercy and pity has made it essentially simple. If it had been otherwise, then children would not have been able to understand and therefore would have been excluded from the experience.

Christ has likened the step of becoming a Christian to that of welcoming a friend into our home. "Behold I stand at the door and knock: if any man hear My voice and open the door, I will come in." How *simple is the condition*—"If any man hear my voice and open the door." How *sure is the consequence*—"I will come in."

Some people think it is presumptuous for anyone to be sure he is a Christian, but surely it is more presumptuous to doubt the Word of Jesus Christ. We can be quite sure that Christ has entered our hearts and lives if we have asked Him to do so, because He promised He would. If you were to ask me how I know that Christ has come into my life, the answer would be simple. "He said He would." Have you asked Him, and are you sure?

What Love Seeks

A garden inclosed

Thursday

Song of Solomon 4:12

What we seek in a loved one is what a gardener would seek in the garden in which he has spent time and toiled. Love seeks in the life of the believer first of all, *fruitfulness*. Everything conducive to fruitfulness had been provided. There are the protecting walls and the flowing waters of the springs. What is fruitfulness in the spiritual meaning of the word? In the New Testament fruitfulness has either to do with character or with service; either the fruit of a Christlike life or the fruit of other Christians resulting from our life and testimony. What an endless variety of fruit will be found in a garden, and at every season different! In the Christian life there is meant to be a wealth of flower, fruit and fragrance.

Something else that love seeks and finds here is *readiness* for anything and anyone! Verse 16 says, "Awake, O north wind; and come, thou south; blow upon my garden, that the spices thereof may flow out. Let my beloved come into his garden, and eat his pleasant fruits." Here is a readiness for any experience and for any presence. The bridegroom says, "I am come into my garden, my sister, my spouse: I have gathered my myrrh with my spice; I have eaten my honeycomb with my honey; I have drunk my wine with my milk." She replies, "Eat, O friends; drink, yea, drink abundantly, O beloved" (5:1). She is willing for anything and for anyone! There is no need to dress up, no need to make special arrangements, no need to tidy away anything. But there is a readiness, through openness to every experience of life and every contact with other lives. Are we ready to welcome the Lord or other people at any time?

Expect to be Persecuted

All that will live godly in Christ Jesus shall suffer persecution

Friday

2 Timothy 3:12

Paul confirms the words of the Lord in John 15:20 when He said, "If they have persecuted Me, they will also persecute you." Why did people persecute Jesus Christ? Why was the only good life, the only perfect life that has ever been lived found intolerable by the society of His day and snuffed out? Was it not simply because the life of Jesus Christ was a rebuke and a condemnation? He Himself said, "If I had not had come . . . they had not had sin: but now they have no cloak for their sin."

His life was a rebuke, His presence intolerable, and so it is still. It is not so much that the Christian lives a better life than an ungodly person. It is rather that a Christian has accepted a relationship with God, through Christ, of obedience and faith. The ungodly person knows he too should have accepted this relationship but has lacked the courage to do so. This acknowledgment of the rightness of the Christian's position creates resentment in the heart of the ungodly. We have been promised persecution, so let us be ready for it.

Fed Up?

I am come that they might have life

Saturday

John 10:10

The surrender that Christ demands from us is not a harsh thing designed to spoil our lives, but an infinitely loving and wise thing designed to bring us into the happiness we seek but so often fail to find. Have we begun to discover that the world's promise of happiness and thrill turns out to be the same kind of sweet wrapped up in a different color of paper?

Have we begun to feel fed up with life? There seems to be so little that really satisfies, so little really worthwhile doing. Jesus Christ can change all that for us. "I am come that they might have life, and that they might have it more abundantly," was His claim. And He meant it. Hundreds of thousands have proved it true.

There is a quality about the happiness Christ gives that never wears out. Instead, it gets deeper and better as we grow in the Christian life—and still there is ever a beyond!

What Compassion Does

When the Lord saw her He had compassion on her

Sunday

Luke 7:11-17

The Christian Church ought to be a caring community motivated by the compassion that motivated Jesus Christ. In this incident we can find three things about compassion and what it should do.

Compassion should see. "When the Lord saw her He had compassion on her." Compassion sees! Notice the tragedy that was observed by Christ. Compassion is observant. It is sensitive to the existence of trouble, pain, suffering, need. We do well to ask ourselves how observant we are. When Christ saw, His sympathy was aroused. He had compassion. Compassion literally means a suffering with. It is not enough to see, we must also feel. Love sometimes feels the sufferings of those loved more heavily than do the sufferers themselves.

Compassion must speak. "He said unto her, Weep not!" What a gentle intrusion the compassion of Christ made! We often want the initiative in caring service to come from others but it must come from us. For here we see that the initiative in caring service came from Christ. We are not to wait until we are asked. What a gracious intention the compassion of Christ had! That intention was simply to lift the burden, to ease the pain, to meet the need. And so, quietly and graciously, compassion moves into action.

Compassion can save. In verse 14 we read of the response, "They that bare him stood still." The response to Christ's compassion was attention from those He wanted to bless. Attention is precisely what *we* need to get from this desperately needy world. Perhaps the indifference of the world is the result of the indifference of the Church. Note the result that compassion sees—there was a total transformation of a situation that had seemed hopeless. That was what happened when the resources of a compassionate Christ were brought to bear upon it.

The Activity of the Love of God

God so loved the world, that He gave . . .

Monday   John 3:16

How ceaselessly active love is! Indeed it refuses to be idle for when we read in John 3:16, "God so loved the world that He gave . . .," we are getting just a glimpse of the activity that the love of God demanded. How far is that love reflected in our lives and in those of our fellow Christians?

Love is unselfish in the giving of its time, its understanding, its sympathy. And it is unceasing in its willingness to be spent for others and for God. I remember a striking tribute paid to a minister of whom it was recorded, "Whenever we saw him cross the street, we thought of a shepherd in quest of souls." We live in days when the educational methods lay great stress upon the value of visual aid, thus acknowledging the fact that what people see is as helpful to them as what they hear.

We in the Church want people outside the fold only to listen, forgetting that all the time they want to look as well. What do they see of the activity of the love of God in you and me?

Impossible!

The tongue can no man tame

Tuesday   James 3:8

You and I might well say, "All right, that lets me out. I am suffering from an incurable disease. Don't ask me to control what I say when the Bible tells me, 'The tongue can no man tame'." But let us read exactly what the Bible does say. "The tongue can no *man* tame." It does not say that the tongue cannot be tamed. It says that no man can do it—and no man can.

What is the answer to this problem? I think we find it in Matthew 12:34 when our Lord says, "Out of the abundance of the heart the mouth speaketh." What your heart is filled with, your tongue will speak of. If your heart is filled with bitterness, your words will be bitter. If your heart is filled with fear, your words will be fearful. But if your heart is filled with Christ, with His love and with His Spirit, your words will be true and gracious, pure and strong.

What is the answer to the problem of our tongue? Surely the answer to the problem of the lips is the Presence in the heart. That's the answer! The prayer that the Word of God has given to us in Psalm 141:3 must also be our constant prayer. "Set a watch, O Lord, before my mouth; keep the door of my lips."

On Being Left Alone

And Jacob was left alone

Wednesday

Genesis 32:24

Silence fell in the heart and life of Jacob at that moment. The family, the herds, the servants and the herdsmen had all gone on ahead. The noise of their going had died away in the darkness. The far-off glow of a fire could be seen, the distant bleat of a sheep and the bark of a dog could be heard, but that was all. Above Jacob was the blue star-spangled dome of the night sky and around him the vast silence of the sleeping earth.

How difficult it is for God to get us quiet and alone today! The busyness of life, the blare of loud-speakers, the glare of the television screen, the voices of the world, all these fill our every waking moment. But it was in the silence that God came to Jacob that night. God still comes where He can find someone quiet enough to listen, and alone enough to heed. "Be still and know that I am God."

Right with God?

How then can man be justified with God?

Job 25:4

There are four things we can say about this question. It is a *universal* question. Wherever men believe in God and whatever God they believe in, the basic question to which they want the answer is, "How can I, as a man, be living in a right relationship with the God I worship?" You are right to want to know the answer to that question.

But it is a *spiritual* question, that is to say God is involved. "How can man be justified with God?" There are two sides to this question, and to its answer. It is not enough, in fact it is utter folly, for anyone to be content with the answer, "Well, this is the way I look at it." Yet this is the position many adopt. But what about the way God looks at it? This is much more important than the way we may look at it. "How can man be justified with God?" If we rely on the way *we* look at this question, the answer that we think is right may be wrong.

It is also a *personal* question, because every single person is aware of his or her unworthiness in the sight of God. We don't need the Bible to tell us that we have all sinned and come short of the glory of God—we know it already. When David talks about his sin in Psalm 51 he speaks about "*my* transgressions, *mine* iniquity, *my* sin." He prays, "Purge *me*, wash *me*." I know I am a sinner, and therefore I am bothered about this relationship with God.

It is also a *vital* question. The whole problem of living is the problem of relationships—between man and man, employer and employee, husband and wife, parent and child. Man's relationship to his environment is becoming increasingly a problem. But the Bible says there is one vital relationship and that is between man and God. Until that basic relationship is right, no other relationship can ever be right. "How can man be justified with God?" Isn't it about time we sorted out that relationship?

Christ's Intolerance

He condemned sin

Romans 8:3

There is one thing of which Jesus Christ is absolutely intolerant and that is "sin." We read in the New Testament that He "condemned sin." Today's trouble is that so many men want to condone what Jesus Christ condemns. Sin pleases men and also pays them, in terms of hard cash. Obviously, those who have accepted Christ into their hearts and lives as Savior are going to find that their values in life are very different from those of people who have not received Him.

This means that the Christian should be different from others who are not Christians. The wrong that modern man permits in his life, either because it pleases him or because it pays him to do so, cannot be permitted in the life of the Christian if it is condemned by Christ. The Bible says, "A scepter of righteousness is the scepter of Thy kingdom. Thou hast loved righteousness, and hated iniquity."

Witnessing Publicly

Saturday

And Jesus turned and said, Who touched My clothes?
Mark 5:30

The healing that this woman received from Jesus personally had to be revealed publicly. In other words, what Christ does in us and for us is not something to be kept to ourselves, it is something that others are bound to know about. We are to let them know about it, and in so doing all the glory will be given to Jesus Christ.

Luke's account of this incident tells us that this woman "declared unto Him before all the people, for what cause she had touched Him, and how she was healed immediately." The people then went away, not thinking what a wonderful experience this woman had had, or what a wonderful person she was, but what a wonderful person Jesus Christ was.

That should be the goal of our witnessing in public. What we have received personally we must reveal publicly!

The Priority of Prayer

Sunday

Away . . . apart . . . alone
Matthew 14:23

One of the problems most of us have is finding time for prayer. Here one can see the *control* the Master exercised as He handled this problem. The demands of the multitude were endless. There were so many of them, and there was so much to be done. It was so in the life of our Lord and it can be so in our lives. So many things clamor for our attention, all of them urgent, legitimate things, and all of them demanding our time, thought and energy. The danger of the multitude was real, yet to our amazement Jesus Christ sent them away. His work did not control Him; He controlled His work. Much had been done, and much remained to be done, but that made no difference to Christ. He sent them away. We watch Him deliberately dismissing the multitude. Do we need to follow His example here? Maybe we do!

Think of the *criticism* the Master evoked. Surely many asked, "Why did He not go on until my turn had come?" So the tongues would wag, but He let them. One thing was supremely needful in the life of Christ which, if neglected, would undermine His whole usefulness. There was criticism, but ignorance inspired it. The people just did not understand and they still don't! There was here also an indifference that quite ignored it. Christ did not allow Himself to be turned from what He knew to be right, just because of the comments and complaints of people. One great saint used to excuse himself from company that stayed too late in his home with the words, "Excuse me but I have an appointment I must keep now." An appointment with His Lord!

We see, too, the *communion* the Master enjoyed. "When He had sent the multitude away He went up into a mountain apart to pray, and when the evening was come He was there alone." Somehow or other we must get apart and alone with our God. Are these words being read by someone in whose life the time of prayer with God has been squeezed right out? You must be absolutely determined that you will get it in. There must be a primacy given to prayer in your life and a privacy found to enjoy it. There are times we can and must pray when we are with others, but our Lord did tell us to get alone with God behind a closed door.

If you are going to secure that, you too must learn how to send the multitude away. You will be able to handle them all the better when you return from that quiet hour with God.

Have You Been to a Convention?

Come ye yourselves apart into a desert place, and rest a while

Monday

Mark 6:31

It would seem as if in these words our Lord gives his seal to the concept of what we know now as "deeper life" conventions. It has been my privilege to minister at a considerable number of these all over the world and they seem to play a vital and important part in the lives of many Christians. The *purpose* behind such a convention is first of all, to leave behind the multitudinous things that fill our minds, burden our hearts, and cloud our vision from one year's end to the other. For at least a few days we are free to devote ourselves undistractedly to the Lord and bring our lives into the light of God's truth and promises, in order that we might become the kind of Christians God means us to become.

The *pattern* of a convention is usually the same. It lasts for several days, and the location is almost always one of beauty, peace and quiet. Day after day, the Christian brings his life into the light of the Word of God, facing the fact of failure in Christian living and the remedy through his union with Christ. He faces, too, the challenge and costliness of such union in a life of total obedience and surrender to the will of God, conscious of the power that resides in the Person of the Holy Spirit. He is aware that all this must finally be expressed in a deepening concern for the world for which Christ died.

Our Lord seemed to think there is a worthwhile time for coming apart and resting a while. Have you ever been to a convention? There are so many. It is worth thinking about and making time to go.

Trials leading to Development

The testing of your faith produces . . . (RSV)

Tuesday

James 1:3

God has a threefold concern with our lives. He is concerned with *what we believe:* He is concerned with *how we behave:* and He is concerned with *what we become.*

What we are matters to God just as much as what we think or what we do. 1 Peter 1:16 says, "Be ye holy; for I am holy." This is true of parental love in human relationships for parents are con-

64

cerned about the kind of people their children become. It is equally true of divine love in spiritual relationships. James is hinting that whatever kind of Christian I am there is always room for improvement. He is thinking of how productive trials can be because of the resulting development. The RSV translation reads, "The testing of your faith produces steadfastness, and let steadfastness have its full effect, (full play—NEB) that you may be perfect and complete, lacking in nothing."

It is only when we face trial and pressure that progress in certain directions is possible, for when we are under pressure three things will be found in our experience. First, there are certain discoveries that we will make—discoveries about ourselves, our unsuspected weaknesses, our failings. We may be unaware of faults that others see until we are under pressure.

Also there will be a sufficiency that we shall prove—the sufficiency of our Savior to meet every need. We can only prove His sufficiency and faithfulness in situations which demand our trusting His grace to meet that kind of need.

There will be an identity we will have. We shall become more and more easily recognizable as Christians; lacking in nothing, wanting nothing, falling short in nothing. No part of our lives will be deficient in any way. There will be a spiritual and moral completeness about our characters which will be the result of patient endurance under trial.

What do you Know of Thirst?

Blessed are they which do hunger and thirst after righteousness for they shall be filled

Wednesday

Matthew 5:6

Thirst is possibly the most intense form of desire. If a man is thirsty he knows two things. In the first place, he is aware of his condition, that he is thirsty. And secondly, he knows what will satisfy his thirst.

This is true in the spiritual world. First there must be a vision—we must have sensed something of the righteousness in Christ. This knowledge, this vision, will come to us either as we come to know Christ through the Scriptures or as we see Him revealed in the lives of those who know Him. Just as a man in the desert may thirst for a spring of cool water, just as a tired housewife may thirst for a cup of refreshing tea, so the soul of the Christian will thirst for that righteousness which is found in Christ.

There is also the thought of the victory we may share—". . . for they shall be filled." The thirst is there because the satisfaction is available. What Christ offers is not a mirage to mock the soul that longs for holiness, but rather the One whose life we can share and whose victory we can enjoy.

The Testing of our Faith

Then said Jesus unto him, Except ye see signs and wonders, ye will not believe

John 4:48

Thursday

To this desperate man, this man so utterly in earnest, Christ said in effect, "Stop a minute while I check up on this faith of yours. Is it really in Me? Except ye see signs and wonders, ye will not believe." Christ was probing the man's faith. Was it really in Christ alone, or in Christ plus something else?

And Christ would still check up on the quality of our faith in Him. He still queries, "Except ye see signs and wonders ye will not believe?" Except you have an ecstasy of emotion, you will not believe! Unless you have a warmth of feeling, you will not believe! Unless you have some sign and wonder, you will not believe!

Christ would ask us, "Where is your faith?" Is it in Him alone or is it in Him plus some sign or wonder? How often we are in danger of looking to the emotional rather than to the spiritual—we want the crutch of emotion to support us, putting our faith in the crutch rather than in Christ. The spectacular appeals more than the spiritual.

But this man was not interested in signs and wonders. He was interested only in Christ. All he did was restate his need, "Sir, come down ere my child die." And then his faith took the final step. Very simply Christ took him as he was. In three words Christ covered this man's need, telling him to go his way. He said, "Thy son liveth." And we read that "the man believed the word that Jesus spake unto him, and he went his way." The man's faith came finally to rest quietly on the word of Jesus Christ. What better place can faith find than that?

Being Born Again

Being born again, not of corruptible seed, but of incorruptible by the word of God, which liveth and abideth for ever

Friday

1 Peter 1:23

Peter writes here of being born again and the place that God's Word has in that conversion experience. Many of us will recall some word of scripture that has been the contact point between the truth of God, the grace of God, and our need—a word that has been trusted, believed and received. It has been indeed a living word to us and in us, and it abides for ever.

Sometimes the Word of God can linger for a long time in our minds before it suddenly comes to life. Years ago, a railway cutting was driven through an area of ground and when summer came that newly made cutting was marked clearly by a vivid splash of scarlet. Thousands of poppy seeds that had been buried for long enough were now exposed to the warmth of the sunshine and the moisture of the rain, and had grown and flowered. So some verses of scripture, heard, learned, almost forgotten, suddenly become the agent to bring to us new life, new grace, new help.

All this is important for us to remember because we live in a day when the preaching of the Word of God is discounted by so many. But the preaching of the Word is like sowing an incorruptible seed. Recently in a series of rallies, testimonies were given by two young ministers who had been converted in my church. Both recalled the occasion of their conversion and both commented that they could not remember a single word of the sermon. But the one thing that had remained was the scripture text which proved to be the very word of God that brought them to new life in Christ. The Word of God is indeed a seed incorruptible "which liveth and abideth for ever."

Are There Back Moves in Life?

I will restore to you the years that the locust hath eaten

Saturday

Joel 2:25

This verse suggests that there *are* back moves in life. The picture that the prophet painted is that of a land left devastated by the advent of a locust horde, as devastated as a life can be after the advent of sin and failure. Then comes the promise: "I will restore to you the years that the locust hath eaten."

67

There are two ways in which God can bring full compensation into a life that has lost so much for so long. First, He can do so by the *profusion of the harvest*. After all, it does not really matter so much how *long* we live, as *how* we live. How many lives have done so much more in the space of a few short years than others which have been lived over a long span of time! God is not governed by our mathematical system! God can do a great deal in a short time.

But there is another way in which God can "restore the lost years." That is by the *perfection of the fruit*. We have all seen fruit that is plentiful but blemished. Through the experiences of failure, God can bring a quality into our lives that might not have been easily achieved any other way. The wilderness can become a garden again.

Illness

Sick, and ye visited me

Sunday   Matthew 25:36

It is a striking truth that there are more people in our hospitals on any Sunday than in our churches. This suggests that our hospitals provide a unique opportunity for evangelism. As we think of this let us remember three things.

Think of the *opportunity that sickness gives.* When we think of hospitals and medical care we find all the world involved. A staggering fact about hospitals is that practically everybody—sooner or later—is found in one of them. If we want to get in touch with people in the name of Christ, contact can be made in our hospitals. Not only do we find all the world here but we have all the time here. The Bible tells us, "Be still, and know that I am God." But stillness, quietness, time and thought are things that most of us seldom experience until we land up in hospital. Then we find that everything is changed and we have ample time to think.

Consider also of the *responsibility that sickness brings.* If it is true that all the world is here and that people have all the time here, then what of the Christian attitude to these people? We can take careful note of how closely related some Christians are to those in the hospital. We know Christian relatives will visit and the minister and chaplain will call, but think of the staff—doctors, surgeons, nurses, orderlies, and other patients. If they are Christians, how alert they ought to be to the responsibility they bear to bring Christ before those who are ill. In a close relationship, Christ ought to be supremely presented in the lives lived. I heard about a Christian nurse who came on duty to be met by a patient's comment, "I am so glad it is you!" Are people who are sick glad to see us because of our kindness, concern, care, and understanding?

The third thought that comes to mind is the *urgency that sickness holds.* There is always a note of urgency about the Gospel. We are told, "Now is the accepted time," and that God's Spirit "shall not always strive." The opportunity in hospitals is always limited. Usually patients don't stay long—they get better and go home. They may be there one week, two weeks, or three weeks, and then they leave. Or if they don't get better, they die. How urgent then the matter becomes! A limited opportunity—and sometimes a lost opportunity. Many of these people are never in church and if the Christian does not make contact while they are in the hospital, they may never have any contact again. What a tremendous call, what a tremendous thrill there is in this area of Christian witness and opportunity!

A King on a Cross

Lord, remember me when Thou comest into Thy kingdom

Monday   Luke 23:42

The dying thief could see and would worship this King marching to His throne. In minutes the centurion, the officer in command of the soldiers, is on his knees, "When the centurion, and they that were with him, . . . saw those things that were done, they feared greatly, saying, truly this was the Son of God." In just a few hours, in the glory of resurrection, Mary would be at His feet naming Him, "Rabboni . . . Master." And then Thomas with his cry of faith, "My Lord and my God." This trickle was to become a flood, and so on earth the exaltation of Christ as King, Lord, and Sovereign began.

What happened on earth is but a reflection of what has already happened in heaven, where "Christ humbled Himself and became obedient unto death, even the death of the cross. Wherefore God also hath highly exalted Him and given Him a name which is above every name, that at the name of Jesus every knee shall bow . . . and that every tongue should confess that Jesus Christ is Lord, to the glory of God the Father."

One of the choicest incidents surrounding the life of the present Queen came in her very early days. Her father, King George VI, died suddenly and tragically when she was in Africa. She seemed then just a slip of a girl but she came back to take up the crown that her father, in death, had laid down. Still living at that time was her grandmother, Queen Mary, one of the most regal and splendid figures that have graced the British royal family. Queen Mary wrote a letter to the young Queen Elizabeth, who had to bear the weight of the crown so early. The letter was full of love and sympathy, but it is not the contents of the letter that seem so important, but rather the way the letter ended. Queen Mary signed the letter to her granddaughter, "Your loving grandmother and devoted subject."

I offer you not an earthly queen; I offer you one who was robed in purple, who wore a crown of thorns and was presented to His people as "Your King." And I want to ask you, "Have you made Him such in your life?"

Lives Blended in Love

Come, my beloved, let us go forth into the field
Song of Solomon 7:11

Tuesday

One of the great words used to describe Christian love and Christian marriage is the word "together." In 1 Peter 3:7, we find the phrase "heirs together." Two lives have become blended together into one so that the concern of each becomes the concern of both. In our verse the blend is so complete that the bride does not speak in the singular any more but in the plural—"let us."

The lovely thing is that she is no longer to be found waiting passively to be summoned or persuaded by her beloved to come and be with him, as in chapter 5. Now she takes the initiative and makes the point that it is then and there that she will be able to demonstrate and express her love. "There will I give thee my loves" (verse 12). Then there will be not only a sharing of love but a showing of love.

Moffat translates the phrase, "Then will I give thee the caresses of love," the caressing touch of the hand or the lips. But just as often, indeed maybe more often, there is the caressing look, the tender glance, in which eyes meet. And in that moment of meeting the message of understanding, of glad recognition, passes between heart and heart, mind and mind. Love is sharing in the purposes of her beloved.

Well Done!

His Lord said unto him, Well done, good and faithful
servant; thou hast been faithful over a few things, I will
make thee ruler over many things: enter thou into the
joy of thy lord

Wednesday

Matthew 25:23

My father was a great cricketer. Often he would recall his cricketing days as captain of the school eleven, and then captain of the
university eleven. He used to say that what really thrilled him
about his cricketing career was not when he had scored another
century and ran in to the pavilion amid the applause of the specta-
tors. Nor was it when he had taken another wicket. But it was
when he went after the match was over to tell his old father how he
had played and heard his, "Well done."

The verdict that crowns the expectancy of the Christian will be
when we get to our heavenly Home and hear our Father say, "Well
done."

Paul had that forward look of expectancy about reaching the
final verdict, the prize-giving day, a look that brought heaven into
view. Paul, of course, realized that although he might go there to
receive the prize, it might also be that the Master would come here
to this earth. So his expectancy was quickened by the thought of
the possible return of Christ. He includes in his letter to Philippi
that from heaven itself one day will come the Savior for whom we
look. The prize-giving day is not far off: that day may come any
time. The coming of the Lord draweth near. May we stand before
the Lamb, when earth and seas are fled, and hear the Judge pronounce our name with blessings on our head.

Reverencing Christ as Lord

Sanctify the Lord God in your hearts

Thursday

1 Peter 3:15

"In your hearts reverence Christ as Lord" is another translation.
We are to reverence Him as Lord not simply with our lips, nor even
now and then in our lives, but constantly in our hearts. There is
therefore a throne room in your heart and mine.

What a delightful man Dr. S. D. Gordon, the well-known author, was! His books were all entitled *Quiet Talks* and when he
spoke, it was usually in a whisper. On one occasion at Keswick he
said, "In every heart there is a throne and a cross; if self is on the

throne, Christ is on the cross; if Christ is on the throne, self is on the cross."

We think of Christ, and rightly so, as exalted in heaven. But the throne He occupies in heaven is surely symbolical of the throne He is to occupy on earth in the hearts of men. We love singing that tremendous hymn, "At the name of Jesus every knee shall bow," but remember, won't you, that there is a verse that goes, "In your hearts enthrone Him"? That is the room in which His throne must stand. "In your hearts reverence Christ as Lord." Is He enthroned there in your heart?

Gethsemane

. . . A place called Gethsemane . . .

Friday   Matthew 26:36

Somehow I think it was quiet in the garden of Gethsemane when the Master went there to face the destiny that awaited Him. How wrong we are to think that spiritual crises must be marked by noise and excitement; that the place of surrender must resound to the crack of the whip as the preacher flogs the people of God. At the hour of the greatest spiritual crisis of all time, it was to a place of quietness that He came.

Then the Son of God, the Son of Man went that little bit further into the stillness of the garden until He came to the place of surrender. It was a place where the sound of a falling leaf might have been heard, or even the sob of a breaking heart. He was alone!

Have you ever come to that place where every other voice has died away into silence so that you may hear the One voice, and make the one choice—"Not My will, but Thine be done"?

The Peace of Surrender

. . . nevertheless not My will, but Thine, be done

Saturday   Luke 22:42

The coming of peace between nations means the cessation of war. The nature of the struggle in the garden of Gethsemane has depths in it which are beyond our understanding. But a desperate struggle took place there to make the Son of God sweat in an agony of prayer like that! But then, with an obedience that was unquestioning and unreserved, the battle stopped and the prayer ceased with the words, "Not My will, but Thine, be done."

Is peace absent from our hearts and lives because the battle is still on? Perhaps it has been going on for weeks, for days, or for years—for far too long! All the time the struggle has continued there has been no peace. Would it not be wonderful if the battle stopped today and we entered into the peace of surrender! It would be so simple, even though so costly, to say what Jesus said in the garden of Gethsemane, "Not My will, but Thine, be done." Will we say it, and say it now? Then we will know the peace that comes through surrender.

Bringing Loveliness into Living

. . .

He will beautify the meek with salvation
Psalm 149:4

Sunday

Here first of all we have the *divine intention*—"He will beautify . . ."

How arrestingly different is this scripture from the absurd statement by the poet Swinburne who speaks of Christ blasphemously as, "O pale Galilean; the world has grown grey from Thy breath." What utter nonsense! Think over this fact—there is a love of beauty that man shares with God. We find beauty everywhere and we want it for ourselves and for those we love. But there is also a loss of beauty that man sees in life. We see it vanishing from the countryside, from the face of a child, from the life of a home.

There is the *divine provision*—"He will beautify the meek *with salvation.*"

God wants to bring back the loveliness into living that has been destroyed by sin, and He does this by what the Bible calls salvation—His saving, healing, transforming activity. Salvation is presented to us in the Bible in two ways; first as a Person, who is of course Jesus Christ. He is to be received as God's love gift to man, given for us on the Cross, given to us through His Spirit.

Salvation is also presented to us as a process. Christ, having been received, must then be released to do what He wills with His own. That may take time, just as the new occupants of a house may take time to transform it into what they want it to be.

There is finally the *divine condition*—"He will beautify *the meek* with salvation."

The only thing that keeps anyone from enjoying all that God in His love is waiting and willing and able to do, is pride. We must be among the meek, the humble. That means two things. We must be humble enough to admit our need, and humble enough to accept God's gift. We are told in the Bible that, "God resisteth the proud but giveth grace to the humble." Is it not strange that man should ever dream of being proud in the presence of God—too proud to accept the gift of Christ who can and will bring back loveliness into living, if we are willing to let Him?

Justified by Grace

Justified freely by His grace

Romans 3:24

Monday

What does this word "grace" tell me? It tells me something about the attitude of my God. It is a *corrective* word and I believe it touches on the basic blunder all of us tend to make. When we try to solve the problem of getting right with God we don't begin with God, we begin with ourselves. We say, "Well, I go to church. I try to live a decent life. I believe I am as good as other people." But if we begin with ourselves, we are beginning at the wrong end. We have to begin with God and His grace to get the Christian answer.

The first step to solving the problem of being right with God is not the discovery of something in ourselves that can constitute a claim on God's favor. It is something in the heart of God that makes a claim on our devotion. If we are going to be justified with God at all, we will be justified by His grace. We must begin with what has been described as "the free unmerited favor of God."

But this word "grace" is not only a corrective word; it is a *destructive* word, because it shatters and destroys our pride and conceit. The Bible says, "There is no difference: for all have sinned, and come short of the glory of God." There is absolutely nothing in us that can constitute any claim whatsoever on God, apart from our need. If we are brought into a right relationship with God it will be because of God's grace—His free unmerited favor—and that's a word that takes a terrific weight off our shoulders. Grace— what a wonderful word that is! The answer to our need begins in the heart of God and reaches right down to each one of us in our sin.

Justified by His Blood

God commendeth His love toward us, in that, while we
were yet sinners, Christ died for us. Much more then,
being now justified by His blood, we shall be saved
from wrath through Him

Tuesday

Romans 5:8, 9

What does this word "blood" mean? It speaks to me of the death of
Christ, and tells me there is nothing I can do about getting myself
right with God. The work has been finished! When we consider the
death of Christ on the cross we find two elements stressed in the
scriptures.

The first is the element of *necessity*. Our Lord said, "As Moses
lifted up the serpent in the wilderness, even so *must* the Son of man
be lifted up: that whosoever believeth in Him should not perish,
but have everlasting life" (John 3:14). Just as Moses had to lift up
the serpent in the wilderness, even so the Son of Man had to be
lifted up on the cross. There is something about the nature of sin
and about the nature of God that required a plan to deal with man's
sin. And the cross tells me that it has been done. The cross does not
imply that God has overlooked sin. It is not that God has said, as it
were, "We will just forget about it," but that God has met the demands of His own law concerning sin, in His own person. Forgiveness is ours at the price of the infinite worth of the Son of God.

We see also the element of *sufficiency*. There is nothing more to
be done. Listen to what the Bible says, "This Man after He had
offered one sacrifice for sins forever, sat down at the right hand of
God." One sacrifice—for sins—for ever! We can't do anything
about that, and God doesn't expect us to. It has all been done. One
of the most tremendous words ever spoken was the word spoken
by our Lord on the cross. After darkness had covered the face of
the earth for those three hours, there suddenly came from His lips
and from His heart that tremendous cry, "It is finished." Finished!

Are you prepared to accept the fact that Christ has atoned for sin
and that God isn't expecting you to do it? Or are you going to insist
still that *you* have to do something? Don't be foolish and try to do
something that has already been done!

75

Justified by Faith

Therefore being justified by faith, we have peace with God through our Lord Jesus Christ

Wednesday

Romans 5:1

Some people find faith elusive, intangible. They wonder why God says that if we are going to be justified at all, it will be by faith. Two thoughts always come to my mind when I think of this word "faith". First, I am reminded of the integrity of personality that God knows He must respect. The solution to the problem of my justification had to respect fully not only the character of God in His holiness but also the personality of man in his moral responsibility. God, having made forgiveness possible through the death of Christ, had also to make it moral.

Justification is not something to be thrust on man whether he wants it or not. Therefore, it had to be made conditional on man's consent. At the same time the condition had to be simple enough to include all and exclude none and to convey no trace of merit to the one fulfilling it. So God puts in this very simple link. If we are going to be justified, it must be by faith. God didn't make the condition on the grounds of moral achievement—that would exclude the weak. He didn't make it on the grounds of material wealth—that would exclude the poor. He didn't make it on the level of intellectual wisdom—that would exclude the simple. He made it on the grounds of simple faith.

The great Dr. Chalmers said, "Faith is like the hand of the beggar that takes the gift while adding nothing to it." And your faith and mine doesn't do anything except appropriate what God offers. Anyone can trust—it is about the only thing that anyone can do. But God says that is what we must do. It is simple, but it is absolutely essential.

The Security Love Enjoys

Leaning upon her beloved

Thursday

Song of Solomon 8:5

We have here the final picture of the bride coming up from the wilderness, leaning upon her beloved. They are walking arm in arm and she is leaning on him. Yet even as she appears thus she is aware of the waywardness of her heart. This relationship has existed before and has been lost before. But the bride has, first of all, the *word on which assurance must rest.* In verse 6 she says, "Set me as a seal upon thine heart, as a seal upon thine arm." Behind this prayer lies an awareness of the need for her beloved. Apart from him, she could do nothing and be nothing. But her need is immediately met by his word of assurance, "Many waters cannot quench love" (verse 7). With that assurance of his unchanging love she rests her heart in peace.

We also see the *effect that assurance will have.* With peace in her heart she can turn and look out on the world and the work awaiting her. She speaks immediately of the need of another, and to this the bridegroom replies that together they will minister to that need. That particular task is then set against the background of the wider work done by so many others in the employment of the bridegroom. This is work of which an account must one day be given— they are workers to whom one day the summons will come. That summons will come even to her and for this she gladly waits. Hasten the day when she hears the summons, "Make haste, my beloved" (verse 14). And so this book ends, as the whole Bible ends, with a prayer of expectation that one day our Lord will come for His own. "Even so, come, Lord Jesus."

Seeking the Unmerited

Friday

Ye love the uppermost seats in the synagogues . . .

Luke 11:43

Our Lord's words imply that the Pharisees were not fit to occupy such seats. There is such a thing as wrongful ambition within the realm of Christian experience. There are men and women who are eager for advancement with their denomination or local church fellowship. They covet positions of prominence and power. They like to be leaders. They are not content to serve; they must command. They must be obeyed. Their ideas are the ideas that everyone else must accept. The rest must dance to the tune they pipe. The convenience of others must give way to their convenience. What these people forget is that there is always a spiritual price for spiritual power.

This sin of ambition shows itself unexpectedly sometimes when we are denied something and our reaction is one of hurt or offense. We go into the sulks or resign altogether from some committee. Oh, the sin of seeking positions of prominence for which we are not spiritually qualified! Are we like the Pharisees in this matter?

The Most Important Question in the World

What shall I do then with Jesus which is called Christ?

Matthew 27:22

He was a clergyman of the Church of England and we met in a Belfast restaurant. I was interested to see that on the lapel of his jacket he was wearing a badge. I had never seen one like it before and I have not seen one since. It was in the shape of a silver question mark. I asked him what the badge meant and he said it stood for, "the most important question in the world." "What is that?" I asked him.

Among the scores of questions that clamor for an answer in our minds, questions about life, about the Bible, about the Church, about society, about death, could there be one question that stood out above all others as the most important question in the world? I believe there is such a question, and so did my clergyman friend. It was first put by a Roman governor nearly two thousand years ago and it is this: "What shall I do then with Jesus which is called Christ?"

Have you answered that question yet? If not, is it not time that you did? It is the most important question in the world. It not only affects this life but also the life that is to come.

A Place Jacob would never Forget

He called the name of the place Bethel

Genesis 28:19

In the tradition of praise found in Scotland the second paraphrase has a very special place in the affection of the people of that country, and has also found its way into the praise of the Christian Church all over the world. It begins by addressing God in these words,

> O God of Bethel! by whose hand
> thy people still are fed;
> Who through this weary pilgrimage
> hast all our Fathers led.

What kind of a place was Bethel?

It was the place of a *vision*. We can read the story of Jacob's first night away from home as he fled from Esau's hatred. That night I am sure he had a twofold vision. It was a vision of his life, of the kind of person he had shown himself to be. The picture was not a pretty one; he was a liar and a deceiver. But it was supremely a vision of his Lord that came to him at Bethel. He saw that in spite of his sin His God had not rejected him. God still had a purpose for his life, and God was still in touch with him.

Bethel was also the place of a *voice*. It was the place where God spoke to him. And God still speaks to men. All of us have surely had that experience. Not that we necessarily hear a voice using words, but God does not need words to get the message through to us. The voice at Jacob's Bethel spoke of a presence, "Behold, I am with thee."

The voice spoke also of a purpose, "I will not leave thee, until I have done that which I have spoken to thee of." The voice spoke of the land that would be his, of the world that would be blessed through him. What a tremendous message for Jacob to get in an hour when he must have been ashamed of his past and afraid of what the future might hold. Have we known such moments? If so, what a wonderful thing to find that God can come to us with a similar message, and tell us that in spite of our sinfulness there is hope!

Bethel was the place of a *vow*. The writer of the second paraphrase does not omit this aspect of the Bethel experience. The second verse takes it up,

> Our vows, our prayers, we now present
> Before thy throne of grace;
> God of our Fathers! be the God
> Of their succeeding race.

What was the reason for Jacob's vow? Surely a realization of his own need. The terms of the vow do not reflect much credit on Jacob, but God was ready to accept the terms. And the vow reached its climax with the words, "If . . . then shall the Lord be my God." How like the vows we have made! The challenge that comes to us when we think of the Bethel experiences we have known is this—have we kept the vow we have made to God?

Abstain

Abstain from fleshly lusts, which war against the soul

1 Peter 2:11

The Christian must learn to abstain from certain things which might damage his spiritual health. Often people hold it as a criticism of the Christian way, almost nourishing a grudge against Jesus Christ, that they are asked to do without certain things. But a moment's thought will show us that this is a principle not confined to the Christian life, and that we cannot excel in anything without denying ourselves a great deal.

Those who would excel in art, medicine, sport or any profession, quickly discover that it means denying themselves much that others will be able to do. The Christian is in this sense no different from anybody else. He may strive for different objectives and the things from which he will abstain may be different, but he shares the principle of denial with anybody who wishes to excel in any area of life.

The Place of Love

At Jesus' feet

Luke 10:39

Love always wants to be near the one loved. Love is never content to remain at a distance. In the life story of Amy Carmichael of Dohnavur, we read of a charming incident when one day Miss Carmichael looked up to see a child standing near her. She stretched out a welcoming hand which the child took saying to her, "I have come." Miss Carmichael asked, "For what?" thinking the child might have some trouble she was bringing to her. But the reply was not the expected one. "Just to love you!" said the child. Is it not true that love always wants to be near the one loved, and to linger there?

I remember hearing Rev. G. R. Harding Wood recount the following incident. A child and her mother went into a church to pray. The child went to the children's corner to say her prayers, while the mother knelt in the church. The mother's prayers were ended, but her daughter's were not. At last her little girl came to her and her mother commented, "You were a long time saying your prayers. What were you doing?" Her daughter replied, "Well, Mummy, I just knelt down and said, 'Dear Jesus,' and He said, 'Dear Barbara,' and then we just loved one another."

Mary was content to be near her Lord. Here is a test we can apply to our professed love for Christ. Are we found at His feet? Is this the place we love? It was the place that Mary loved.

A Worthy Walk

That ye might walk worthy of the Lord

Colossians 1:10

Wednesday

Worthy of all that He is, worthy of all that He has given. If we call Christ our Lord, does our way of life illustrate and vindicate that name adequately and worthily? Does it commend Christ? If we call Him Lord, do others see that He is, indeed, Lord of our lives? If He was full of grace as well as truth, do our lives reveal these two qualities? So many Christians are full of truth but destitute of grace. If He, as God, is both love and light, do our lives reflect both love and light? Do we live in a manner befitting those in whose hearts Christ dwells by His Spirit?

Paul's prayer is that the walk with God of these Colossian Christians might be worthy of Him; that others looking at them might see Christ portrayed in lives possessed by Him.

A little girl was busy drawing one Sunday afternoon and when her mother asked her what she was drawing she replied, "I am drawing God." To which the mother said, "You can't draw God because you have never seen Him and nobody knows what He looks like." The little girl replied, "But they will when I have finished drawing Him." What picture of Jesus Christ do other people see as they look at us?

One–Talent Failure

Then he which had received the one talent came and said . . .

Matthew 25:24-26

Thursday

It is worth noting that in this tremendous parable the realm of failure selected by Christ was that of the one–talent man. When the parable opens we read of those who received five talents, two talents, and one talent. We might have expected Christ to deal with the failures of those who had the greatest opportunities and the greatest responsibilities—those who had received five talents.

But no, the emphasis of the story lies on the one-talent man. Therefore, the parable speaks particularly to those of us whose opportunities seem limited and whose responsibilities seem small. How searching this is because at once it brings so many of us within the range of its truth. If I were speaking to you about the great opportunities a man can miss, many of you might relax and say, "Well, this is not for me. I have none of these opportunities, for my opportunities, like my gifts, are very few." But this parable centers around those whose opportunities, like their gifts, are few. And that brings most of us within its range.

How searching the parable is and how serious; serious because there are so many of us. Failure among the one-talent people, when added together, can mean failure on a very big scale!

 ## What shall We do?

Pilate saith unto them, What shall I do then with Jesus which is called Christ?

Matthew 27:22

Friday

Pilate was a man who was afraid to do the right thing by Jesus Christ in the way so many other people are afraid. We can note three facets of this fear. First, there was the *fact of the Person he faced.* This was an encounter Pilate knew he could not avoid; sooner or later he had to be brought face to face with Christ, and that hour had come. There was also an evasion that Pilate found he could not achieve. He tried desperately to hand over the issue to others—to Herod, to anybody—rather than make the decision himself. But Christ was brought back. He could not escape Him.

Secondly, there was his *fear of the people he knew.* Their motives were bad. He knew that hate, envy, and fear had driven them to bring Christ to him to have Him executed, and the meaning of their words was crystal clear to him! They threatened to cause trouble if he didn't do what they wished. This is often the position in which we find ourselves. The motives of those who hate Christ are not worthy ones, and the meaning of their words is quite plain to us—they are going to make it rough if we don't toe the line.

Thirdly, we see the *farce of the protest he made.* Some action was inevitable: he had either to say yes or no, and finally he said "yes" to the crowd's demands. This action was inexcusable. Pilate had to do something and what he did was tragically wrong.

Behold, Your King!

Then came Jesus forth, wearing the crown of thorns,
and the purple robe . . . And Pilate saith unto the Jews,
Behold your king!

Saturday

John 19:5, 14

If contempt and cynicism tinged the color of his words, was there not also the uncanny and uneasy feeling that what he was saying was the sober truth. Christ was being presented in mockery as king. But what happened at that moment was merely bringing into sharp and clear focus a fact that had been becoming apparent ever since His birth at Bethlehem.

I find in the record of the life of our Lord a sovereignty that men felt whenever they met Him. When the wise men came at His birth they found the answer to their question, "Where is He that is born King?" to be but a babe in Bethlehem. Yet we read that "when they were come into the house, they saw the young child with Mary His mother, and fell down and worshiped Him." Thus it was at the beginning of His life and thus it was at the end.

On the cross itself the penitent thief turned to the dying Son of God with the prayer, "Lord, remember me when Thou comest into Thy kingdom." At the hour when the hatred of man had done its worst, when even the disciples had forsaken Him and fled, the dying thief suddenly saw that this Christ was no criminal going to His doom but a king marching to His throne. In Bethlehem, at Calvary, and in between, the sovereignty of Christ seemed to break through the disguise of His humanity and men felt it.

Illustration

That which we have seen

Sunday

1 John 1:1

All communication has a visible aspect and John writes about the impression left on him by the Lord's ministry. He not only heard a message: he saw a Man. So often we want people to listen and they want to look as well. We are living in a day when visual aids are regarded as essential and when the most powerful factor in shaping the minds of people is television. It is powerful because it appeals not only to the ear but also to the eye.

What did John see in Jesus Christ? I think he saw first, the *activity of the love of Christ.* We glory in John 3:16, "God so loved the world, that He gave," but we seldom live that out or demonstrate it. The love and concern of God were seen in the ministry and miracles of our Lord, and that concern covered the whole man.

Some evangelicals have distorted the message and tried to make out that the Gospel is simply concerned with the souls of men, but this is not what the Bible says. 1 Thessalonians 5:23 tells us, "I pray God your whole spirit and soul and body be preserved blameless." Our Lord said that even "the very hairs of your head are all numbered" (Matthew 10:30). Is this one reason why communism makes an appeal to so many of the backward nations? Communism at least professes a concern for the well-being of the whole man.

But John saw not only the activity of the love of Christ; he saw the *adequacy of the power of Christ.* Then, as now, Christ came face to face with problems that baffled the minds of men. He faced a vast arena of human needs, but He brought to bear upon that need a power that healed the hurts of men. We know that neither humanism nor materialism can solve the basic needs of men: they need salvation in Christ, they need power and resources greater than their own. Can that power be seen in our lives? We claim that we are saved, but what have we been saved from?

The third thing that John saw that brought him through faith into fellowship was the *agony and the passion of Christ.* This John would never forget; the very cross itself. How Christ suffered there! John realized that complete identification with the needs of men means identification with man's sin. On the cross Christ was bearing the burden in that great redemptive act of divine love.

How far have we accepted the price of a similar identification? Are we getting under the burden, not simply of the material or social needs of men, but of their spiritual needs? How far are we really under the burden of the sin of the world, not in that uniquely redemptive sense in which Christ bore that burden, but in identification with the will of God in Christ? That means that we too will have to suffer, and that our lives will not be self-centered but characterized by a deep concern for others.

Visual Aids

We beheld His glory

Monday

John 1:14

Today we hear a great deal about visual aids in education and the Church itself is turning to them more and more. We have films and filmstrips, flannelgraphs and object talks. This is but a recognition of the vital importance of illustration in the work of teaching. This concept also comes with a note of tremendous challenge to all Christians. Do we illustrate in our lives the message we proclaim? Do we illustrate the Gospel or do we caricature it? Have you ever come across the saying, "If every Christian was the same as me, what sort of church would my church be?" Well, what sort of church would it be? There ought to be a clear illustration in the life of every Christian of the Christian Gospel.

John 1:14 is one of the most remarkable verses in the New Testament. We read, "The Word was made flesh, and dwelt among us, (and we beheld His glory, the glory as of the only begotten of the Father,) full of grace and truth." How closely John had lived to His Lord, and for how long—yet in the closeness of that intimacy never once did he discern a flaw in the character of his Lord. At the end of those years of close fellowship his testimony was, "We beheld His glory."

Made More Useful

. . . the God of all comfort; Who comforteth us in all our tribulation, that we may be able to comfort them which are in any trouble, by the comfort wherewith we ourselves are comforted by God

Tuesday   2 Corinthians 1:3, 4

We read here of a discovery Paul has made about God—He is the God of all comfort. As Paul thought of all the trouble he had been through he realized that there was value emerging from it. Having suffered, he would be able to help others who were suffering. He would now have a new sympathy with those in trouble, and there would be a new testimony that he could bear. Having experienced God's sustaining grace, he could with confidence tell others that they, too, would experience God's sustaining grace.

This brought a greater usefulness, unquestionably, to Paul's ministry. He was conscious of the fact that there was a purpose to be served which lay beyond himself and his sufferings. They would enable him to touch and bless other lives.

Professor William Barclay quotes Barrie as saying about his own mother who lost her favorite son, "That is where my mother got her soft eyes and why mothers come to her when they have lost a child." What a difference it makes when we can say, "I have been there. I know what you are going through, and I know just how God's grace sustains." So Paul could see a positive gain in his ministry through his sufferings.

Perhaps through our troubles we will find as Paul did, a greater usefulness in God's service.

Why?

Why then is all this befallen us?

Judges 6:13

For seven long years the forces of Midian had impoverished the people of God. These alien forces, unchallenged and undisputed, had gone up and down the land to destroy and rob. They were like a locust horde. The story of their undisputed supremacy and greed is told in the opening verses of this chapter. The children of Israel had retreated into the dens and caves of the mountains. When Gideon is introduced to us here, he is a frightened man threshing his wheat by the winepress to hide it from the Midianites. But all the time he was asking, "Why has this befallen us? We are God's chosen people: it isn't right. Our destiny is not that we should be impoverished and enslaved by the oppressors."

Is this not something that moves our hearts as we look around? Is this really the way God meant things to be? The forces of evil seem quite unchallenged while we hide away in our little groups. In the heart of Gideon was a voice that would not be silenced, asking, "Why?—Why?" He was a man with a deep concern. Does it concern you that your church is as it is? Does it trouble you? Is an empty church to the glory of God? When you see folk pouring out of the Bingo Hall and a trickle coming out of the church, does it bother you? Are you concerned that this is all the following that the Lord of glory has?

Rev. John Stott, in one of his books on evangelism, lists among the motives for evangelism a concern for the glory of God. This was Gideon's concern. Is it ours?

Hungry for Souls

I have meat to eat that ye know not of . . . My meat is to do the will of Him that sent Me, and to finish His work

John 4:32, 34

Here Christ was saying in effect, "As you hunger for food, so I hunger for the spiritual well-being of men, for the fulfillment of the redemptive purpose and will of my Father." The setting is the meeting of the Master with a woman whose whole life was in a tangle. Reading the whole story through, we can sense two things.

In the first place, there is the *stimulus of need.* As Christ sensed the need of the woman, so He longed to satisfy it. Are we as sensitive to the spiritual need of others as the Master was? Do we long to see that need met? Or are we like the disciples, preoccupied with other things, however legitimate? Are we blinded by prejudice? "The Jews have no dealings with the Samaritans."

We see also the *satisfaction of success,* of service. The woman had gone, to return later with the whole city. The disciples had returned thinking they would find a hungry man, but He was hungry no longer. Satisfaction at a deeper level had filled Him with content. Are we "hungry for souls"?

The Communion Love Would Have

Let me see thy countenance, let me hear thy voice; for sweet is thy voice, and thy countenance (or face) is comely

Friday   Song of Solomon 2:14

You can be a companion to someone without having communion with them. But God wants communion too—not someone simply to share the work but someone to share His thoughts, His desires, His caring, and the hurting that may come to Him as well as the joys and the gladness.

It is this identity of heart and mind leading to communion and sharing that love seeks and desires. It would seem as if, in the very creation of man, this is what God wanted from man. Sin intervened and that fellowship was broken, but in salvation that fellowship is meant to be restored. Salvation, then, is not simply lifting away the guilt and penalty of sin; it is that which makes possible a communion of heart and mind based upon a common love.

God looks for those with whom He can communicate, hearts and lives that are responsive to the faintest whisper, to the changing moods. We need Him—that's true: but He needs us too. We want Him—that's true: but He wants us too.

The Companion Love Would Have

Rise up, my love, my fair one, and come away
Song of Solomon 2:10

Saturday

The bridegroom has work to do, a road to travel, plans to execute, but he wants someone with him and that someone is the bride of his choice. The time is opportune. What lovely words are used to describe it in verse 11: "For, lo, the winter is past, the rain is over and gone; The flowers appear on the earth; the time of the singing of birds is come, and the voice of the turtle is heard in our land; The fig tree putteth forth her green figs, and the vines with the tender grape give a good smell. Arise, my love, my fair one, and come away." Companionship is an integral part of love, to know that there is a sharing of everything.

As I read these words, "For, lo, the winter is past . . .," I wonder if they might have a special meaning for us as a nation, as a Church. Has the long spiritual winter of hardness of heart and coldness gone? Is new life beginning to show itself? Has the time of the singing of birds come? Is there a new spirit of praise abroad? Is this such a time? Is the Lord saying to us, "Arise, come away; the winter is past"?

Think what a companion the bride would be to him. Oh, how God has wonderfully ennobled human life by having this same relationship with us! I suppose God could do all His work alone; but that is not His way. From the very beginning we find God reaching men through men, and so it was in the great commission that our Lord gave. "All power is given unto Me in heaven and in earth. Go ye therefore, and teach all nations." The early Christians were called "laborers together with God." The companions of God—that is what the Lord wants us to be in this relationship of love; companions in compassion, those who will go with Him and show His caring love to the whole world.

A Mighty Man of Valor

The Lord is with thee, thou mighty man of valour
Judges 6:12

Sunday

The story of Gideon has always fascinated the minds of men. "A mighty man of valour." What an incredible statement it was to make to a man who was so frightened of the enemies that he was threshing his wheat by the winepress to hide it from the enemy! Was it a joke? But, God saw fine points about this man which made him in the end the instrument of a mighty deliverance.

There was a *sorrow that concerned him* and there were two aspects to this sorrow. On the one hand there were the personal problems of his people. They were impoverished and oppressed and Gideon found himself asking the question, "Why then is all this befallen us?" He was a man who was willing to ask questions and who refused to accept things as they were. There were also the spiritual problems to his faith. "Where be all His miracles which our fathers told us of?" If God was with them, if they were God's people and if God had done great things for the nation in the past, why was God not doing something now? He was a man who was concerned.

Then came a *summons to challenge him*. All that Gideon had to say was in complaint against God, but Gideon found to his amazement that while he was saying to God, "Why don't you do something?" God was saying the same to him. "Why don't *you* do something?" The summons that came to him was first to offer his life. What a challenge that was—but it was one that he met! The challenge was also to obey his Lord. In the first instance, that obedience lay within the sphere of his own life. He was told by God to throw down the altar of Baal that stood in the grounds of his own home. And Gideon did what God told him. Even though he did it by night, because he was afraid to do it by day, he did it!

In the end, there was a *success that crowned him*. As a result of his obedience we are told that the Spirit of the Lord came upon Gideon (verse 34). It is obvious that if anything was to be done, he would need divine help to do it and divine help came. In his success we see first that the design for his task was accepted! That design was God's. Never was a stranger battle fought in a stranger way than Gideon's battle! But to the smallest detail he went about it in the way God told him. Is it any wonder that the story ends with the defeat of his foes? The great army of the Midianites was put to flight by a handful of men, three hundred to be precise, waving torches and shouting, "The sword of the Lord and of Gideon." God's work done in God's way, in the end achieves God's purposes. Is this a lesson we need to learn? Maybe in learning it we may find that some of us are people God wants to use in carrying out His purposes to bring deliverance to the people.

Christian Living in the Home

Wives . . . husbands . . . children . . .

Monday

Colossians 3:18, 19, 20

We often forget that there are practical implications of living the Christian life that affect the people in our homes. We Christians are genuinely concerned about our relationships with God and the world around; perhaps also our relationships with other Christians. But so often we ignore our relationships with the other people in our homes.

Paul is speaking here of wives, husbands, or parents and children. All these relationships are to be brought under scrutiny. Why should this be? Surely for one reason, because of the presence of Christ in the heart. And that presence is not just in the hearts of those in the home but in the home itself.

One of the loveliest religious paintings I have ever seen hangs in St. Mary's Episcopal Church, Edinburgh. It is called quite simply, "The Presence." The artist depicts a long view from the door of the cathedral through the empty nave to the chancel, where there is a glow of light around the communion table. Many brought up in the High Anglican tradition maintain that the presence of Christ is to be found there—on the altar, in the sacrament—but the artist thought otherwise.

Right in the foreground of the picture, in the shadow, the artist painted a woman, crouching over the first line of chairs nearest the door. She is weeping, and standing beside her with His hand on her shoulder is the Christ. His presence is experienced not in the distance at the communion table but where the troubled, humbled, concerned heart is. How practical then are the implications of the indwelling Christ, affecting not simply our worship in the sanctuary but our relationships in the home.

Too Soon to Quit

Take heed to the ministry which thou hast received in the Lord, that thou fulfill it

Tuesday

Colossians 4:17

This man apparently faced the temptation to resign, to step down, to quit. The NEB translates these words, "Attend to the duty entrusted to you in the Lord's service, and discharge it to the full." That was the thrust of what Paul was saying—don't quit.

In a book given to me many years ago by the late Dr. Raymond Edmund, President of Wheaton College at that time, there is a chapter entitled, "The Disciplines of Life." One of these Dr. Edmund called, "The Discipline of Determination." He relates that when Henry Ford was asked for the secret of a successful life he replied, "If you start a thing, finish it." When Henry Ford was enthusiastically making his first car in a little brick building in the alley behind his home, suddenly the whole thing turned sour and the thrill and excitement evaporated. He thought he had gone far enough with that car and could see now how to build a second, better one. What was the use of forcing himself to complete this first one? But force himself he did and later told how he discovered that he learned more and more about his second car by completing his first one. He realized that the temptation had not really been to do a better job, but to quit doing anything.

Dr. Edmund makes this comment: "It is almost always too soon to quit." Quitting, he says, makes a dead end of many a road often just as it is about to open. Why did Archippus want to give up, to quit? He could have had very worthy reasons. Perhaps things were not going as well as they had when Epaphras had been there. Perhaps people were talking about him. Perhaps, because of his faults, he was being discredited, discouraged and disheartened and people knew it.

Is this something for us to take to heart? "It is almost always too soon to quit."

Something that Lasts

The Word of God, which liveth and abideth for ever
1 Peter 1:23

Wednesday

Peter speaks of the Word of God as "an incorruptible seed," of a word which "liveth and abideth for ever." Many influences which contribute to our spiritual experience are not lasting. We think of the influence of a friendship. Most of us, at one time or another in our lives, have come to owe more than we can tell to the help of a Christian friend more deeply taught in the things of the Spirit than ourselves. Then circumstances separated us from that one.

Or perhaps we owed a tremendous debt to the ministry of a certain church until we left that church, or there was a change of minister. It may be that we owed a great deal to our home until we lost our parents or left the home. These things all played their part in our spiritual development, but the sadness of them all was that they did not "abide for ever."

How different the ministry of the Word! It is vital that in every Christian this abiding ministry should be exercised. It is comforting to the worker to know that the seed of the Word which he has been able to plant is an incorruptible seed, that it will endure and abide for ever. The one who has been ministered to is blessed by knowing that the same wealth—indeed a far greater wealth of ministry—can be found in the Word itself. The Word of God endures and this enduring quality alone makes the Bible indispensable in our spiritual experience.

The Life that Wins

For to me to live is Christ

Thursday

Philippians 1:21

I shall never forget the day, as a young Christian, that a booklet entitled *The Life that Wins* came into my hand. The number published has long since exceeded the million mark, and I don't think it cost more in those days than two or three pence.

Dr. Charles Turnbull, the author, describes how, although he was a long-time believer actively engaged in Christian work, there came to his life a new concept of Christ—almost, to quote his own words, "a new Christ." This new experience of Christ simply transformed his life and made it more satisfying to him and more pleasing to his Lord. The very title of the booklet made a tremendous appeal to me—*The Life that Wins*.

I wonder how many of us live a winning life? Or is it instead a losing battle? The opening words were very stimulating and exciting. Dr. Turnbull wrote, "There is only one life that wins and that life is the life of Jesus Christ. Every man may have that life; every man may live that life. I do not mean that every man may be Christlike, I mean something very much better than that. I do not mean that a man may always have Christ's help, I mean something better than that. I do not mean that man may have power from Christ, I mean something much better than that. I do not mean that a man should be merely saved from his sins and kept from sinning, I mean something better even than that."

What could be better than all these things, for these are the things all of us long for? My curiosity was aroused and I read on. Words like these began to stand out: "The resources of the Christian life, my friends, are just Jesus Christ . . ." "Jesus Christ does not want us just to work for Him; He wants us to let Him do His work through us." Again, "Remember that Christ Himself is better than any of His blessings, better than the power, or the victory, or the service He grants." *The Life that Wins.* What was the verse that lay at the heart of this experience? It is a verse of six words, of one syllable each: "To me to live is Christ."

We don't Know the Name

There cometh a woman of Samaria

Friday   John 4:7

A great deal of the work of the Church from the time of Christ onward has been done by people whose names we don't know. The boy with his forgotten lunch; the child taken up into the arms of the Master; the woman at the well of Sychar; the owner of the colt; the owner of the upper room—we don't know their names. How many there are whose names are never mentioned in the New Testament!

But it is worth noting that there never seemed to be any doubt in the mind of the Master that the service asked would be rendered. The ministry of the unnamed seemed to have a quality of reliability about it. Nor does there ever seem to have been any delay in the work of the Master. The triumphal entry into Jerusalem was not postponed; the Last Supper did not start late.

This ministry of the unnamed draws its dignity and finds its reward from one simple fact, that it secured the presence of the Master and furthered His purposes. Great will be the reward of the unnamed upon earth when one day they are named in heaven before angels and men.

God has no Favorites

Ye all are partakers of my grace

Saturday   Philippians 1:7

These words might better be rendered, "Ye all are partakers with me of grace." Now this is a profound truth and a very wonderful one, that all Christians are partakers of the same life. Lydia, the wealthy business woman, did not receive a special brand of spiritual life that was suited to her high social standing. Nor did the degraded, demented, devil-possessed slave girl get a spiritual life of inferior quality suited to her social status! Nor did the civil servant, the jailor, get a different kind suited to him! The Christ they received was the same, the one Christ. And if the color of a man's skin is yellow or brown, the Christ he receives is the same Christ received by those whose skins are white. Let us hold on to this truth, that we are all partakers of the same life. It is a wonderful fact of experience. It is a glorious truth.

Professor Blaiklock referred to this at the Keswick Convention. When he set out from Auckland University on his sabbatical year, he felt so thankful to God for Christian fellowship, and so sorry for his unbelieving colleagues who had set out on a similar world tour. He explained: "You see, wherever I travel, I have friends. Wherever they go, they meet strangers. I don't—I meet other members of the family."

In my own world travels it was perfectly wonderful to experience this fellowship. Whether I went to Australia, New Zealand, Honolulu, the States, South Africa, Rhodesia, Kenya or Uganda, it didn't matter. I would be introduced to some Christian, a stranger to me but born again of the Spirit of God, and within five minutes we felt as if we had known each other for years! Why? Because of a life common to the fellowship. Differences of educational background or social standing don't matter basically. There should be no such thing as snobbery within the Christian Church. I can't be snobbish about my Christ and look down on one who is indwelt by the same Christ! It would be impertinence and blasphemy if I did! The one bond that binds us together is Christ.

Marching Orders

Go ye therefore, and teach all nations, baptizing them in the name of the Father, and of the Son, and of the Holy Ghost

Matthew 28:18-20

Sunday

How familiar we all are with the words of our text for today. The last words of Jesus Christ in what is called the Great Commission: "All power is given unto Me in heaven and in earth. Go ye therefore, and teach all nations . . . and, lo, I am with you alway even unto the end of the world." It is a commission some of us are in danger of applying only to missionaries who go abroad. If we do so we forget the fact that the words were a directive to the whole Church!

94

Behind these words I can see a *throne* at which we all must bow. Jesus Christ said, "All power is given unto Me." It is worthwhile facing up to His right to the throne. We are told elsewhere that "God also hath highly exalted Him, and given Him a name which is above every name: That at the name of Jesus every knee should bow, . . . and that every tongue should confess that Jesus Christ is Lord." He has the right in His very being. He is God. If we admit His right to the throne, then surely we must accept His reign from the throne. This means that His will should be controlling and directing every moment of our time, every aspect of our lives. Like Paul we say constantly, "Lord, what wilt Thou have me to do?"

There is also the *task* in which we all must share. Christ's marching orders were that we are to go and we are to make disciples. There is an initiative for us to take. We are to go, not wait for them to come to us. So often the complaint of the Church is, "They won't come." But who said they would? Is Christ's complaint, "They won't go"? The intention we must have is to "make disciples." A disciple is a learner. It is God's intention and should be our intention, too, that others should learn about Christ from our lips and through our lives.

To crown everything, we find here a *truth* by which we all must live. That truth lies in the words, "Lo, I am with you alway." We will not be alone, for He will be with us. His resources, His wisdom, His courage, His strength and His love will be ours. Whom God calls, He enables; whom God sends, He equips. So we need not be afraid. In Mark's gospel we are told that "they went forth . . . the Lord working with them." They went! He worked! And that being so, what place was there left for fear?

Are You Hated?

If the world hate you, ye know that it hated Me before it hated you

John 15:18

Monday

We need to remember that Jesus was hated, and the reason He gives is found in verse 22 of this chapter: "If I had not come and spoken unto them, they had not had sin but now they have no cloak for their sin." Jesus was hated just because He was good and because His goodness revealed the sins of men. And when sin pleases or sin pays, men hate to have it shown.

When the sins of men are exposed by the righteous living of another life, they are faced with only two possible lines of action:

they can either resent it or they can repent of it, and most folk don't like to repent! It is too humbling, too hurting to pride. Jesus was hated, and the amazing fact is that goodness and righteousness are not popular. If you are going to live a life in which you let the Holy Spirit fill you, don't think you are going to be popular. "Marvel not," says John, "if the world hate you." This is the echo of what our Lord had said Himself. "If the world hate you, ye know that it hated Me before it hated you. If ye were of the world, the world would love his own; but because ye are not of the world, but I have chosen you out of the world, therefore the world hateth you."

This hostility was experienced by the Lord and it led finally to the Cross where the only man who ever lived a perfect life was found to be intolerable to the religious society in which He lived. So they killed Him, not because He was bad but because they couldn't stand His goodness; and as we become like Him, they won't stand our goodness either. Yes, Jesus was hated, and we can expect to be hated if we are like Him.

Our Bodies Wear Out

For which cause we faint not; but though our outward man perish, yet the inward man is renewed day by day
2 Corinthians 4:16

Tuesday

Paul speaks of "our outward man" perishing, and we need to face the fact that physically this body of ours is not going to last for ever. It does wonderfully well to last so long and it does this because, we are told, every seven years or so our body completely renews itself! But there comes a time when even the body itself seems to run out of spares. We discover that our sight is not so keen, our hearing is not so good. We don't seem to have the same amount of energy; we can't walk so far; we can't do so much.

In Paul's case all this had been accelerated by the hardships he endured in the service of Christ. Indeed, Paul was just getting worn out and this was something he was prepared to accept. Paul did not live and work as if he would do it for ever. His outward man was perishing!

Have we recognized this? Our outward man, our physical body won't last for ever; and what happens when it does finally wear out? Paul's answer is that although the body may get worn out and old, the man who dwells within the body doesn't. The outer shell may not get younger but the man doesn't stop growing. The Christian keeps on growing in his experience of God's ways, in his knowledge of God's Word, in his likeness to God's Son, in his usefulness in God's work, in his conformity to God's will.

Bringing the Wanderer Back

Let him know, that he which converteth the sinner from
the error of his way shall save a soul from death, and
shall hide a multitude of sins

Wednesday

James 5:20

There are two thoughts here: first of all, a possibility is admitted that a Christian can wander away from the truth. It comes as a note of solemn warning when James writes in verse 19, "If any of you do err from the truth"—anyone. There is no single Christian, however experienced or inexperienced, however keen or apathetic, whose life is not open to this danger of falling away from the truth.

James points out how this begins in the mind of the defaulter. It begins by thinking wrongly concerning God, concerning sin, concerning others, concerning himself. What he thinks in his mind begins to show itself in his ways. Thinking wrongly, he begins to live wrongly.

There is also a responsibility to be accepted. Someone must bring him back—anyone—not just an elder or a pastor, but somebody, anybody. The condition of this backslider has been observed and someone must become concerned and make the resolve that love always makes, to help bring that Christian back. And the reward, to quote James, is that a person who does this "shall save a soul from death, and shall hide a multitude of sins." The phrase, "save a soul from death," is not easy to understand.

Rev. A. J. Motyer suggests that James is explaining that the only convincing evidence to the watching world of the reality of a person's conversion is his way of life, and that when a person backslides the reality of his conversion is brought into doubt and question. His restoration vindicates the previous testimony. In the eyes of the watching and doubting world, this person's conversion is seen to be genuine; thus the soul is saved from death in the eyes of the watching world.

The second phrase, "shall hide a multitude of sins," means a multitude of potential sins. Restoring a backsliding Christian is a work that can cut short a potential tragedy of immeasurable depth and replace it with a life of incalculable fruitfulness.

My Master

Jesus saith unto her, Mary. She turned herself, and saith
unto Him, Rabboni; which is to say, Master

Thursday   John 20:16

I recall a very godly lady whom I loved and revered and whose
Christian counsel meant much to me when I was young. She was an
elderly widow but was approachable in the delightful way that
some elderly folk are. Don't think that there is always a generation
gap—there need be none. What I remember most vividly is that she
always dressed in black and wore a gold brooch. That brooch
spelled out the letters of one word—Rabboni—Master.

Could you ladies wear a brooch like that? And if you did, would
it demonstrate the whole basic principle of your life? I am sure it
did in the life of the lady I am thinking about.

Sometimes I wonder what happened to that brooch. I wonder
who is wearing it now, and if she wears it as my friend wore it,
bearing witness that Christ was not only her Savior but her
Master.

Our Inheritance

To an inheritance incorruptible, and undefiled, and that
fadeth not away, reserved in heaven for you

Friday   1 Peter 1:4

Peter is speaking of the nature and character of the Christian's hope
which looks beyond the trials of this life to the life to come. Incorruptible means that it is beyond the reach of death. How often
death takes away our joy. But there will be no death there, and our
joy will be endless.

Undefiled—it is beyond the taint of sin. How often sin robs us of
our joy. Sin enters into the loveliest of lives and tarnishes and
spoils. But there is no sin there, so our joy will be unclouded.

The inheritance fadeth not away—it is beyond the blight of
change. How often things change, things that are beyond our control. Circumstances suddenly alter; the life that we thought we
were going to live is suddenly snatched away from us. There will
not be that kind of change there.

This inheritance too is safe. It is "kept in heaven for you." The
Christian hope is based upon a certainty, upon a promise that God
has made. That is why the Christian can rejoice, even in the darkest
hour, because his hope is certain.

The Damage that Words can do to Life

Fire . . . Poison . . .

James 3:5, 8

James, that essentially practical Christian, describes the effect of words as being like fire and poison, damaging and destructive. There is, however, a subtle distinction between the two in that damage by fire tends to be accidental while damage by poison tends to be deliberate.

This is certainly true of the damage done by our tongues. A great deal of it is accidental. Sometimes a whole life has been devastated spiritually or morally by an apparently chance word. But the use of poison suggests some act which is both secretive and deliberate. So there can be an intentional use of words which are designed to destroy, to damage, to spread and to ruin. Often such words are spoken secretively, behind a person's back and without their knowledge.

How much we need to pray the prayer of the psalmist, "O Lord . . . Keep the door of my lips."

What is the Gospel?

I am not ashamed of the gospel of Christ . . .

Romans 1:16

Firstly, Paul shows it is "unto salvation," so the apostle is speaking of the *existence of a danger.* Man needs to be saved, for two reasons. First is the sinfulness of man. Man is born a sinner with a heredity of sin that goes right back to the time when man's first parents sinned. Second is the seriousness of sin. Sin is a fact, an inconvenient fact with all sorts of implications and complications. But these are not merely social and personal, they are spiritual. Sin involves God, and separation from God. "The wages of sin is death," and death is not cessation, it is separation.

The Gospel is "the power of God," and Paul sees the Gospel as the *experience of a dynamic.* The Greek word for "power" is the word from which we get our word dynamite. The Gospel speaks of the power of God at work in human history—in creation, in revelation and supremely in redemption. The dying of Jesus was a "doing" by God. Something was accomplished there that made forgiveness possible. The Gospel speaks also of the power of God at work in human hearts, in lives opened to receive the life of the risen Christ by the Spirit who counteracts the power of sin that has infected our very nature.

Paul insists that the Gospel is available "to every one that believeth," and in it Paul sees the *emergence of a decision*. It is a decision to trust, just about the only thing that everyone can do. But there is the necessity for a decision. Everyone can trust, but everyone must, who wants to be saved. Just as a sick man may, but also must trust a surgeon for health, so a sinful man may and also must trust the Savior for salvation. It would be an immoral thing if salvation was not conditional. Although there is a condition, God has made it such a simple thing that the door is wide open and "whosoever will may come."

Kept Unspotted

Pure religion and undefiled before God and the Father is this, To visit the fatherless and widows in their affliction, and to keep himself unspotted from the world
James 1:27

Monday

James indicates here that when we are truly and fully Christian there will be created in us a likeness to God, for the life and love of the Spirit is there. So James illustrates from two areas of human need that should evoke our compassion. He speaks of the fatherless and the widows.

What James is really getting at is that if our lives are authentically Christian, they will be characterized by a great concern for others. This caring is not just a meticulous observance of detail in religious habit, but a compelling compassion which cares for others. He is not concerned with talking but caring. Also, there will be a real sensitivity to anything that might grieve the love of God, for the God who is love is also light. We are told, "God is light, and in Him is no darkness at all."

I remember so clearly a mother saying of her daughter, "She is a perfectionist." This is true of God. He longs that our lives should be completely acceptable to Him. This is, of course, a mark of love, for love is always seeking perfection.

If a mother loves her unborn child, every little garment she prepares will have the same standard—perfection. When a bride is preparing for her wedding, she will have the same standard—perfection. And when God looks at our lives, there is one thing He desires above everything else, and that is perfection. "Be ye therefore perfect, even as your Father which is in heaven is perfect."

Is the Sermon Important?

They that worship Him, must worship Him in spirit and in truth

John 4:24

There has been a tendency in some quarters to decry the place of the sermon in the services of the Church. The emphasis must be on worship, we are told. I would make the strongest possible plea for us to recognize that the Word of God, rightly preached, is in itself an essential part of worship. Jesus Christ laid down a golden rule concerning worship: "They that worship God must worship Him in spirit *and in truth.*" Surely that means in part that we cannot worship God, give Him His worth in our lives, unless we think of Him truly, and are rightly related to Him. The whole purpose of the preaching of the Word of God is to secure these two objectives.

I believe with all my heart that for many people the highest point of worship is found at the end of a sermon when the soul bows down responsively before the living God, knowing Him more fully and seeking to honor Him more wholly than was possible before the sermon began. Worship cannot rest upon either ignorance or insubordination.

Does God Get Tired of Waiting?

. . . No more Jacob, but Israel

Genesis 32:28

God was saying in effect, "Jacob, you haven't changed in the last twenty years since you left home and this just will not do. It's not good enough. It simply has to stop." I wonder if we sometimes exhaust the long-suffering and patience of God. He gets tired of the shoddy kind of Christian lives we live and then He steps in with some shattering experience and encounter and says bluntly, "This has got to stop."

Jacob, like every Christian, had a purpose to fulfill in God's redemptive plan for the world. God just could not afford to have that plan wrecked by one man's compromise, so He broke into that shabby life in a shattering experience. He sought to end the old way and to lift the life to a new level. "No more Jacob . . . but Israel." He was no longer to live shabbily but to live royally, having the privilege of intimacy with the throne of God and wielding power

101

among men. "The sun rose upon him." It was the dawn of a new day, a new life.

Hope

The Lord Jesus Christ, which is our hope

Thursday   1 Timothy 1:1

Hope in the Christian sense of the word is not hope as we use it in common speech. It is not a vague hope but rather a confident expectancy that what is required, what has been promised, what is desired, will be provided. And in the turmoil of Christian service, Paul and Timothy shared a confidence in Christ that nothing could change. They were, therefore, ready to attempt anything that Christ asked them to attempt. They were prepared to endure anything that obedience to Christ called them to endure. They were confident in the message they proclaimed. They were confident in the Master they served.

In the face of the greatest difficulties they moved forward with hope, saying in effect, "Christ in you, the hope of glory." It was because they shared this confidence that they were able to enjoy fellowship in a deep way. It was not a case of one being confident and the other despairing. Both were confident, prepared to take the initiative, prepared to make the venture, prepared to tackle the task, prepared to endure the battle—confident in Christ's ability and His faithfulness.

How desperately we need in the fellowship of the Church today this note of ringing confidence: too often it is missing. There are those who are confident in Christ but there are so many others who see only the difficulties and can only raise problems. Let us each remember individually that Jesus Christ is our hope.

Prayerfulness

I exhort therefore, that, . . . prayers . . . be made for all men

Friday   1 Timothy 2:1

Paul would say here that all men must be prayed for. We need to remember that every Christian lives at the center of a series of expanding circles of contact. There are the contacts in our homes, those with our families and relations. There is a circle of contacts where we work, where we worship, where we spend our leisure time. All those whom we encounter are involved in this redemptive purpose of the will of God, that they should be saved. And if they are to be saved, then they must be prayed for.

I think one of the tragedies of the Church today and in the life of the average Christian is that we do not take the ministry of prayer seriously. Surely here is one area of life in which the promises of God can, and should be tested and proved. The old jingle says that "Satan flees when he sees the weakest saint upon his knees." The tragedy is that he doesn't flee very often because he doesn't see us very often on our knees!

Do you remember the words of the hymn about prayer which begins, "There is an eye that never sleeps beneath the wing of night?" The last two verses are tremendous. I wonder if we really believe them.

> But there's a power which man can wield
>   When mortal aid is vain,
> That eye, that arm, that love, to reach,
>   that listening ear to gain.
>
> That power is prayer, which soars on high,
>   Through Jesus to the throne,
> And moves the hand which moves the world,
>   To bring salvation down.

No wonder Paul speaks of prayer as the most important thing in the life of a servant of God.

What are we Made For?

Thou hast created all things, and for Thy pleasure they are and were created

Revelation 4:11

Saturday

Christianity states emphatically that man is made for God. Just as the bird is made for the air, as flowers are made for the sun, as fish are made for water, so man is made for God. "For Thy pleasure they are and were created." Here the Bible and the much maligned and neglected Shorter Cathechism agree, "Man's chief end is to glorify God and to enjoy Him for ever."

From the Christian point of view, a bad man is a man who is not living for God. This kind of man is a "sinner" in the Bible meaning of the word. This matches Christ's answer to the question, "What is the first and great commandment?" His answer was, "Thou shalt love the Lord Thy God with all thy heart, and with all thy soul, and with all thy mind and with all thy strength." To fail to do this is to fail in the real and ultimate purpose for which we are alive at all. To break the greatest commandment is to commit the greatest sin.

The Lord's Table

What mean ye by this service?

Exodus 12:26

Sunday

Both the Old and New Testaments had a service of remembrance at the center of their worship, and this question asked in the Old Testament can equally well be asked in the New Testament. The answer is at least threefold.

The service of Holy Communion is one of *worship*, and worship means giving a person his worth. In this service the Person of Christ is central, since everything about this service speaks of and points to Jesus Christ. But not only is the person of Christ central; His passion is too, for we are compelled to think of Him crucified, dying for the sins of the world. Unless we see Him as Savior, we are not giving Him His worth in our minds.

This service is also one of *witness*. Paul tells us in 1 Corinthians 11:26, "Ye do shew (or proclaim) the Lord's death till He come." We proclaim our faith in the Christ who died; not simply the fact of Christ's death, but our faith in the Christ who died. We also proclaim our fellowship with others of like faith, a fellowship that transcends all barriers of color, race, and class. We are bearing witness to the faith we have placed in Him and to the fellowship we have found in Him.

There is a great sense of *wonder* when we think of the Host who will preside. How rightly we speak of the Lord's Table for it is the *Lord's* Table and not ours since He who provides presides as the Divine Son of God once crucified for our sins, but now raised from the dead, alive for evermore and most truly in our midst. There is always wonder when we think of the guests who are present, all sinners, but sinners saved by grace.

104

Temptation, not Sin

. . . in all points tempted like as we are, yet without sin
Hebrews 4:15

Monday

It is important to remember that temptation is never sin, for our Lord was "in all points tempted like as we are, yet without sin." The fact that you and I are tempted does not mean that we are bad, but that we are important. The danger is, however, that we allow temptation to become sin. Sin lives next door to temptation and only a step will take us from the one to the other. That is the step of desire and decision.

The second thought we have in scripture, and an assuring one, is that God will not allow us to be tempted above what we are able to bear (1 Corinthians 10:13). There is a tremendous assurance here for us that God knows exactly how much we can stand, and God's sovereign grace and care will see that we are never tempted to excess.

Canon Guy King tells the story of a small boy in a shop who was being loaded with goods by his father. As the lad waited for more, an onlooker said, "You can't carry any more than you have got." To which the answer came, "Daddy knows how much I can carry." It is a great thought, is it not, that our heavenly Father knows just exactly how heavy a load we can bear, and He will see to it that it is never exceeded.

John Blanchard commenting on this verse in 1 Corinthians 10:13 says it tells us three things about temptation—it is *common* to man, it is *controlled* by God, it is *conquerable* by us through Christ.

The Extravagance of Love

That your love may abound yet more and more
Philippians 1:9

Tuesday

Paul prays for that profusion which is the measure of love. The picture is of a bucket not only full itself but with water pouring over on every side—cascading over. Love is a great giver.

In the margin of the Bible of Mary Slessor, the great Scottish missionary, there is this definition of love: "Love = to live for." There is always a note of extravagance about love, extravagance in the giving of its time, the spending of its money, the use of its strength. Love never asks, "How little may I?" but always, "How much can I?"

In the Bible, Mary's love for her Master made her bring a gift to Him that was described as "very costly." We might do well to pause and ask ourselves how far our love for Christ and His Church bears this authentic mark today.

Advance and Counter-Attack

And Believers were the more added to the Lord,
multitudes both of men and women

Acts 5:14

There was the advance of the Church, but the counter-attack follows swiftly for we read in verse 17 of this chapter, "The high priest rose up." Where there is blessing there will be battle. Also in this verse we see the anger of the Sadducees against the Apostles; in verse 18 comes their arrest and then after their miraculous deliverance we learn from verse 28 of their rebuke. Later in verse 35 we read of the hatred that was shown towards them. Not one of these pressures would be easy to meet and when they all have to be met at one time how difficult to go on advancing.

We can see two things blending in the minds of the early Church. First, the *resolve* to continue. In verse 29 they affirm, "We ought to obey God rather than men." The greatness of God demands that we obey Him. By comparison what is man? How sad and pathetic it is that so often we allow our actions, our lives, our conduct, even our destinies to be molded and determined by what some insignificant person or group of persons might think or say. The goodness of God, too, demands that I obey Him. That so great a God should have done so much for me means that not only logic but love will be the motivating force in my life.

Then we learn of their *rejoicing*. For the first time in the history of the church, we encounter actual physical suffering and violence. The Jewish authorities had the apostles beaten (verse 40), then they threatened them and finally let them go. Do we then read of moans, regrets, resignations, or retreat? No! "They departed, rejoicing that they were counted worthy to suffer shame for His name." Their Lord had suffered, and now they were suffering. They were following in His steps; their experience was that of which He had spoken in Matthew 5:11, "Happy are ye, when men shall revile you and persecute you."

Happy? Of course they were. Suffering is the hallmark of sanctity, of likeness to Christ. No wonder they rejoiced!

Hopeless

O wretched man that I am! who shall deliver me?
Romans 7:24

Thursday

Jesus Christ takes a hopeless view of human nature and in doing this goes much deeper in His diagnosis than any other person. He recognizes that while some of the remedies suggested by men may be valuable, they are not essential. Education is one such remedy, the improvement of living standards is another, the passing of just and equitable laws is another. But Jesus Christ probes deeper. He says that nothing less than a new birth will meet the situation. Human nature is naturally bad, and man's supreme need is a new nature. Christ's word to the individual is, "Ye must be born again."

Just as heredity plays its part in the physical and mental make-up of man, so in the spiritual part of his being heredity has bestowed on man a warped nature. It can be traced right back to the first sin of man's first parents, and has been passed down by heredity. As a result, man is "born in sin." There is nothing sinful about his birth, but there is something sinful about him at his birth. Sin is in his very make-up; he has a "traitor" within his own personality which betrays him from within.

It is beyond man's power to control this tendency, so he is compelled to recognize that "whosoever committeth sin is the servant of sin." This sin also condemns him in the sight of God for "the wages of sin is death." The diagnosis of Christ may be severe but the remedy is sure. In the cross is the forgiveness we need, while in the life of the risen Christ is the new nature, the new power for which we crave, imparted by the Holy Spirit to every believing heart willing to receive Him. "As many as received Him to them He gave power to become the sons of God" (John 1:12).

Giving Pleasure

That ye might walk worthy of the Lord unto all pleasing
Colossians 1:10

Friday

That little word "all" has crept in again. Does it mean in all areas or at all times or in all places? Surely it means that they are to live an outward open way of life that just delights the heart of the Savior who loves them.

107

There is a finer point here that we must not miss. The force of the word translated "pleasing" carries with it the sense of anticipation, a walk that does not wait until it is told what will please but, because of its insight of love, will anticipate what pleases.

The word is always used in a bad sense in Classical Greek, to describe a cringing subservience, a fawning attitude, that is always trying to curry favor with someone else. But grace has a wonderful way of taking such words and transforming them. Here the thought is of a sensitivity that anticipates the wish or the needs of the one loved, and so gives pleasure and delight—a life that loves to plan surprises to give pleasure.

Paul is concerned about the pleasure we give to the Lord. What a thing to pray for! Do our lives just delight Him? They ought to.

A Spreading Fragrance

We are unto God a sweet savor of Christ

Saturday
2 Corinthians 2:15

J. B. Phillips translates the verse, "Through us spreads the fragrance of the knowledge of Him everywhere. We Christians have the unmistakable scent (or fragrance) of Christ."

Rita Snowden tells a delightful story of holidaying in Devon. She was sitting at the window in the house where she was staying and suddenly the air seemed to fill with fragrance. It was so noticeable, so striking, that she asked herself where on earth it could be coming from. She looked out of the window and all she could see were ordinary people walking up and down the street. She went out and the fragrance was stronger than ever. So she inquired, "Where does this fragrance come from?" The hostess of the house said, "Don't you know? These people all work in a perfume factory. They live in the fragrance all day and when they come out at lunchtime they bring the fragrance with them."

Do we bear the fragrance of Christ so that wherever we go there is something different about us that makes people want to follow and find the secret? "We Christians," said Paul, "have the unmistakable fragrance of Christ." I wonder if we do!

The Whole Armor of God

. . . Put on the whole armor of God, that ye may be able to stand against the wiles of the devil . . .

Ephesians 6:10-18

Dr. Alexander Whyte, a great Scottish preacher from St. George's Church, Edinburgh, once called the Christian life, "A sair fecht," a hard fight. He was telling the truth. The note of conflict is found everywhere in the Bible. This passage tells of God's provision for the battle.

First—these verses speak of our *engagement with the enemy of God.* If there is a battle, there must be an enemy. Paul speaks of who this person is! In verse 11, the enemy stands unmasked—it is the Devil himself. Ranged beneath him are the ranks of those who carry out his commands (verse 12). We also see the purpose of this enemy. His "wiles" warn us that he seeks to deceive; his "flaming darts" warn us that he seeks to destroy!

Secondly—these verses speak of our *equipment from the armory of God.* It is important to note that it is the armor *of God.* There is an obligation we must face here—to put on the whole armor of God. I must have my life girded about with the truth of God and know the protection of the righteousness of Christ. I must stand firmly in and on the peace with God which is the Gospel, and know the safe protection not of *my* faith, but of God's faithfulness. That Salvation which is Christ must protect and control my life and I must wield the Sword of the Spirit, the Word of God. There is also an explanation here for why defeat is sometimes ours. Is it because we have not put on the armor of God, the *whole* armor of God? Or is it because we are running away from the foe, thus exposing our backs—for which no armor is provided?

Finally—these verses speak of our *enjoyment of the victory of God.* Nowhere is there any thought of either defeat or retreat. Instead, we see a confidence that is unshaken. "Be strong in the Lord, and in the power of His might." There is also a dependence that is unbroken. "Praying always with all prayer," like Christian in *The Pilgrim's Progress,* we can go forth "harnessed from head to foot."

Is Your Christian Experience Stale?

I count not myself to have apprehended

Philippians 3:13

Monday

. . . As Paul looked back down the years of his long Christian experience of wonderful service and great success, he said, "I count not myself to have apprehended." In effect, he said, "You know, when I look back along the way I have come, I feel as if I have hardly started, and all I want to do concerning that which is behind is to forget it. So I forget the things that are behind and press on."

I believe we can learn from him a very important lesson in the matter of rejoicing. There is real danger of resting on the past, of relying on what God did yesterday for our satisfaction today. We try to get the fun and sparkle of Christian experience, when all the time we are living on stale grace. Once it was very wonderful, but now it is not new.

Do you remember the experience of the children of Israel recorded in Exodus 16? They were told to collect manna every morning, early in the day, because when the sun was up it would melt away. In verse 20 of that chapter we read of those who were lazy and thought that they would try to "slip a fast one" over on God and Moses. They tried to keep their manna from one day till the next. But we read that it "bred worms, and stank."

I believe some Christians don't have a singing experience because they have a "stinking" one! It's so old that it smells! They are living on stale grace, if there can be such a thing! Their Christian experience is all old. It's all past. It's all finished. They are trying to drag along this stale grace with them! No wonder they can't sing!

A cake can be very lovely when it is fresh. I don't know of any lovelier household smell than the smell of freshly baked homemade bread. What a lovely fragrance it gives when you come into the house! I like fresh cake, and I like new bread . . . But I don't like stale cake, and I don't like stale bread. Have you ever gone to the bread box and taken the bread out, only to find that it was covered with mold because it had been there so long?

Is your *grace* moldy? Is your Christian experience stale? I believe this is one reason why many Christians are not rejoicing—they are spiritually stale. There is nothing new about them. Yet they were called to "walk in newness of life."

110

Spiritual Sponges

He that believeth on Me . . . out of his belly shall flow rivers of living water

Tuesday

John 7:38

What a difference there is between a river and a sponge! Yet there are some Christians that we can only liken to spiritual sponges. This kind of Christian loves to hear the simple Gospel and delights in attendance at meetings and conventions. The "sponges" sit and listen and soak up all that they hear—and that is the end of it. It just doesn't enter their thoughts that there should be an outworking of what they have received in a disciplined and effective life of prayer or of sacrificial service. They are quite happy to listen, to taste, to approve or to criticize.

The sponge, however, does not come in to the list of metaphors used in scripture to describe the life of the believer. I read instead of a "well of water springing up" and also "rivers of living water" flowing out of the inner being of the real Christian. Let us pray that our churches may be delivered from the tragedy of the spiritual sponge. These people need to be squeezed until it hurts and until they learn that what they have received, they have received in order that they may share it with others.

The Intimacy on which Love is Resolved

Tell me, O thou whom my soul loveth, where thou feedest, where thou makest thy flock to rest at noon: for why should I be as one that turneth aside by the flocks of thy companions?

Wednesday

Song of Solomon 1:7

The bride's heart is drawn out in longing and love to her shepherd king and that love has the insight which knows that love demands a sharing of the whole of life. "Where," she asks, "does my beloved lead his flock to pasture?" "I must accompany him if I am to know him, and love him. His companions will not suffice: I must be with him." It would seem as if, overwhelmed with a sense of her own unworthiness, she had, for the moment, lost him. She cries out to him and the answer comes back from the daughters of Jerusalem, "Go where the work is being done, and you will find him there. You will come to know him there and in that deepening fellowship will come deepening love." How right they were.

It is sometimes only when you work with people that you get to know them. The wife of a surgeon may know her husband as a man, as a father, as a husband, but she doesn't know him wholly or fully—not as the patients or the nurses know him. She doesn't know him as a surgeon. She would have to be his patient, she would have to work with him.

I once heard of a young minister whose wife was reported to be an atheist. If that report is true then God help the minister! What kind of love can there be if there is not a unity of purpose? The bride knows this. She knows that loving him means going where he goes, caring for what he cares, toiling where he toils. So it is in the Christian life. If you would know your Lord and then love your Lord, you must work with Him and share the great concern of His love for the needs of men.

The Privacy Love Demands

The king hath brought me into his chambers: we will be glad and rejoice in thee

Song of Solomon 1:4

Thursday

Hudson Taylor makes a choice comment on this verse in his matchless little commentary called *Union and Communion.* He writes, "Not first to the banqueting house—that will come later—but first to be alone with himself." Then he asks the question, "Could we be content to meet a loved one only in public?" How perfect! How true!

Yet, how does this work out in our spiritual relationship with Christ? We think of meeting Him in a service, but what about meeting Him alone? Is it not true that sometimes we go with dragging feet and count the minutes that seem to pass so slowly while we are with our Bibles or on our knees? And then, having done what duty demands and propriety requires, we hurry away, glad to think our duty is done.

But how can we love unless we know? And how can we know unless we linger in His presence? It was said of Mary of Bethany, who loved her Lord beyond dispute, that "she sat at Jesus' feet and heard His word" (Luke 10:39). That was the place she loved—near Him. And that was the voice she loved—the voice that sounded like music in her ears.

How can we love, how can we know, unless we linger in the same place, listening to the same voice and looking into the same face?

112

Unconditional Surrender

Whosoever he be of you that forsaketh not all that he hath, he cannot be My disciple

Luke 14:33

All that we are as well as all that we have must be handed over to Him. This surrender covers the way we earn our money as well as the way we spend it. It covers home, children, time, gifts, ambitions, body, life and soul. Everything is to be surrendered to His control. "Yield yourselves unto God" . . . "Seek ye first the kingdom of God" . . . "Present your bodies a living sacrifice"—so the verses multiply.

One result this surrender produces is that while everything goes under His control, some things will go out of our lives. Everything that is sinful will have to go—not because God wants to spoil our lives or to rob us of happiness, but for the very opposite reason. It is because sin is always the enemy of man's deepest and truest happiness and good that God wants to put it out of our lives.

Christ the Gardener

Supposing Him to be the gardener

John 20:15

Charles Spurgeon has a sermon on this text in which he lets his imagination follow Mary in the mistake she made, and derives from her mistaken concept of Christ certain truths that are helpful indeed. I can't remember anything Spurgeon said about this text but there are some thoughts that linger in my mind.

If Christ indeed be the Gardener of our souls then His is the hand that plants; and His mind will have much to do with preparing the soil, and then planting the seed. His hand will be the hand that prunes. The reason for pruning is not to hurt but to help the plant, and the results from pruning will be a finer blossom or a greater harvest of fruit.

If He be the Gardener of our souls then His will be the hand that plucks. The whole garden is under the rule of the gardener, and he therefore has his rights. If he chooses to pluck a blossom, just in bud, in full bloom, or withered and old, that is his right. Let us take this blunder of Mary's and see if there is not a blessing hidden in it. If your life is under the hands of the Gardener of our souls, then surely all will be well.

Moved with Compassion

And Jesus went forth, and saw a great multitude, and was moved with compassion toward them, and He healed their sick

Sunday

Matthew 14:14

It is frequently said about our Lord that He was "moved with compassion." It means literally, "suffering with." It is used in the Old Testament about God as "gracious and full of compassion." To have compassion means to care deeply and feelingly. So there must always be a heart that compassion fills!

If compassion is to be shown there must be a person through whom it may be shown. The realities of human need must be faced. It was when Jesus *saw* that He *felt*. Aware of the need of people He met, whether physical or spiritual, He was deeply stirred. Then, having seen, He cared. The resources of that divine love must be felt by men and women in their need today, through those whose hearts and lives possess that same divine life and love. In Romans 5:5, Paul tells us that with the life of the Spirit comes the love of the Spirit.

Added to the *heart that compassion fills* must be the *hands that compassion needs.* Compassion not only sees and feels; compassion also acts. In Matthew 20:34 we read that Jesus, moved with compassion, put forth His hand and touched—the eyes of the blind, the skin of the leper, the bier on which the widow's dead son was being carried for burial. There is always an activity that compassion demands. It must act. Maybe it will act differently in different situations. It may give, may pray, or may speak—but act it must. In addition, there is a proximity that compassion desires. It always seeks to identify itself with the suffering as if to say, "I am here, I am with you, I am feeling with you and for you."

The result of all this will surely be the *hope that compassion brings.* Whenever there is a caring heart with caring hands these will bring a message of hope. The loneliness of so many needy hearts and lives will be relieved, and the helplessness ended. When another comes, new resources are brought to bear upon the problem. And if these resources are His resources, then there is hope indeed, for "with God all things are possible."

The Devil—The Deceiver

The Devil . . . which deceiveth the whole world
Revelation 12:9

Monday

The Bible speaks of the enemy of our souls as one who "deceiveth the whole world" and in another scripture we read that he was a liar from the beginning. He still is. How clever his approach can be! Veiled in language which professes a concern for our happiness, it can be accompanied by the fairest of promises. That was the approach he made to our first parents in the garden of Eden. "Hath God said, 'Ye shall not eat of every tree . . .?'" "And the serpent said . . . 'Ye shall not surely die . . . in the day ye shall eat thereof, . . . ye shall be as gods . . . .'"

It has been said that in time of war truth is the first casualty. This is certainly true in the spiritual warfare. There is only one answer to deceit, and that is truth. We have that in the Word of God—the truth about sin, the truth about happiness, the truth about ourselves, the truth about God. How vital it is that every Christian should be steeped in the Word of God so that we are not deceived by the enemy of our souls.

Reverencing the Unwanted

Ye build the sepulchers of the prophets, and your
fathers killed them
Luke 11:47

Tuesday

Matthew adds the touch, "and garnish," or decorate and make ornate the sepulchers of the prophets that your fathers killed. And I think that what our Lord has in mind is, "and you would do the same if they were alive today." Is this not the sin of paying lip tribute to something that basically we do not want?

Sometimes a church has been mightily blessed of God under a great ministry. Succeeding generations may pay lip tribute to the greatness of the past, but if that same preacher were to come back and preach the messages that made the church great, many would gladly respect the memory of the man's greatness, but would bitterly resent the ministry if it searched them as it had searched their fathers.

We pay lip service to the need for revival and even pray for it, but if it came, would we welcome it? Do you see what our Lord is getting at here? We pay lip service to tradition, to memory because it is conveniently remote and leaves us unchallenged. But if the memory of the past became a ministry of the present, we would resent and resist it with all our powers.

Dressing Attractively or Expensively

. . . in modest apparel . . .

Wednesday

1 Timothy 2:9

The wish of a woman to be attractive is a distinctive feminine characteristic. While most men love old clothes, old jackets, and old hats, ladies love new ones. It may well be part of the very nature of a woman to love to be attractive, but this can have its repercussions in the life of a church. And Paul is concerned about an extravagant and expensive ostentation in the matter of dress.

Of course a Christian woman's hair will be well cared for, and of course she will be nicely dressed, but the hour and place of worship is neither the time nor the place to display what money can buy. When we come to worship and have fellowship, we do not want to draw other people's attention to ourselves. That is why Paul says here that the adornment of a Christian woman is not a matter of elaborate coiffure, expensive clothes, or valuable jewelry, but the living of a good life.

Paul's concern is that attention should not be drawn to the Christian but rather to the Christian's Master and Lord. And the real attraction that will draw people to Christ lies in our attitudes and our actions.

Unworthy

Depart from me; for I am a sinful man, O Lord

Thursday

Luke 5:8

Simon Peter had just shared in a wonderful miracle. Something tremendous had been achieved and accomplished and he had a part in it. Yet his final reaction was not that he was a wonderful man but that he was totally unworthy. A man who is used to the limit of God's purpose for him and through him will never have any thoughts of pride, will never be unkindly critical towards others. The one thought that dominates the heart of such a man is the glory and grace of his Master and the utter and absolute unworthiness of his own heart. "Depart from me; for I am a sinful man, O Lord," was Simon Peter's response.

One of Scotland's greatest saints, Robert Murray McCheyne, once wrote, "What a minister is on his knees, in secret before God Almighty, that he is, and no more." Although McCheyne wrote that about a minister, he could have written it about any Christian. What you are in secret on your knees before God Almighty, that you are and no more. I don't think that any Christian who applied those words honestly to his own heart and life in the light of God's word could say anything other than what Peter said that day long ago, when in the dust and on his face he knelt before his Lord and said, "Depart from me; for I am a sinful man."

The man who dwells often and long in the presence of his Lord can never be proud of himself although he will know most truly how to glory in his Lord.

Love's Perfection

That ye may be sincere and without offense . . . being filled with the fruits of righteousness, which are by Jesus Christ, unto the glory and praise of God

Friday   Philippians 1:10, 11

Here is the standard that love sets—perfection. We are frightened of that word, but God isn't. We shall never achieve it by human resources, but we can at least aspire to it. Perfection! Here is a mother stitching the tiny garments for her first baby. What is her standard? It is perfection. Here is a girl going out to meet her sweetheart. She spends a long time in front of the mirror before she goes out. What's her standard? Perfection. Mind you, no girl can ever achieve it, but how hard she tries! Here is a bride going to her wedding. How long does she take to get ready on this great day of her life? She takes hours! What's her standard? Perfection.

If it is true that some of us evangelicals have reached the stage where we think that sin just doesn't matter, let us look, listen, and learn. The standard that love sets is perfection—not necessarily of achievement but always of intention.

And here is the secret that love has. For Paul comes back, as he always does, to the source and secret of it all. He doesn't vaguely say, "That ye may be sincere and without offense . . . being filled with the fruits of righteousness." He goes on to say, "Which are by Jesus Christ unto the glory and praise of God." He comes back to where he began. He began "in Christ," and all that they are going to be and do will be "by Christ." Everything that you and I are as

117

Christians begins with Christ. And all we shall ever be will be due to Christ, and so all the praise and glory will go to Him.

The Direction that Words can Give to Life

Bits . . . Helm . . .

Saturday

James 3:3, 4

Why is it our words are so important? Surely it is because of the direction they can give to life. James likens them to the bit that guides the horse and the helm that guides the ship. How insignificant they may seem! The bit is tiny compared with the size of the horse and so is the helm compared with the size of the ship.

We may think our words are so tiny and insignificant that they do not matter. They tumble out of our mouths like snowflakes out of the sky, and just as the snowflake falls on to the river and vanishes so we think our words just disappear, but they do not. They may seem insignificant, but they are important. They give direction to life.

This is true in the experience of the individual soul as well as of society. Possibly one of the greatest needs today is for the Christian Church to become vocal. In the Psalms we read, "Let the redeemed of the Lord say so," which might be translated freely, "Let Christians speak out." The tragedy is that too often fear silences our tongues, and no direction is given to those who need it so badly.

A Walled Garden

A garden inclosed

Sunday

Song of Solomon 4:12

The Song of Solomon is admittedly a difficult book, but many have found in it a mine of spiritual wealth and truth. The relationship of love between the bride and bridegroom has been interpreted as throwing light upon the relationship between Christ and His bride, the Church. In this verse the bride is described as being "a garden inclosed," or as we would say, "a walled garden."

A walled garden suggests a *privacy from observation* that love can enjoy. A glimpse may be had of the garden through a gate in the wall, but the greater part of the garden is hidden from view. Here, surely, we have a truth concerning the inwardness of the

Christian experience. For just as the gardener moves about unseen within the garden, so Christ lives and dwells within the soul of the believer. Here we have a searching text for our Christian experience. Too often we are more concerned about maintaining the outward appearance than the inward and hidden relationships of faith.

A walled garden suggests a *variety of occupations* that love will find. How differently the gardener is at work in such a garden. Now it will be to sow the seed; now the spade of change will dig deeply and turn the soil of our lives; now the gardener will come with the pruning knife; then he will be busy gathering and burning the rubbish. How constantly he will be found at work in such a garden. If ever you come across a beautiful garden, you know that someone has been constantly at work in it. So, too, Christ will work in our lives.

A walled garden suggests a *hospitality to others* that love will dispense. There will be a sharing of the produce, be it flowers, fruit or vegetables. Those who come with empty hands will go away laden with the good things that love will lavish on them. Then there will be praises sung of the gardener. "Herein is my Father glorified, that ye bear much fruit." So said Jesus Christ in John 15. I wonder sometimes how often or how seldom the praises of the Gardener are sung by those who have been enriched by the "fruit of the Spirit" which they have found in our lives?

Diversity

Now there are diversities of gifts, but the same Spirit
1 Corinthians 12:4

Monday

There is a diversity of experience concerning the gifts of the Spirit, and right away we face a head-on collision between the teaching of scripture and the teaching of some Christians. How often I have met Christians who want to impose a uniformity where the Word of God has laid down a diversity. They maintain that unless a Christian has one particular gift, either he cannot be a Christian or he cannot truly be filled with the Spirit.

But listen to what the Bible says here. In verses 4, 5, and 6 of this chapter the word comes again and again—diversity, diversity, diversity. In verses 8-10 the same diversity is stressed—"to one is given," "to another," "to another," "to another." In verses 29 and 30 the whole section ends with a series of rhetorical questions to which the implied answer is "No." "Are all apostles?" No! "Are all prophets?" No! "Are all teachers?" No! "Are all workers of miracles?" No! "Have all the gifts of healing?" No! "Do all speak with tongues?" No! "Do all interpret?" No!

Where the Bible says, "No!" I dare not, I must not, say "Yes." Otherwise, I am surely sinning against the very Spirit who inspired the Scriptures, and in whose name I claim to speak.

When Will Jesus Come?

Of that day and hour knoweth no man, no, not the angels of heaven, but My Father only

Tuesday

Matthew 24:36

One thing certain about the Second Coming of Christ is that the time of His coming will not be disclosed to men. There is nothing clearer from the teaching of our Lord than this simple fact. It is one of the things stated repeatedly in the chapter from which today's verse comes.

In verse 39, drawing a parallel between the coming of the flood and His own Second Coming, our Lord said, "They knew not until the flood came, and took them all away." Then in verse 42, He said, "Watch therefore: for ye know not what hour your Lord doth come." And in verse 44, "In such an hour as ye think not the Son of man cometh." Again in verse 50 we are told, "The Lord of that servant shall come in a day when he looketh not for Him."

At the end of the parable of the wise and foolish virgins recounted for us in chapter 25 we read, "Watch therefore, for ye know neither the day nor the hour wherein the Son of man cometh." Before the Lord ascended up into heaven one of the last things He said was, "It is not for you to know the times or the seasons, which the Father hath put in His own power." In His own inscrutable wisdom God has determined that the time of our Lord's Second Coming will not be disclosed. We must hold that steadily in our minds. To ignore it is certainly going to lead us into error and bring the wonder of Christ's Second Coming that we cherish and treasure into disrepute, discrediting it in the eyes of both Christians and non-believers.

One thing we do know—He will come. But when, we do not know; therefore we must be ready.

A Basic Problem

How to perform that which is good I find not
Romans 7:18

Surely we have here one of the basic problems of human life. Some people assume that man will do the right thing if he knows what is right. For them, the way to remedy the moral evils of the world is to teach people what is right, with the result that they will do it— education is the remedy! But it is obvious from human experience that man's problem is not just to *know* what is right.

Our problem is that when we do know what is right, we are not willing to do what is right, and even if we are willing to do it we are not able to do it! We have neither the desire nor the strength. Christianity recognizes an element of truth in this approach to the problem of modern man's moral dilemma, but will not agree that it is the whole truth.

Others also base their diagnosis upon a happy confidence in the so-called inherent goodness of man. They take the line that the real root and source of moral evil in the world lies in man's environment. This approach is a social one, the argument being that if you can only give people enough things you will remove the cause of moral evil. The answer is to be found along the line of higher wages, better houses, a higher standard of living.

Here again the facts of experience run counter to this solution. If it were really true that environment is the one decisive factor, then we could assume that those people living in the best environments with the highest wages and the nicest houses would be the best, most upright people. But experience simply does not bear this out. Indeed, some of the choicest characters are often found in the most difficult surroundings.

A Decisive Battle

Then thou shalt make thy way prosperous, and then
thou shalt have good success
Joshua 1:8

The decisive battle in the second world war was the battle of the Atlantic. When Britain lay helpless, unequipped and alone, a stream of supplies started to come across the Atlantic from the United States. The German submarines and raiders made an all-out attack to cut Britain off from the States because that would have

121

cut off supplies. If the battle of the Atlantic had been lost, the war would have been lost. If we lose the battle of communication between our souls and God, maintained through His Word and prayer, then we have lost the spiritual war.

If we want to have good success and if we want to make our way prosperous, God makes the condition absolutely plain. "This book of the law shall not depart out of thy mouth: but thou shalt meditate therein day and night, that thou mayest observe to do according to all that is written therein." We are required to study the Word, and we must obey it. With the lines of communication wide open, the supplies of God's grace and truth can flow in. Then we shall make our way prosperous and then we shall have good success.

Paul and Timothy

Paul . . . unto Timothy

Friday

1 Timothy 1:1, 2

The partnership, or friendship, between Paul and Timothy is one of the loveliest of all the partnerships recorded in the history of the Church. It is all the more remarkable because of the wide gap in age between the two men, in all probability a gap of about thirty years. We hear much today about the generation gap in our society but in the partnership between these two men, the gap was bridged by Christ. It happens so still.

I can recall two friendships that meant much to me in my late teens and early twenties, with people who were at least as far removed from me in age as Paul was from Timothy. One was with the late Bishop Taylor Smith who was in his seventies, and the other with the godly widow of the late Rev. Gordon Watt. Mrs. Watt was at least in her seventies if not in her eighties. I suppose one explanation is that the development of spiritual maturity and spiritual affinity is determined by factors other than the mere passage of time. All of us have known some Christians to grow spiritually at a rate, which, in a matter of months, has taken them far beyond others whose Christian life could be measured in years.

The opening two verses of this letter give us some insight into the quality of deep fellowship in the service of the Gospel that meant so much to Paul and Timothy, and also through them to the whole Church of Jesus Christ. That is the kind of deep fellowship to which Amy Wilson Carmichael referred in her later years as being of the "innermost inner sort." In one of her letters, feeling that more and more of her close friends had gone on before her she wrote, "There are so few of the innermost inner sort left."

In the Hands of the Potter

As the clay is in the potter's hand, so are ye in Mine hand

Jeremiah 18:1-6

Many Christians may know this passage in Jeremiah where the relationship between God and His people is presented in an acted parable. Many preachers base their message to the unbeliever upon the truth here that a life marred by sin can be made new again. That is of course true, but the first application is to the believer.

The pressure of the hands of God molds our lives, like clay in the hands of a potter. We sometimes experience this pressure inwardly through *conviction.* Psalm 32:4 says, "Day and night Thy hand was heavy upon me." Perhaps this was a conviction about something the Psalmist should stop doing, or start doing. Alternatively, the pressure is sometimes felt outwardly through *circumstances.* How often circumstances quite beyond our control shape and mold our lives. In Psalm 31:15, the Psalmist says, "My times are in Thy hand."

We know there is a purpose in the mind of God, for in verse 3 we are told that the potter "wrought a work on the wheels." Gradually revealed in the clay of our humanity is the purpose in the mind of God. God's purposes, like the potter's, are almost always two. One is *loveliness,* the desire to create something lovely. In Psalm 149:4 we read, "He will beautify the meek with salvation." The other purpose is *usefulness.* In John 15:16, Christ said, "I have chosen you, and ordained you, that ye should go and bring forth fruit, and that your fruit should remain."

How patient is the love of God. In verse 4 we are told that the vessel was marred in the hand of the potter—so he cast it away? No! "So he made it again another vessel, as seemed good to the potter to make it." Here we have the *changelessness* of God's love. "I have loved thee with an everlasting love," says the Lord in Jeremiah 31:3. But we also need to remember the *costliness* of God's love. Forgiveness may be free to the sinner but it cost the Savior His life. The marred vessel can look up into the marred visage of the Son of God and see there, and there alone, the assurance of the forgiving love of God.

The Ministry of Grateful Love

And the house was filled with the odor of the ointment
John 12:1-11

This incident in Bethany is surely one of the choicest of all incidents in the life of Jesus Christ. At the time when the hatred of men was to do its worst, the love of Mary shone out most brightly.

Think of the *quality that marks the ministry of love*. There is the sheer extravagance of it. Mary's offering was "very costly." Love is extravagant in the price it is willing to pay, in the time it is willing to give, in the strength it is willing to spend. Love never thinks in terms of how little, but always in terms of how much. There is always a sweet fragrance to it—we are told that the fragrance of the ointment "filled the house." It was an attractive, expensive, pervasive fragrance. Are not the most fragrant memories in life the memories of places and people with whom we associate love?

Think of the *sympathy that guides the ministry of love*. They say that love is blind. It may be blind to faults, but not to thoughts. Love is filled with knowledge and with insight. Mary knew because she loved. See the ministry her wisdom revealed. She knew that the mind of her Lord was preoccupied with His imminent death and she wanted Him to realize that she knew. See the welcome her ministry received. How grateful Jesus was! When Judas dared to criticize, there was surely an edge to Jesus' words, "Leave her alone." To give and to receive such a ministry is beyond the price of rubies.

Think of the *memory that crowns the ministry of love*. In the account of this incident in Mark and Matthew, Christ said of it, "Wheresoever this gospel shall be preached throughout the whole world, this also that she hath done shall be spoken of for a memorial of her." Love gives, love knows, and love lasts. This deed of love was to be an enduring memory, it was to be an enriching memory. Someone has said, "Love ever gives, forgives and lives and ever stands with open hands and while it lives it gives. For this is love's prerogative, to give and give and give!"

The Fragrance of Love

The house was filled with the fragrance of the ointment
Monday   John 12:3 RSV

What are the most fragrant words in our vocabulary? What word is there more fragrant than the word, "Mother"? What names are there more fragrant in our minds than the names of those whom we love? And what name is there more fragrant than the name of Jesus? In that name love reaches its highest perfection.

What are the most fragrant memories of life? Are they not those which come back to us again and again with such sweetness—the memories of love? Is this not the reason why the memories of our childhood are among the most fragrant to us, because it was during our childhood that we were surrounded with love and affection?

What shall we say of life in the spiritual realm? What lives are most fragrant in the life of the Church? Not necessarily the most orthodox, the most important, but surely those lives that simply lavish their strength, their time, and their love in the cause of Jesus Christ. What about our own lives? We may be absolutely orthodox, we may even hold office; but is there a fragrance about our lives and our testimonies that people simply cannot evade? Does the "fragrance of the ointment" fill the house?

The Mind of Christ

Let this mind be in you, which was also in Christ Jesus
Tuesday   Philippians 2:5

What is the mind of Christ? What is the way of Christ that you and I must follow if we are to discover the secret of maintaining unity? He is the One who was truly God and yet truly man. He followed the path of utter selflessness, holding on to nothing as His right, but instead accepting the uttermost depths of degradation in the purpose of God and in His love for the world. Being in the form of God, He became obedient in an ever-descending scale of humiliation until He became obedient unto death. And this death was not even an ordinary death; it was "the death of the cross."

The thought which comes with a note of tremendous challenge is that the mind which was in Christ was a mind which set no limit to the amount of injury it was prepared to receive. Christ set no limit to His sufferings. Christ never said to the Father, "I will go so far

125

and no further." He couldn't have gone further than He went; He couldn't have suffered more than He did; He couldn't have been more insulted and degraded than He was. He, being in the form of God, had the right to all the adoration and all the worship and all the praise and all the obedience of the whole human race; yet He took the sum total of their disobedience and their hatred—He took it all.

Let that mind be in you. When our injuries and insults and wrongs exceed the injuries and insults and wrongs of our Master, perhaps then we have the right to call a halt. But not until then. What causes a break in fellowship between Christians? An unforgiving spirit. We cannot set a limit to the injury we are prepared to take from someone, to the criticism we are prepared to bear, to how much comment and gossip and talk we will allow. The very moment we set a limit, the moment we nurture an unforgiving spirit, the song dies.

Speaking to One Another

Then they that feared the Lord spake often one to another

Malachi 3:16

Wednesday

This was a favorite text of Bishop Taylor Smith, who described Christian fellowship as being like a game of tennis. When one person serves the ball over the net, the other returns it. There is constant interchange between the two sides of the net. The challenge of Christian fellowship is that we must give as well as receive.

Fellowship has been described as a living intercourse between personalities. This is challenging, for what have we to give? We feel we know so little; yet, however little we know, we should give what we have even if our contribution takes the form of questioning rather than sharing positively our experience and knowledge.

What keeps us back from this giving in fellowship? Perhaps sometimes it is the fear of displaying our ignorance. So many of us pose as being better Christians than we are, or of knowing more than we do. The result is a superficial fellowship, which is a mere face-saving device. On the other hand, we may hold back from giving in fellowship through fear of evoking criticism. If we really said what we thought or believed, others would criticize us. Let us pray that we may be delivered from a failure to give and receive in fellowship; and let us encourage others to give by abstaining from criticizing them when they do speak.

May we be in the company of those who speak often one to another. We are told in Malachi that "the Lord hearkened, and heard it," and was so delighted that He wrote it all down.

Before God

I charge thee therefore before God . . . preach the Word
2 Timothy 4:1, 2

Thursday

The minister of the Gospel is a man who must know what it is to stand and live in the presence of God. There is nothing new about this. It was true of the Old Testament prophets. Elijah, speaking to Obadiah, said, "As the Lord of hosts liveth, before whom I stand." The place of a servant was always in the presence of his master.

There are surely at least two reasons why the minister of the Gospel should be found in the presence of God. First, so that he may perceive the will of God both for himself and for others, and that he may do what God wants him to do and go where God wants him to go. There is a wonderful picture of this relationship in Psalm 123:2 where we read, "As the eyes of servants look unto the hand of their masters, and as the eyes of a maiden look unto the hand of her mistress; so our eyes wait upon the Lord our God."

Another reason is found in the fact that when he is in the presence of God, the Word of God can be received by him. "Preach the word" was Paul's counsel to this young minister Timothy. The minister of the Gospel has been put in trust with the Gospel, to use Paul's great phrase. He has been entrusted with a message—God's word to man. God's word is heard supremely in Christ who is the Word. In 2 Corinthians 5:19 Paul calls the Gospel, "the word of reconciliation," and Paul calls himself and all others like him, "ambassadors for Christ." He is not inventing a message but simply delivering it in its completeness.

When Paul took his farewell of the elders of the Church at Ephesus, he was able to say, "I have not shunned to declare unto you all the counsel of God." That is why a minister must be found in the presence of God, and remain there.

127

Sinning by Doing Nothing

To him that knoweth to do good, and doeth it not, to him it is sin

Friday

James 4:17

I wonder how far we ever go in our thinking as we try to assess where the most serious aspect of failure or, to put it more bluntly, of sin is found in the lives of Christian people. None of us would go so far as to say that there is no failure or little failure, but where it is found?

The area of failure today—and a vast area it is—lies in one aspect of Christian living to which the vast majority of us scarcely give a thought, and concerning which we have scarcely a twinge of conscience. The key to it lies in the words of our text for today, "To him that knoweth to do good, and doeth it not, to him it is sin." Or, to put it in other words, the failure of the Christian today lies not so much in doing what he knows to be wrong as in not doing what he knows to be right.

Let me throw this into sharp focus. If we met a man reeling along the road in a state of drunkenness we should, I expect, sense the tragedy of it and feel something of the misery that kind of failure can cause. But might not we ourselves be walking along a road in a state of prayerlessness? Does that not cause just as much misery as drunkenness? "To him that knoweth to do good, and doeth it not, to him it is sin."

Fitting In To a Plan

The foreknowledge of God

Saturday

1 Peter 1:2

The Christian is the object of God's thought and concern. That is not only true now but stretching right back into the eternal counsels of God. God has been thinking of the Christian for a long time—planning for us, providing for us, and when we actually were born, dealing with us. This fact makes the imagination stagger. The Christian matters so tremendously to God that God has been thinking of him from back in the vastness of eternity itself.

This has echoes in Paul's letters. He writes in Ephesians 2:10, "We are his workmanship, created in Christ Jesus unto good works, which God hath before ordained that we should walk in them." This verse can mean two things. It may mean that there is a

128

pattern of good works within which God expects every Christian to move. Or it may mean that God has a specific plan for each individual Christian which God wants that one to enter into and fulfill. I think both interpretations are possible.

God has not only a place for us but a plan for us. In Isaiah 43:1, God says, "Fear not: for I have redeemed thee, I have called thee by thy name; thou art mine." And our Lord speaks of the intimate concern of God for the individual in the words, "Even the very hairs of your head are all numbered" (Luke 12:7). This is indeed a tremendous truth. It brings a sense of assurance, too, that my life is the object of the thought and concern of a gracious, loving, heavenly Father.

More Bearers of the Burden Wanted

They shall bear the burden with thee

Sunday   Exodus 18:22

It is worthwhile to ask ourselves if we are part of the burden of the work of God or if we are under the burden. Someone once said that every Christian is either a missionary or a mission field. Are we part of the problem or part of the answer? This passage could have been written today about the situation so often found in the Church where the famous words of Churchill could be applied, "Never was so much owed by so many to so few." Moses was in danger of facing a breakdown. If we read the chapter through, we will find that it is fascinatingly up to date.

We must recognize that there are *limits in the work of God that should be sensed.* Limits, that is, to what one man can do. There are limits imposed by the time that one man has. Even if he uses all the time he has, there is just not enough time for one man to do everything. Most of my life I have worked a six-day week with about ninety hours of work clocked up! It makes the claims of some unions today look a little strange to me. There are also limits imposed by strength. With the best will in the world and with all the time available being used, the strength is still not there to tackle and finish the work that has to be done.

We must accept that there are *loads in the work of God that need to be shared.* This is obvious when we see the size of the task. There are so many things to be done, so many lives to be reached. Moses was at it (verse 13) "from the morning unto the evening"—and still the work was not done! There must, therefore, be a sharing of the task. What wise words were spoken by Jethro, "This thing is too heavy for thee; thou art not able to perform it thyself alone . . . provide . . . able men . . . and they shall bear the burden with thee." How many there are in the fellowship of the Church who are perfectly able to share the load, but may have never been asked or thought of offering.

We must admit that there are *lives in the work of God that could be saved.* There are tragedies that could be avoided. "Thou wilt surely wear away" was the warning given to Moses. It is not unknown for ministers and missionaries to have breakdowns due to overwork, and for lives to be shortened by sudden death. Someone once said that in our churches we have men capable of running big businesses but in the church we give them the job of licking stamps. Where is the efficiency we could achieve? So we come back to where we began. As a Christian, are you a missionary or are you a mission field? Are you under the burden or part of it? Are you part of the problem or part of the answer? It is worth reading Exodus 18 and then asking and answering these questions.

A Hindered Walk

Ye did run well; who did hinder you?

Monday

Galatians 5:7

The late Bishop Taylor Smith had a wonderful gift for drawing profound spiritual lessons from events of complete simplicity in the lives of ordinary people. One such incident happened when he was attending the Keswick Convention. As he walked along the road, a group of young people walked towards him. When they were still some distance away, one girl stopped, took off her shoe, shook out a stone that was obviously uncomfortable for her, and replaced the shoe on her foot. Then the group continued walking towards the Bishop. When he met them the Bishop stopped them and said to the girl who had taken off her shoe, "That's right—never let anything hinder your walk." Those young folk would never forget that word.

"Never let anything hinder your walk." I don't expect the stone the girl shook out was a big one—it doesn't take a big stone in a shoe to make our walk uncomfortable. And it doesn't take a big thing that is wrong in our lives to make our walk uncomfortable. Too often Christians allow something or someone to hinder their walk. They need to follow the example of that girl and shake it out of their lives.

Is there something in our lives that needs to be shaken out? If we could shake it out today, we would be able to walk better, more comfortably, more easily, with greater freedom, and more worthily of our Lord tomorrow.

What About Your Appetite?

Blessed are they which do hunger and thirst . . .

Matthew 5:6

Tuesday

I want to think about the importance of having a good appetite. "I'm not hungry." These words and the action of the child who pushes away his plate immediately suggest to the mother that the child is not well. A good appetite goes with good health.

The same is true in the realm of the spiritual life of a Christian. The Christian should have a good appetite for Scripture. In 1 Peter 2:2 we read, "As newborn babes, desire the sincere milk of the word, that ye may grow thereby." How hungry are we for the Word of God? This is the nourishment that has been provided for our health.

In the realm of nutrition there are dangers—we may not get enough, we may not get the right food, we may not have regular meals. The nourishment God has provided is designed for development as well as health. It is provided in order "that ye may grow thereby." The Christian is meant to grow as well as to live. What a tragedy it is when a baby does not develop! There are too many Christians who remain "babies in Christ."

Justified by Works

Ye see then how that by works a man is justified, and not by faith only

James 2:24

Wednesday

What does James mean? At first sight it would seem as if he contradicts the teaching of the New Testament that we are justified by faith. But of course James isn't as stupid as that. I have never understood why Martin Luther called this epistle "an epistle of straw." What James is saying is not that God accepts us *because* we are good but on terms which ensure that we *become* good!

Let's think just for a moment of the dependence that faith shows. What is this faith? Faith must be faith in Christ. It is important to get this clear; it is not a matter of believing that Christ died for our sins. That would be a purely intellectual assent to a historical fact, not saving faith. It means believing *in* the Christ who died for our sins and who now lives. That is saving faith.

Saving faith is not believing in an event but relying on a Person. It is that blend of reliance and obedience which looks away from itself to Christ. And in utter dependence and total weakness, it puts total confidence in the work, the word and the will of that Christ who died and lives. Just as a sick person puts his faith in a surgeon with the resources and skill necessary to restore him to health, the sinner puts his faith in the Savior and all the resources of that crucified, risen and living Lord become available to him.

The dependence that faith shows will lead to the difference that people see. "Ye see then how that by works a man is justified, and not by faith only." James is not, of course, denying the importance of faith; he is demanding the evidence of it. He says in effect, "If you put your faith and confidence in the living Christ who died for your sins, there is bound to be a difference in the way you live, and I want to see that."

Of course there will be a difference. When I put my faith in a surgeon, it means not only my dependence upon his ability but my obedience to his authority. I start doing what he tells me. And I will do that with Christ. It is not simply relying on the fact that Christ died, but it is relying on and being obedient to the Christ who died and is alive. And that is bound to make a difference.

Preaching in the Home

The church in thy house

Thursday

Philemon 2

There is a choice incident in the life of the great preacher, Dr. Campbell Morgan. His sons grew up to be preachers too. On one occasion when all the family were gathered together, a visitor looked around the family circle and asked one of the sons, "Who is the best preacher in the family?" Without any hesitation he replied, "Mother." Have we not made a blunder in excluding our homes and the people who live there from the claims and service of Jesus Christ? How the number of bases from which the Holy Spirit could operate would be multiplied if each of us considered our home one of these bases.

There are many Christian homes in the average congregation but many of these the Lord would like to use much more than He is permitted to. The members of a church fellowship participate in the life of the church, but in the early Church there were no church buildings so what happened took place in the homes of Christians. A home used for this purpose need not be large and the numbers with whom it is shared need not be great; but what a fruitful fellowship and wonderful witness could come from homes where the preachers are mothers, housewives, fathers and even children.

We can always have at least a congregation of one when we have a friend in our home. Our chair can become a pulpit, and the teapot can be part of the equipment we will use. With the chair and the teapot and mouths consecrated to the service of Jesus Christ, what effective preaching can happen in the home!

The Need for Endurance

Be strong in the grace that is in Christ Jesus

Friday   2 Timothy 2:1

Paul knew that Timothy, a naturally shy, timid and shrinking disposition, would require this call and challenge possibly more than most people. It would be difficult for him to demonstrate that quality of toughness that Christian service demands. Bishop Handley Moule points out that "if we are Christ's, indeed we are called not to a holiday but to a campaign and our tent is pitched upon a field of battle." How desperately we need to recapture this note in our Christian living and service today—to remember that the life of Christian service is a rough life which calls for endurance.

I have never forgotten the sense of shock that came at the close of a great missionary gathering in London some years ago when the final speaker, one of the most outstanding missionary statesmen of that time, ended a masterly address on the task confronting the Church today with an appalling anti-climax. He concluded with a call and challenge to youth to respond in obedience to the cry of the world in need and then added these words, "Anyway, it is such fun." Fun!

I compared those words with the words of Paul in Galatians 6:17, "Henceforth let no man trouble me: for I bear in my body the marks of the Lord Jesus." Paul is concerned that Timothy should be prepared to take his "share of suffering as a good soldier of Christ Jesus." This is the translation found in the RSV of the words which appear in the KJV as "endure hardness." The phrase, "your share of suffering," reminds Timothy that he is not the only one who will suffer, but that all Christians are called upon to suffer as good soldiers of Jesus Christ.

So there is the summons, "Be strong," and here is the secret, "in the grace that is in Christ Jesus." "Timothy," writes Paul in effect, "you will never be able to endure in the strength you have but only in the strength that Christ will give you by His grace." The NEB translates this verse, "Take strength from the grace of God which is ours in Christ Jesus."

The Agony of Prayer

Epaphras . . . always laboring fervently for you in prayers

Saturday   Colossians 4:12

The word translated "laboring" is a word from which we get our word "agonize." It is taken straight out of the vocabulary of the sports arena where it was used to describe the wrestling and striving of combatants. Prayer, for Epaphras, was a strenuous affair. It would be, first of all, a battle to get to the place of prayer. Is this not a struggle for all of us? We have to find the time and get to the place where we can pray.

In one sense, prayer is the very atmosphere in which we live and breathe; but our Lord said that prayer was also something that had to be done behind a closed door. So many things crowd in upon our lives that we have a great struggle to get behind that door. Even our Lord found it a battle. In Matthew 14:23, we read that our Lord had to "send the multitudes away" before He was able to go up into the mountain apart to pray. So, for Epaphras it would be a struggle to get to the place of prayer and then a battle when he got there. Paul describes him as "always laboring fervently for you in prayers." For this man, prayer was something that was both continuous and strenuous. Is this not what our Lord said prayer was like?

In the parable in Luke 11, our Lord said that prayer was like a man hammering on a door at midnight and shouting until his request was granted. Do we know what it is to battle in prayer?

Together

Heirs together of the grace of life

1 Peter 3:7

With these words the Bible describes the essential meaning of Christian marriage. The key is possibly the word, "together." What contributes to this experience of "togetherness" in married love?

There is a *life shared together.* It is a different life from that of the ordinary person, because it is a Divine life. It is the very life of the Lord Jesus Christ indwelling each and both by the Spirit of God. It is a living bond that brings and then binds together two lives into a wonderful unity; and just because it is a different life, we find that it is also a demanding life. It's standards are infinitely higher than those of ordinary people because the standards are set by Christ Himself; and these are demanding both in what we are to attain to and what we are to abstain from.

There is a *love shown together.* There is a new concern for others and for God. Love is always looking outward and the unselfishness of true love will characterize the lives of these brought together in Christian marriage. Their hearts and their homes will always be open to the needs of others. There is a new constraint. "The love of Christ constraineth us." What a compulsive force love is. It can take hold and control and dominate and motivate a life in a way that is quite irresistible.

There is a *Lord served together.* This means that the Word of God will be studied together. The importance of both partners reading the Word of God is that both should be finding out what the will of the Lord is. That makes it possible for the will of God to be sought together. If two are to remain together, they must be traveling spiritually at the same pace. If one lags behind the other, they will in the end drift apart from each other.

I believe the Christian home is a special target for attacks from the enemy of men's souls. It is such a strong witness, especially in these days when the home has become one of the most common areas of human failure. Christian couples must see that togetherness is secured and then guarded. A Christian husband can get so engrossed in his Christian work that, unconsciously, he finds himself slipping away from his wife and his home. The Christian wife can become so engrossed in the cares of running a home that, if she is not careful, she will drift away from her Lord and her husband. The key ingredient of a happy Christian home is the "togetherness" that it maintains.

Like a Tree

The righteous shall flourish like the palm tree . . .

Psalm 92:12

"For every tree growing up there is a tree growing down." As real as the tree that can be seen is the tree that can't be seen, and the hidden tree is the secret of the visible one. That hidden tree growing down draws its sustenance and its nourishment from a hidden supply. It is impossible to grow in grace and in the knowledge of the Lord without a daily time of quiet with Him over His Word. If you were to ask me, "What is the primary problem that lies at the root of a withered Christian experience?" I think I would reply (after counseling thousands of Christians and knowing my own heart), "It is the neglect of the daily hour of communion with God in prayer." We just cannot do without it. There must be nourishment for the soul.

I was interested to find that John Wesley and the late Dr. W. E. Sangster, the great Methodist preacher, both came to the same resolve in their lives. They both determined to give the first hour of each day to God. It need not be the first hour that we give to God, although it ought always to be the best hour. But if we do spend time with God and have a tree growing down, we need not worry too much about the tree growing up.

Persecuted

. . . scattered . . .

1 Peter 1:1

The Christians, like the Jews, were scattered because of persecution. In Acts 11:19 we read, "Now they which were scattered abroad upon the persecution that arose about Stephen travelled as far . . ." This bears out what the Lord had said would happen. In John 15, He warns the disciples, "Because ye are not of the world, . . . the world hateth you," and the reason He gives in verse 22 is, "If I had not come . . . they had not had sin: but now they have no cloak for their sin."

There is nothing human pride resents so much as rebuke, and this rebuke sometimes is administered, not by the lips, but by the life of another. The basic reason the Christian is not liked is because the Christ-rejecting man knows that the Christian had the humility,

136

grace, and courage to do what he himself should have done and has failed to do—namely, to accept Christ into his life and to obey Him.

To find too that the Christian treats as worthless what he values doesn't help matters. The only way to compensate for the sense of inferiority felt when meeting a Christian is to belittle the Christian by finding fault with him. He gets angry with the person who humiliates his own pride. I was brought up with the idea that to get angry is foolish in every way. If they are in the wrong they can't afford to be angry: if they are in the right they have no need to be!

When do Things Happen?

And it came to pass, that, as they went, they were cleansed

Luke 17:14

In their obedience to Christ's command, the lepers found a pathway leading to an experience of His power. The history of the Church leaves no room to doubt the reality of men's experience of God. Why is it then that for so many of us that experience is almost nil? This sentence in the story of the healing of the lepers by our Lord reveals the reason. We are told that "as they went, they were cleansed." The experience of Christ's healing power did not come until they were obedient. He said, "Go," and as they did what He said they were cleansed.

Obedience is always the gateway to our experience of the power of Christ. We may have been spiritually stuck for weeks, for months, for years. The tragedy is that we usually know where progress stopped. It was at that place where we were disobedient to the will of God. We did not yield to God on some point or other, and spiritually we have not moved one step further on. How can we experience the power of God? Simply by doing what He tells us to do. With our obedience will come the experience.

Love's Wise Insight

That your love may abound yet more and more in all knowledge and in all judgment; that ye may approve things that are excellent

Philippians 1:9

Here we see that perception which guides the ministry of love. Phillips' translation reads, "A love that is full of knowledge and wise

137

insight." Two things are involved—knowledge and wise insight. The first, "knowledge," speaks of the *intimacy in which love grows.* "That your love may abound yet more and more in all knowledge." One of the fundamental blunders many Christians make is that of attempting to love a Lord they do not know. If love is to abound it must do so in the environment of knowledge, and it is here that we see the significance of our daily quiet time.

Not only do we see the intimacy in which love grows, but also the *insight by which love knows.* The wise insight of love! How much clumsy and bungling Christian work there is today which is not guided by the wise insight of love. Here Paul is thinking of a love which doesn't need to be told because it knows. Are you that kind of Christian?

The Spiritual Flirt

Present your bodies . . . unto God

Friday

Romans 12:1

A flirt is someone who wants to get all the amusement, excitement, and entertainment out of love without any thought or desire for the responsibilities of the marriage to which that love is the summons. There is, of course, a thrill and an excitement attached to certain aspects that come within the orbit of the normal Christian life. There is the thrill of big meetings and crusades, of listening to a great preacher; or maybe there is the enjoyment of holiday house-parties, the wonder of the fellowship of a great convention. Many of these things bring a rich and full measure of happiness and joy to the Christian. But to make these things alone the goal of Christian living is a travesty of the Christian life, just as a flirt is a travesty of a lover.

Marriage speaks of self-denial, sacrifice, service, of a hundred and one things that fall under the title of duty rather than pleasure. And the Christian life, lived in union with Christ, is also marked by many of these things. Marriage speaks of dusting, cooking, washing up, mending clothes, crying children, straitened finances, liberty foregone, of a score of things that are accepted by love and turned to good account. Such things have little of what the world calls glamor. Similarly, in the Christian life there is laboring in prayer and teaching children in the Sunday School, the hard work that has to be done in every living church but has no publicity and no praise. The flirt never touches these, and often does not know they exist. May we be saved from the temptation to be just a spiritual flirt!

Good News

I am not ashamed of the Gospel of Christ

Saturday

Romans 1:16

Paul was not ashamed of the good news that he had to proclaim to men, news that had its focus and center and power in the person of Jesus Christ.

Some years ago a Christian Commando Campaign was held by the churches in Edinburgh. Christian Commandos went to their people where they could find them, instead of waiting for the people to come to them in the churches. An Edinburgh evening paper reported one such visit to a public house. The Christian Commando, thinking he was making a wise opening for conversation, said to a man propping up the bar, "If Jesus Christ was here speaking to you, what would He ask you to give to Him?" The man's reply revealed a greater understanding of the nature of the Christian Gospel than the Christian Commando's question, for the man replied in these words, "If Jesus Christ was here speaking to me, He would not ask me to give Him anything. He would want to give me something."

Is this not the very heart of the good news of the Christian Gospel which centers in the Cross of Christ? It tells us what Christ has done for us and what, in the light of that, God waits to give to us. So many people reverse this. They think Christianity consists of man doing something for God in his own strength, and man in his condescending kindness giving to God the trivial areas of his life.

Briefing for Battle

And, behold, there stood a man

Sunday

Joshua 5:13

Joshua very sensibly had gone out to do some reconnaisance of the situation confronting him. He wanted to take a good look at Jericho and instead found himself looking at Jesus!

Think of the *reassessment of his task* that this interview meant for Joshua. The problem that concerned him was obvious enough, the fortified and defended city of Jericho, an obstacle to any further advance. Christians are not unfamiliar with massive problems that seem to make any further advance impossible. But the Presence that confronted him was a surprise. Joshua had to learn that the basic problem was not with Jericho, but with his Lord, with Jesus, who confronts us all as "Captain of the Lord's host!"

Think of the *readjustment in his life* that this interview asked of Joshua. It was right and proper that Joshua fell on his face and asked the question, "What saith my Lord unto His servant?" How startled, however, Joshua must have been when the reply revealed that the Lord's concern had nothing to do with Jericho at all, but with Joshua himself. Something in Joshua needed adjustment. "Loose thy shoe from off thy foot." The assent to His Lord's control came at once as we read, "And Joshua did so." What would have happened if Joshua had refused to do what his Lord required, if he had insisted that it was Jericho that he wanted to hear about?

Think of the *reassurance from his Lord.* Only after Joshua's obedience concerning something in his own life did the Lord deal with Jericho. Joshua learned that the intention of the Lord concerning Jericho was summed up in one word, "victory." What had been a problem to Joshua was no problem to Jesus. "I have given unto thine hand Jericho." But Joshua then had to listen to the instructions that his Lord gave. They were strange instructions which, when carried out, brought the promised victory. Is the lesson here for us that we too need to follow His orders if victory is to be ours?

Knowing Means Loving

That I may know Him

Monday

Philippians 3:10

You just can't love a person you don't really know. I shall never forget the light that suddenly blazed across the Christian path for me when I stumbled over that great verse in Philippians 3:10. It is a verse I write practically every time I am asked to sign my name. "That I may know Him, and the power of His resurrection, and the fellowship of His sufferings."

I realized that the Christian's first concern must be to know his Lord, not what he can get from his Lord. At that time in my life, as a young Christian, I wanted power. I wanted power for service, power for victory. Through this verse I suddenly discovered that I had things mixed up and in the wrong order. The first thing Paul determined to do was to know his Lord, not to get anything from Him.

Some Christians are rather like the girl who only dates a boy to see what he will give her—a box of chocolates, a bottle of perfume, or dinner in a restaurant somewhere. All she is interested in are the gifts, not the boy himself. This kind of Christian doesn't even want to get to know the Lord. All he wants is what Jesus will give to him. But getting to know Him means getting to love Him.

So it was that I discovered the Bible truth behind a common cliché among evangelical Christians, but a profound truth all the same. I discovered the meaning of "the expulsive power of a new affection." Again we see the necessity for that daily quiet time—for it is there that we come to know Him.

The Unreaped Corners

And when ye reap the harvest of your land, thou shalt not wholly reap the corners of thy field

Leviticus 19:9

Tuesday

Here we have God's counsel not only for harvesting crops of the farm, but for life itself. We face the lesson that we must not claim all that we possess. That unreaped corner in the field of golden grain is as much the farmer's as all the rest he is reaping. It is grown on his land, he purchased the seed and sowed it, he watched and weeded the crop until it ripened from green to gold. The whole field is his.

But, "No!" God says, "Leave something for others—leave something for Me." This principle applies to life. The unreaped corner is a denial of selfishness. We all know people who lack consideration for others. What they possess, they claim—firmly, politely and if need be, fiercely! It may be their home or their children but how possessive their attitude can be, especially when the children begin to catch a vision of the world's need and see that life means service for others.

There are two things in our lives that we especially claim as our own. The first is our time—but God steps in here and says, "Six days shalt thou labor, . . . but the seventh day is the sabbath of the Lord thy God." Every day is really His but all He asks is one day out of seven. The second is our money. "It is mine," we say. "I can spend it as I choose." Can we? God has the right to all, but He only claims one tenth. Do we give to God as little as we dare, or as much

141

as we can? A seventh of our time, a tenth of our money are His. That unreaped corner is not for us, it is for Him and for others.

Coming to Christ

To whom coming

1 Peter 2:4

This opening phrase in verse 4 is most significant. Peter is going to say much about the Church, but he begins with Christ and speaks of those who have "come to Christ." Having come to Christ, they then find they have entered the Church. Some theologians, so called, reverse the order: in their minds the church somehow or other brings us to Christ and we become Christians through the sacraments or through membership in the church.

But the New Testament order is the reverse of this—we come to Christ first, and as we come to Him we enter the Church. This phrase, "come to Christ," is one which some people scorn! It sounds too simple to "come to Christ," but simplicity is the very heart of God's revelation of Himself in Christ. Coming to Christ surely means being aware of our need of Him, accepting His claims to meet that need, trusting in His merits in the sight of God, and experiencing His risen life, and His gift to us through the Holy Spirit. To become part of the Church of Jesus Christ, we must first come to Jesus Christ.

A Matter of Evaluation

Less honorable . . . more abundant honor . . .

1 Corinthians 12:23

Paul wants to deal with a very foolish way in which some Christians think. From verse 22 on, he deals with the question of evaluation. Paul points out that in the physical body some of the most important functions are carried out by the least attractive members: their functional value is much more important than their physical appearance. A girl may have a beautiful face but it will soon be much more important to her husband if she can cook a decent meal.

We see this in society. The people who keep our street tidy are really of much greater importance than the pop singers who fill our

142

screens, and yet we despise the one and admire the other. So it can happen in the matter of the gifts of the Spirit. The person who has one special gift could be tempted to look rather pityingly upon the Christian who has not that particular gift. Paul says in effect, "God has in the physical creation of our body attributed a vital importance to organs which do not particularly impress the observer with their beauty." I have never yet heard anybody say about a beautiful girl, "Hasn't she got a healthy liver, or kidneys!" but without a liver or kidneys, beautiful or not, she couldn't live.

So, too, in the body of the Church, essential and important gifts are being exercised that evoke no comment, get no publicity, arouse no envy, and yet without them the work of the Church would grind to a halt tomorrow. The tragedy is that these very Christians are sometimes despised as inferior. What a strange standard of evaluation some of us have.

Are you Drifting?

Lest we drift away from it (RSV)

Friday   Hebrews 2:1

Some of us have known the pleasure of idly drifting in a boat on a lovely summer's day. But drifting can be dangerous. It is possible to drift spiritually and morally. Think of the powerful currents that can take hold of our lives and carry us along unless we make the effort to control the direction in which we are traveling. There is the current of social opinion. The Bible calls it "walking according to the course of this world." There is the current of personal desire, doing the things that we want. What a tremendously strong current that is!

The currents are powerful, and the consequences of drifting can be perilous. By drifting we can land ourselves in real danger. By doing nothing and just giving ourselves to the currents that bear us along, we can drift a long, long way. How many Christians there are who used to be deeply involved in the work of the church but who have drifted so long and so far that these things are all out of sight. They never meant to get that distance away but have taken that direction through laziness, weakness or cowardice.

There are two courses possible for us. We can either continue to drift or we can make up our mind that we are going to cease to drift, and start pulling on the oars with God's help to get back where we ought to be. Have you been drifting? If so, is it not time

143

you stopped and began to move back to where you used to be in Christian things?

The Obedience of the Servant

The Spirit suffered them not

Acts 16:7

Whether there would be a church at all in Philippi depended upon Paul's obedience. And his obedience was twofold in its character.

First of all, God closed a door. "After they were come to Mysia, they assayed to go into Bithynia: but the Spirit suffered them not" (Acts 16:7). That is, God said to Paul and Silas, "There is something you are not to do. Don't do it." Paul accepted the closure of that door.

But with the closing of one door, another door opened. A vision appeared to Paul in the night. "There stood a man of Macedonia, and prayed him, saying, 'Come over into Macedonia, and help us.' And after he had seen the vision, immediately we endeavored to go into Macedonia, assuredly gathering that the Lord had called us for to preach the gospel unto them."

I believe there is something for us to learn from this. Are we not suffering today from an overfamiliarity with the truth of the forgiveness of sins? We have almost come to the position where we think it doesn't really matter whether we obey God or not. It doesn't matter very much if we don't do something God has told us to do. After all, we can simply turn to 1 John 1:9 and claim the promise, "If we confess our sins, He (God) is faithful and just to forgive us *our* sins, and to cleanse us from all unrighteousness." We are in serious danger of taking the attitude which says, "It doesn't matter if I sin."

The one lesson that stands out vividly in this particular passage is that the work of God depends upon the will of God and ultimately upon obedience to God. It matters profoundly if you and I are obedient or disobedient to the will of God. I think we can say that in evangelical circles today the whole issue that God has with the Church does not lie in the realm of our ignorance, for we *know* so much. It is our obedience that is at fault. We don't *do* the will of God!

How much does the situation in your hospital, your church, your school, your business, your factory, your shop, your home, turn upon your obedience? There may be people that God is wanting to reach whom He cannot reach because He cannot get to them through you.

How a Christian rises from His Knees

Thine is the Kingdom, and the power, and the glory, for ever. Amen

Sunday

Matthew 6:13

How often do we stop to think over what these familiar words mean as we rise from our knees after saying them?

"Thine is the kingdom." The Christian rises from his knees *committed to the will of God!* The king reigns and rules and is to be obeyed. Here is but an added confirmation of the earlier words, "Thy will be done." There are always alternatives we can find to the will of God; we can do what others do, or we can do what we like. But while these may at times be acceptable, to the Christian the decisive consideration is what He says. And this is the imperative the Christian will face, happily and eagerly.

"Thine is the power." The Christian rises from his knees *confident in the power of God.* That power was received when the new life of Christ came into the life of the sinner. "Ye shall receive power, after that the Holy Ghost is come upon you" was the final great promise of Christ to His own. But the power that has been received is a power that must be released. The Holy Spirit must be allowed to do in our lives what He has come to do and to be in our lives. Our consent will mean that He has been received; His control will mean that He has been released.

"Thine is the Glory." The Christian rises from his knees *concerned for the glory of God!* Think for a moment of the dishonor to God which the Christian is distressed to see. His will defied, His Word unread, His day desecrated, His house left empty, His Son rejected! On every hand there are those who say they believe in God but fail to give Him the honor due to His name. This the Christian cannot bear to see, and so the mind of the Christian is set on the vindication of God. Someone has said that "a concern for the glory of God is the ultimate motive for Christian living and Christian witness."

145

A Fellowship that was Dependable and Reliable

I thank my God upon every remembrance of you . . .
for your fellowship in the Gospel from the first day until now

Philippians 1:3,5

Are people grateful for your fellowship because it is reliable and dependable? Or are they disappointed with your unreliability? We seem to be living in days when dependability and responsibility are almost forgotten features of life. It seems to be so in industry. Can your boss depend on you? Is he glad that you are his secretary? Is your Sunday School superintendent grateful that you work with him to further the Gospel among the children? Are you so reliable and so faithful that he thanks God on every remembrance of you? Is your minister thankful that you're one of his flock? Does he know that you are going to be at the prayer meeting come rain, come wind? Is he grateful for your fellowship in furthering the Gospel from the first day until now?

Here was a fellowship that had been proved and tested. We want this kind of Christianity. I called once to see the matron of a big London hospital about some aspect of Christian work. She told me she had recently been at the annual meeting of the Nurses' Christian Fellowship in that hospital where one nurse gave her testimony about what a difference Christ made in her life. But all the time the girl was speaking, the matron was remembering what supervisors had said about the same nurse in the ward and the kind of examination results she was producing. The two didn't match—her testimony and her life. Are people grateful for you?

Do You Know Him?

That I may know Him

Philippians 3:10

Here is the goal of all Christian endeavor, of all Christian experience. The first thing, the all-important thing, is to know Christ.

So many of us get things out of order. Sometimes we put power first; sometimes we put blessing first; sometimes we put success first; sometimes we put the fullness of the Spirit first. If we put anything else first, we are wrong. "That I may know Him"—that is what matters.

Incidentally, this would help many in their thinking about the Holy Spirit. I have never forgotten some words of my principal at theological college. He was a deeply-taught Bible student, a sane and godly Christian man. We were young theological students with all the enthusiasm and lack of balance that is the mark of youth. It cannot be easy, as principal of a Bible or theological college, to keep under control a lot of young men as restless and undisciplined as wild horses.

There are movements that sometimes pass through such a college. There were men who were longing for the baptism of the Holy Spirit, as they called it. Others sought the fullness of the Holy Spirit. Still others sought for a second, third, or fourth blessing! They had all kinds of ambitions. But the principal said something like this: "You can always test any claimed blessing of the Holy Spirit by asking the following question: 'Does it bring me to a deeper knowledge of Christ?'"

If an experience doesn't bring me to a deeper knowledge of Christ, it is not the work of the Spirit of God. Why? Because we read of that very same Holy Spirit, "He shall testify of me." "He shall glorify me." Christ said that about the Spirit of God. What matters is not, "Am I excited? Am I moved?" but, "Do I know Christ more?" If you don't know Christ more after a so-called experience of the Spirit of God, then question the validity of that experience right away.

Equipment for Witness

They were all filled with the Holy Ghost, and began to speak with other tongues, as the Spirit gave them utterance

Wednesday   Acts 2:4

We will not deal here with the phrase, "with other tongues," which seems to have been a unique experience on the Day of Pentecost when the crowds heard the apostles speak in their own language. There was no need for any interpretation. But we do want to note one thing that happened when the Holy Spirit took possession of Christians: their mouths were opened. We read this again and again. They were "filled" and then they spoke.

But even here care is needed. Some people are in danger of assuming that whenever a Christian is filled with the Spirit this will result in tremendous blessing, and thousands will be converted to faith in Christ as happened in Jerusalem on the Day of Pentecost, and later in Samaria. But in scripture, big movements of this nature are confined to a few occasions. Was Paul not filled with the Spirit when he went to Athens? How many responded there? Was Paul not filled with the Spirit when he went to Corinth? How many were converted there? Surely Paul was continually being filled with the Spirit, and yet in the greater part of his missionary journeys the response seems to have been small.

The reason for the exceptional responses in Jerusalem and Samaria was surely that these were fields where the seed had been well sown and well tended by the earlier ministry of Christ Himself and there was a great harvest to reap. Yes, we will be equipped for witness when we are filled with the Spirit. We will find we can speak with understanding and with power, but let's not think that thousands will necessarily be brought to Christ. It didn't happen then, so why should it happen now?

Suffering as a Christian

For as the sufferings of Christ abound in us, so our consolation also aboundeth by Christ

2 Corinthians 1:5

Thursday

In the opening verses of Paul's second letter to the church at Corinth he speaks of the way in which "the sufferings of Christ abound in us." He tells the church how he found that to serve Jesus Christ meant receiving the same kind of treatment Christ had received. There are certain sufferings that come our way, just as they came Christ's way. These sufferings come to us because we are Christians. Christians share the very life of Christ; they live the same way, they are concerned about the same things, they suffer in the same way.

The suffering of Christ came to Him mainly along two lines. First, suffering came to Him from the hands of men because of the resentment His life provoked as it convicted them of their failure, and because they rejected His message. Suffering also came to Him through His acceptance of the will of God in achieving redemption for the world. This acceptance of the will of God for Him meant bearing the burden of the world's sin in His atoning death.

Suffering for Christ is something which the true Christian will have to face in life. In Colossians 1:24, Paul also speaks of "filling up that which is lacking of the affliction of Christ," and in Hebrews 13:13 the writer speaks of going outside the camp "bearing His reproach." We need to remember that the badge of the Christian is not a cushion but a cross. One commentator quotes the words of

Samuel Rutherford when writing to a friend: "God has called you to Christ's side and the wind is now in Christ's face in this land; and seeing you are with Him you cannot expect the leeward side nor the sunny side of the brae."

The Response Love Gets

Behold king Solomon

Friday

Song of Solomon 3:11

Preoccupation with the splendor of the king possesses the heart and mind of the bride. Although she is sharing it all with him, and all that he has is hers, her thoughts now are not so much of what he gives but of who he is. So in verse 11 the bride says, "Go forth, O ye daughters of Zion, and behold King Solomon with the crown wherewith his mother crowned him in the day of his espousals, and in the day of the gladness of his heart." What a tremendous word of testimony this is—"Go forth, . . . and behold the king . . . crowned."

It reminds me of that tremendous opening scene of the Passion Play at Oberammergau when, all of a sudden, the courtyard fills with hundreds of people, all singing. They are pointing and looking in one direction from which, through the crowd, emerges the figure of Christ, riding on a donkey. The words of their song are, "Hail to Thee! Hail! O David's Son! Hail to Thee! Hail! The Father's throne belongs to Thee." It is the same thought—"Behold the King crowned." Here it seems as if at last the bride's heart realizes just who the bridegroom is. The wealth with which he has enriched her, the splendor and majesty that belong to him, the position she now shares with him, all overwhelm her with glory; and in a sense of utter self-forgetfulness she enthrones him too as king and lord in her heart. If he is sharing all that his love has to give, she will respond with all the love she has to give. And in that mutual self-giving there comes an experience of joy that sets their hearts a-singing.

What love shares! Surely this is one of those amazing truths whose familiarity dulls our sense of wonder, that we simple folk are nevertheless lifted up into that environment where all the glory, majesty, and wonder of God's grace in Christ is ours.

Is There a Prayer Meeting in Your Church?

. . . many were gathered together praying

Saturday

Acts 12:12

Behind every revival that has marked the life and history of the Church has been the prayer of some of God's faithful people. It seems that one of the most urgent needs in the life of the Church today is that prayer be given its right place—not only in the life of the individual Christian, but also in the corporate life of the Church's fellowship, worship and service.

It is a tragedy that so many churches have given up even attempting a meeting for prayer during the week, and that where it is attempted so few are to be found there at prayer. There is something radically wrong with a church's sense of spiritual values when fifty to a hundred will turn out for a meeting of a social character, and only five to fourteen come to a meeting of such a specifically spiritual character as a prayer meeting.

Very often one of the features of a true revival is that the attendances at weekly prayer meeting so increase that they exceed the numbers previously found attending the normal services of worship on Sunday! Does your church have a prayer meeting? Do you attend it as often as you can? If there is not a prayer meeting have you ever thought of asking for one to be started? In the early Church we read of "many . . . gathered together praying."

Failure Need Never be Final

Jesus saith unto him, Feed My lambs

Sunday

John 21:15

The scene by the lakeside after the resurrection of Jesus which led to the restoration of Simon Peter is surely one of the most beautiful scenes in the New Testament. Think of the *tragedy that Christ sensed* in Simon Peter. There was of course the *disgrace* that was well known; for everyone knew about his denial of his Lord with oaths and curses. But there was also the *despair* that was unknown to all except Christ.

When Simon Peter said to the rest, "I go fishing," was that just evidence of a hidden despair and blackness? Had he fallen so low that he could never rise up again? But Christ wanted him, and Christ was seeking him. So we can note also the *honesty that Christ sought* from Simon Peter. There was something that Christ wanted to face alone with him and so He drew him aside. Surely the deeper crises in our spiritual experience are not public affairs but private matters between the soul and Christ. There was also something that Christ wanted to find alive in him. Christ was anxious to discern if love still lingered when all else had disappeared. He found it to be so in those great words of Peter, "Lord, Thou knowest all things; Thou knowest that I love thee."

As a result there was now the *destiny that Christ shared* with Simon Peter. What a surprise that new responsibility must have been. Simon Peter, the man no church would ever have chosen for a minister, was nonetheless chosen by God, and the secret of his new reliability would be the love he had for his Lord. When all else had gone, this remained, and that was enough for Christ.

What a tremendous truth it is that failure need never be final. As long as there is, lingering in our hearts, a love for Christ, then Christ will take us and use us again in His service.

Surrendered

Yield yourselves unto God, as those that are alive from the dead, and your members as instruments of righteousness unto God

Monday   Romans 6:13

The thought underlying these words is that of action taken decisively, once and for all. There has to come a time when in one moment, one place and one action we crown Christ Lord of all. We "yield ourselves to Him as God."

Evan Hopkins, a great teacher at the Keswick Convention, used to say that yielding means three things. It means *ceasing to resist*— to resist the claims and the voice of God. Just as a girl who has resisted the approach of love finally gives in and gives herself to the love of a man in marriage, so we are to cease resisting the pleadings of the love of God in Christ. Have some of us been resisting the lordship of Christ in our hearts? We don't mind giving Him this or that bit of life, but that inner throne room—No. We have a notice on that particular door—'No admittance—Private.'

But the Lordship of Christ means *ceasing to withhold* and to allow every area in our lives to come under His control. Yielding means *ceasing to struggle*. It means giving ourselves without reserve to Him and to receive in return the riches of His love and grace. Yielding is an unseen action in our hearts proclaiming His Lordship in our lives. It happens at that moment when we place the crown upon His head. In every reign there is a moment of coronation. Has that moment come in our life with Christ?

When Guilt is Denied

If we say that we have not sinned, we make Him a liar, and His word is not in us

Tuesday   1 John 1:10

This verse always used to bother me. It seemed to me so stupid. Who on earth would ever dream of saying that they had not sinned? Then one day as I was reading the familiar words, I suddenly realized that we have to put the emphasis where I am sure John meant it. If we put the emphasis on the word "sinned," we get the meaning. "If we say we have not *sinned* we make God a liar, and His word is not in us."

John is not concerned with people who actually deny that they ever sin, but with those who claim that the sin they do commit is not sin at all and therefore deny that they are guilty. John means that there are times when we are not prepared to admit anything wrong about what we are doing.

Today more than ever we find people in this precise position and maintaining it. We call this age the age of permissiveness, and what permissiveness has at its very heart is the denial of guilt. Men change the labels and say things that God's law condemns are not sins. Labels can be changed but that doesn't change what is inside, and sin in the sight of God is still sin. The people to whom John is referring rejected the condemnation and judgment of God upon the sins they were committing.

We are told that "God sending His own Son in the likeness of sinful flesh, and for sin, condemned sin in the flesh." If is true that there is a *guilt these men denied,* then that leads to a *grace that these men had discarded.* If there is no guilt there is no sin; if there is no sin there is no need for a Savior. These people were adopting a position which simply made God a liar and said that God's whole plan of salvation was irrelevant and meaningless, and that the Gospel of God's saving grace in Jesus Christ was nothing but a quack remedy for an illness that never existed. What a fantastic situation; and what a tragic destination for those who walk in the darkness.

Are We Willing?

At thy word I will

Luke 5:5

How those five words could change our lives if we dared to utter them honestly and without reserve to Jesus Christ! How tremendously challenging and exciting our Christian experience would become instead of being the rather humdrum sort of thing that many of us know, month after month, year after year.

One of the first lessons of Christian experience that we have to learn is that of instant obedience to the will of God. Delayed obedience can become disobedience. So often we have arguments and reasons for disobeying, just as Peter may have had, but our own ways prove to be fruitless endeavor, while His way, however unpromising it may seem in advance, always proves blessed and fruitful. Are we ready to say every day, at any time, "At Thy word I will"?

It is worth noting that the Master was asking for obedience just then. The disciples might have asked Him to wait until the nets were mended or until they had been able to get fresh ones along. But no, the nets they had used all night, torn as they were and half mended, were the nets they were to use. One of the miracles of the grace of God is what He is able to do with the torn nets of lives that are surrendered to Him. He uses men and women who, though far from perfect as yet, are nevertheless obedient to the voice of the Master they love. The responsibility for guidance is always His. The responsibility for obedience is always ours.

The Need for a Decision

Multitudes in the valley of decision

Joel 3:14

In this verse we come face to face with a word that lies at the very heart of the Christian Gospel. It brings out an emphasis that so many people seem to resent. Paul says that the Gospel of Christ is "the power of God unto salvation to every one that believeth." It is difficult to understand why people get upset about the challenge to make a decision concerning Jesus Christ. It seems so essentially reasonable.

The need to make a decision finds its place in every other realm of life. The captain of a cricket team decides who is to bat first. A lady buying a hat decides ultimately which out of many she will purchase. A child wanting to spend his pocket-money decides what he is going to buy. A man facing life decides what he is going to be. Everyone in almost every relationship of life is accustomed to making decisions.

Why then should we think that the spiritual realm of life is to be excluded? Why should we think that Christianity is to be experienced as a result of intellectual and individual drift? We surely don't expect to become Christians by chance—clearly it must be by choice. Such an emphasis on the need for a decision is eminently reasonable, and it is also essentially ethical.

If the whole plan of salvation is to have a moral foundation—for man is a moral being with the power of choice—then man must be able to choose. Salvation can't be forced on man or the integrity of human personality will be destroyed. So it is that what Christ did for us and can be to us and in us becomes ours in personal experience when we put our trust in Him, just as all the skill and ability of a brilliant surgeon becomes ours when we put ourselves into his hands.

Quarrelsome Women

Friday

I beseech Euodias, and beseech Syntyche, that they be of the same mind in the Lord

Philippians 4:2

Euodias and Syntyche have achieved immortality just because they quarreled! They are described by Paul as those who had labored with him. I don't think they were just members of the rank and file of the church; in all probability they were people of some prominence, but they weren't on speaking terms. They were not "of the same mind" in the Lord. Some serious difference between them was causing trouble and anxiety in the church and Paul said the trouble must be dealt with. So we see that sometimes prominent people have problems in relationships.

Here the problem persisted, suggested by the words in verse 5 where Paul speaks of, "your moderation." The meaning of that word as Handley Moule suggests is, "Let your yieldingness be known unto all men." The fact that you disagree is widely known but let your "yieldingness"—the fact that you are willing to give way, to be gracious—be known too unto all men. I think the lack of yieldingness implies that this situation had existed for a considerable time.

How strange it is and how inconsistent about Christian living at an executive level that sometimes Christians in high office are out of fellowship with each other. And the facts get widely known just because they are so prominent. It is still more strange that such a situation can go on year after year. There is a warning here for some of us. We must avoid the danger of assuming that because we are growing up in our responsibilities in the church and because God is using us that we are getting beyond the need of correction. Those who instruct others or hold responsible offices are sometimes so accustomed to telling other people what they ought to do that they fail to stop and think that perhaps they need to be told what they ought to do!

Secret Sorrows

Behold, he had sackcloth within upon his flesh
2 Kings 6:30

Saturday

These were desperate days within the besieged city of Samaria. The people had been reduced to cannabalism and the king, on a tour of inspection, suddenly realized how desperate the plight of the people was. He rent his clothes and we are told that, "Behold, he had sackcloth within upon his flesh." The discovery that the people of Samaria made concerning their king was as startling as it was unexpected. Who would have dreamed that beneath the rich apparel there would be found the coarse and constant irritation of the sackcloth within?

But how often in life we, too, have made a similar discovery concerning the hidden sorrows and secret trials of other people. Some chance wind of circumstances reveals the sackcloth within. This discovery must have had a transforming effect upon the judgment the people passed on the king. They must have had their thoughts about him. Did he care? Was he indifferent? This discovery threw a sudden and revealing light upon a man whom they had been judging in their daily conversation; and how superficial now their judgment would seem to be!

The king was wearing sackcloth, that's true, but he didn't have to. He could have remained aloof and indifferent to the troubles of his people but he chose not to. He preferred to be constantly reminded of their troubles. Does this conduct of the king rebuke us?

Do we seek to escape from the troubles of others, or do we, like the king, share them? Like our Master, but in another way, we may bear in our bodies the sins of the world. The king did not shirk his duty. Do we?

The Sufficiency of God

The vessels were full

Sunday   2 Kings 4:6

I like to think that the miracles, whether in the Old or New Testament, are simply parables in action. If that is so, then this miracle has some lovely truths to teach us about the sufficiency of God.

This widow has some things in common with most of us. There were demands that she could not meet. Through the death of her husband and the claims of the creditors she was in danger of losing her sons who would have to go into servitude to work off the debts—quite a sensible arrangement in some ways, but causing her great distress. There was also the disgrace that she could not bear, for her husband had been in the service of the living God and it would not bring any credit to the name of the Lord if such a state of affairs became known. So it is with many of us, facing not just the threat of servitude, but the slavery of it, and feeling that such living is not worthy of the name of the Lord.

The woman was also in touch with God for we read, "She cried unto Elisha." She was a wise woman to take her troubles there. But how searching were the words of God in the two questions asked through His servant. The first was, "What do you want?" and the second, "What have you got?" What we want is revealed in the prayers we offer and what we have is made plain in scripture. If we are Christians, we have our "pot of oil." We may be tempted to think like the woman that we have nothing; but she remembered that she did have something and so must we. We have the Holy Spirit! How simple were the ways of God for the widow! She had to take what she had and, with the gathered empty vessels, allow God to show her what He could do with what she already had. We need to learn the same lesson—that the Spirit of God does not lack power but only the opportunity in our lives.

She was in earnest with herself. We know that because of the hiddenness and the thoroughness of her obedience. In faith she did exactly what she had been told to do until there was not a vessel more. We have received the Holy Spirit—now we must release Him to do in our lives what He has been given to accomplish there. Remember that what she did, she did behind closed doors. Do we need to learn that the secrets of spiritual sufficiency have no public audience?

What a Let Down

Now when Paul and his company loosed from Paphos,
they came to Perga in Pamphylia: and John departing
from them returned to Jerusalem

Monday   Acts 13:13

The exact circumstances surrounding the defection of Mark are not clear but the consequences of his defection (Acts 15:36ff.) suggest that in Paul's view, at any rate, it was inexcusable. Perhaps he just could not stand the pace, or the dangers and hardships, and so he went home.

I wonder if too much had been asked of John Mark too soon! I wonder if people assumed that just because he came from a family with relatives such as Barnabas, John Mark, a much younger Christian, could therefore come up to that same level! Were others pushing him too far, too fast, too soon? All I know is that such things can and too often do happen. A girl or a boy with a spiritual home background is pushed too far, too soon, and then tragedy strikes. They are not ready for it, can't take it and so walk out on it all.

When Barnabas suggests later on that Mark be given another chance, Paul will have none of it and replaces Mark and Barnabas with Silas and later on Luke. But how wonderful that there was someone who did have time for John Mark. "And Barnabas took him." Barnabas parted with Paul so that he might link up with John Mark. John Mark, who never became the preacher that his mother may have wanted him to be, later became the writer instead and gave us the priceless gift of the Gospel that bears his name. Perhaps God wants us to do something quite different from what others expect of us; and perhaps He will give a Barnabas to take us by the hand and lead us into that new service.

Like a Mighty Army

A good soldier of Jesus Christ

Tuesday   2 Timothy 2:3

"Like a might army moves the Church of God." These are great

157

words out of a great hymn, but to be in an army calls for courage. And our nation today desperately needs men and women who will throw off the laziness and slackness which grips so many lives, who will dare to live in the light of what they believe about God and Jesus Christ, about sin and salvation. We need people who will live out what they believe and, in so doing, lead others who are in the dark and looking for a better way to a truer happiness and a richer life.

But others will only find this as Christians accept the challenge of their own faith, show the courage that faith demands, and confess by lip and life before the world from which they differ, but to which they have so much to give—so much for which it is searching blindly.

Well-Wishing Achieves Little

Thirty-two thousand

Wednesday   Judges 7:3

Gideon declared war against the oppressor and summoned the nation to his side. Thirty-two thousand who wished him well responded. The cause of Jesus Christ has never lacked its well-wishers, but mere well-wishing seldom achieves anything.

A twofold test sifted the well-wishers then and does so now. The first test was that of *fearfulness.* "Whosoever is fearful and afraid, let him return." There is much that has never been attempted because of fear—fear of failing, fear of what people might say, fear that it would be too difficult, fear of not being able to see it through.

The second test was that of *casualness.* This test took place by the stream. Only a handful were so pressed by the urgency of the hour that they scarcely paused. The rest got down lazily and thankfully to the business of drinking. The same spirit is abroad today— what's the hurry, why be so keen? How many fail this test and scarcely know that they have been found wanting.

Being in a Minority

Three hundred men

Judges 7:6

Only three hundred men to tackle a vast army and to deliver a whole nation! But is it not true that God always works with a minority? Democracy needs a majority but Deity is content with a minority!

Let us never then be discouraged if we find ourselves in such a company, but let us remember the three hundred of Gideon. Let us remember the twelve of the Master. Let us remember the two of Jonathan—Jonathan and his armor-bearer, who encouraged one another with the words in 1 Samuel 14:6, "Come and let us go . . . it may be that the Lord will work for us: for there is no restraint to the Lord to save by many or by few."

So it was that Gideon's three hundred routed the Midianites; Jonathan and his armor-bearer routed the Philistines; and so it was that the twelve of the Master turned the world upside down. We may be in a minority but even one with God is really a majority!

Stand Fast!

. . . That ye stand fast in one spirit, with one mind striving together for the faith of the Gospel; and in nothing terrified by your adversaries: . . .

Philippians 1:27, 28

Nothing brings more confusion, more disorder and more disunity into Christian fellowship than a large-scale retreat on a section of the front. It means a break in the line. One of the simple elementary tactics of warfare is divide, and then destroy. Break the unity, and then make the most of the disunity. Paul said to this church, "When you are facing pressure from without, from the world or from the devil, don't retreat. Stand fast. Don't give way."

We are living in a day when the Christian Church, by and large, is on the retreat. We are giving ground—right, left, and center. Disunity is creeping into our Christian fellowships. Why is it that people retreat? Always because they don't want to suffer. They don't want to be laughed at; they don't want to be thought peculiar; they don't want to be criticized; they don't want to be ridiculed. So they give way, and they give in. Paul said, "Remember this. It's part of your privilege. When you are facing the opposition

159

and the ceaseless pressure from the world and the devil, it is part of your privilege as a Christian to suffer."

We must not think that the only thing about being a Christian is believing; it is suffering too. Paul said, "Unto you it is given in the behalf of Christ, not only to believe on Him, but also to suffer for His sake: (1:29).

If you want to be popular, if you want to be a hail-fellow-well-met in the crowd where you work, then stop thinking about being a real Christian! Our Lord said, "The servant is not greater than his Lord. If they have persecuted Me, they will also persecute you." Once you are sure that you have ground upon which you must stand, (some Christians stand upon ground that they needn't stand on) then stand, and stand together.

Impossible

I cannot speak: for I am a child

Saturday

Jeremiah 1:6

I wonder whether you feel that the very thought of God using you as a spiritual influence to touch hundreds and thousands of people is quite ridiculous. When you meet the challenge of God's will and God's purpose your reply, like Jeremiah's, is, "I cannot speak, for I am a child."

I have never forgotten the story of Bishop Taylor Smith's call to the ministry, a call that came to him when he was just a lad. He had gone with a friend to a church in Carlisle which adjoined the cathedral. They arrived late and during the service a voice suddenly seemed to say to him, "Go to the Cathedral." This seemed a crazy thing to do for the service had hardly started yet apparently he was not to stay until it finished. The voice was so clear that he got up and went. The service in the Cathedral began a little later than that in the church and when he arrived the first lesson was just being read. And what was the lesson? "The word of the Lord came unto Jeremiah . . ." and John Taylor Smith was called by God into His service; a man who said, "I cannot speak: I am a child."

The amazing thing is that God seems to delight in using the people who think they are of no real use at all. If you think you are a great Christian, just the kind of person that God ought to be using, then you are the kind of person that He will never use. But if you can't believe that God could ever use you to do anything, then you are just the kind of person that He will use.

Paul says, "God hath chosen the foolish things of the world to confound the wise; and God hath chosen the weak things of the world to confound the things which are mighty: and the base things of the world, and things which are despised, hath God chosen, yea, and things which are not, to bring to nought things that are: That no flesh should glory in his presence."

An Unexplored World

Bring . . . the books

2 Timothy 4:13

An unexplored world for so many Christians is the world of Christian books. How many so-called Christians seldom, if ever, read any books about the Christian faith. If they do, the Bible is the only one, and that is often only read fitfully. We have to be careful, of course, in our choice of books, especially if we are young Christians. We do well to be guided by the author's, or publisher's name to be sure that we are going to read something that will be helpful. Every book that is religious is not necessarily Christian. But there are excellent reasons why good books are such valuable aids to Christian faith and life.

The intimacies of the Christian life are exposed in many books. Here we can find secrets of the victories of the saints. The problems they faced are so often like the problems we face, and the answers they found could well be the answers for which we ourselves are looking. We can find too the stimulus of vision. When we read and learn what God has done for others and through others, we find ourselves challenged as to whether God could do the same for us and through us. Books of Christian biography are surprisingly stimulating along these lines.

The realities of the Christian faith are explained in books. There is a reticence due to ignorance of which so many of us are guilty. We seldom talk about our faith to others because we don't really know ourselves what it is. We also need to face up to the importance of instruction which so many of us need. We usually hear a sermon only once and forget most of it, but a book can be read over and over again until we have really mastered its contents.

We benefit from ministries of the Christian Church. But ministers, pastors, vicars, rectors vary in their preaching ability. Some may be good but others are not as good, and some are really bad! By reading the books of really great preachers we can all enjoy the

161

greatest sermons ever preached. When death silences their voices, as in time it must, their books go on speaking. When distance separates them from us, the book brings the distant preacher into our home. Sunday is a wonderful opportunity to explore this unknown world.

The Sound of a Voice we Love

Mary . . . heard His word

Luke 10:39

To listen and to learn from the Master was Mary's supreme delight. To hear His voice meant everything to her. How much some voices mean to us! It may be the voice of some servant of God who has been greatly used as a means of grace to our own souls. We owe them such a debt, and we bear them such a love in Christ that the very sound of their voice is music to our ears. I can think of one such voice that I heard first in the tent at Keswick, a voice that has been stilled now in death.

This is why letters from home and from loved ones mean so much. As we read the written word we hear the speaking voice. But does God's voice mean as much to us as that? When the time comes for us to make our way to His feet do we go with dragging feet and with reluctant hearts? Or do we go eagerly and expectantly? The place of love is found at the feet of Jesus and the voice of love is heard there.

Baptized into One Body

For by one spirit we are all baptized into one body

1 Corinthians 12:13

Paul stresses here that the baptism in or with the Holy Spirit is a baptism into the body of Christ, into one body. The word translated in the Authorized Version "by" the Holy Ghost in Greek is the word "en," exactly the same word as is found in Matthew 3:11 which says, "I baptize you with water." Similarly in Acts 1:5. It is not a baptism by the Holy Spirit here, and a baptism by Jesus Christ there; it is a baptism with the Holy Spirit by Christ.

It is obvious that Paul here is referring to an initial experience and a universal one which every Christian in the Corinthian

162

Church had shared. He does not say that some of them had been baptized with the Holy Spirit and others had not, but they had *all* been baptized—good, bad and indifferent Christians as they were. They had all been baptized with the Holy Spirit into one body and here the purpose is stated clearly. The baptism with the Holy Spirit is the baptism into one body, the body of Christ.

The Christian in the New Testament is never told he *must be* baptized with the Holy Spirit; he is told that he *has been* baptized with the Holy Spirit. We never read in the New Testament that just some have been baptized with the Holy Spirit and that others have not, but we find that all have been baptized with the Spirit into the body of Christ and brought into union with Him. The baptism with the Holy Spirit in the New Testament has to do with something that happens at conversion; the Holy Spirit is uniting us to Christ, uniting us to one another, and creating a living, spiritual bond that has brought into existence a new, living community. This is the body of Christ, through which the Person of Christ will be seen, and through which the purposes of Christ are to be served.

The baptism with the Holy Spirit in the New Testament is always an initial experience, it is always a universal experience, it is always a spiritual experience. We never read of Christians seeking it, but always of a Christian sharing it, and sharing it with all other Christians. "You shall be baptized with the Holy Ghost" is the promise before Pentecost. You *have been* baptized with the Holy Ghost is the statement after Pentecost.

Think on these Things

Wednesday

Finally, brethren, whatsoever things are true,
whatsoever things are honest, whatsoever things are
just, whatsoever things are pure, whatsoever things are
lovely, whatsoever things are of good report; if there be
any virtue, and if there be any praise, think on these things
Philippians 4:8

Don't let your thought life become a kind of gossip shop. There are some Christians who, even if they don't gossip to one another, gossip to themselves. They allow all the unkind and sometimes the untrue, the unfair, the impure, and the unclean to circulate in their minds. The thought life is tremendously important, not just in this context but in every aspect of Christian work. If you think unkindly of a person or in an unfriendly way, that inner attitude which has become the constant attitude in your mind is something they are bound to sense when you meet them.

This is relevant in personal work and soul-winning work. The average Christian can be very zealous and very faithful in trying to reach the unconverted and the unsaved, but his efforts are doomed to failure before he begins if his attitude of mind to unconverted people is a critical one. "This person doesn't go to church. Isn't that terrible?" "This person never reads his Bible. I think that is frightful." "This person lives a kind of life that is absolutely godless. I think that is appalling." If you come into contact with a person you think is dreadful, frightful, and appalling, and you try to win that person for Christ, how does that person react? People know instinctively the moment they meet us how we feel about them. So if our attitude is critical, we never get anywhere with them.

Bishop Taylor Smith once told me, "When I meet a person I have never met before and I feel in my heart I must bear some sort of witness or testimony, I don't assume that they are unconverted. I may find out in a matter of minutes that they are not, but when I first meet them I assume that they are in full agreement with my outlook. This means that in my mind I am not approaching them critically or censoriously. I am approaching them with an attitude which is friendly and we are at ease with one another right away." We do well to follow the Bishop here and to remember that our Lord was called "the Friend of sinners" and not their critic.

Witnessing

Ye shall be witnesses

Thursday

Acts 1:8

A witness is someone who says what he knows. Christianity is meant to be talked about, not just by those in the pulpits, but by everyone who names the name of Christ. That is how it spread at the beginning. We read in the New Testament that when persecution broke out the Christians were scattered and that they went everywhere "preaching the word."

I don't mean by this that we impose on people whom we do not know and ask them intimate questions about their souls. But I do mean that when our faith is challenged, as it most certainly will be, or when the name of Christ comes up in conversation, then we have *got* to speak up. Other people who think differently are far from backward in expressing their points of view.

What the Church needs desperately today is that the thousands and thousands of ordinary people found in her ranks should not be ashamed to "say a good word for Jesus Christ."

Man Needs to be Saved

I am not ashamed of the Gospel of Christ: for it is the power of God unto salvation to every one that believeth

Romans 1:16

Friday

When Paul describes the Christian Gospel as being "the power of God unto salvation to every one that believeth," the word "salvation" is a strong word. It is not a word invented by any particular brand of Christianity but a word that is stamped with the authority of Jesus Christ Himself who said that He came "to seek and to *save* that which was lost." The word found its way into the language of the gospels at the very commencement of His life on earth. The message that came to Joseph concerning the child that was to be born was, "Thou shalt call His name Jesus: for He shall save His people from their sins." The Gospel does not say that men need just to be helped or that they need to be advised, or strengthened, or guided. It says they need to be saved.

Whenever we use the word "saved," it carries with it a sense of urgency, a sense of desperation, an awareness of danger. For example, I could say—and say truly—that penicillin has saved my life. Some years ago when I developed blood poisoning, the numerous and frequent injections of penicillin I received literally did save my life. By contrast, some years earlier, before the discovery of penicillin, my elder sister fell ill with the same disease. At that time there was no certain cure for it, and within a few days she died.

So there is in Christianity this note of urgency, this note of seriousness. Indeed it is a note that is beginning to find its way more and more into the thinking of men today. In this atomic age man's powers of destruction are so extensive and terrifying that it would seem almost as if all human life might be destroyed in a moment of time. But man needs supremely to be saved from sin—its guilt, its power, and its presence.

Love's Desire

*Then took Mary a pound of ointment of spikenard,
very costly*

Saturday

John 12:3

Love's desire is always to share the burden and to enter into the experience of those it loves. How could Mary show her Lord that she knew what was in His mind and burdening His Spirit? How could she tell Him that He would not be alone in the sacrifice that He was going to make? It was this desire of her love which made her bring that costly alabaster box of ointment and lavish it on Him. She would not allow Him to remain uncomforted, and so she brought her best—almost her all! Prodigal the gift might be, wasteful it might seem, but how welcome it was to the heart of Christ! When the cold voice of criticism spoke, "Why was not this ointment sold for three hundred pence, and given to the poor?" Christ broke in sharply, almost harshly, "Let her alone: against the day of my burying hath she kept this."

Yes, love discerns and love desires to enter into the very heart and mind and experience of those it loves. How much clumsy and awkward piety there is in the Church today! What need there is for Christian living that is sensitive to the mind of God. How much we hurt because we blunder! We may be keen and zealous for Christ, but we are clumsy and rough in our handling of men. If we are going to become more sensitive and more discerning, we have to get to know the Lord better. We must spend more time at His feet as Mary did.

Could You not do This?

Couldest not thou watch one hour?

Sunday

Mark 14:37

This reproach of Christ in the garden of Gethsemane was spoken to His disciples and particularly to Peter, who had failed in the ministry of prayer. It is a reproach of which someone has said that "every word is an arrow whose point is dipped in wounded love."

Think of the *immensity of the debt!*

"Couldest *thou*"—the words were addressed to Simon Peter and behind them would seem an awareness in the mind of the Master of all that this disciple owed Him. Think of the privileges Peter had known, the experiences he had shared in the ministry of Christ!

166

Think of the profession he had made! And yet, he fails. We, too, are similarly indebted to Christ. Do we fail?

Think of the *modesty of the demand!*

"Couldest thou not *watch*?" That was all that Christ asked—to watch and pray. It was not very much. He might have asked so much more, but He didn't. He might have asked Peter to share His humiliation, the agony of the cross, the scourging and the suffering—but He didn't. He just asked him to pray. And that is what He asks of us.

Think of the *brevity of the duration!*

"Couldest thou not watch *one hour*?" How quickly an hour can pass—sixty minutes and how quickly they fly! How gladly we give an hour when we want to. A girl will give an hour to her lover, a man will give an hour to his garden, the mother will give an hour to her children. We will spend an hour watching the television. But how little time we give to Him. Is this an area of failure that we need to face up to? Christ still asks the same question, "Couldest thou not watch one hour, with me?" Matthew adds those two words, "with me," in his account. Surely they reveal the intensity of Christ's desire for our companionship and for our cooperation in the work of redemption. How often do we disappoint Him?

Are You a Spiritual Tramp?

. . . wandering stars . . .

Monday   Jude 13

There are some Christians that can best be described as "spiritual tramps." The tramp is a person who has no fixed place of abode. There are Christians who are in the same state spiritually. A tramp has a carefree sort of existence. He wanders wherever his fancy may take him. But his is rather a useless kind of existence. How many spiritual tramps there are to be found in our cities! They wander around from church to church, listening to this preacher or that preacher just as their fancy takes them. Theirs is a carefree sort of life. They know nothing of the responsibilities and drudgeries of a home, and little of life's achievements. The only record they leave behind them is that of the journeys they have taken, the churches they have visited, the preachers they have heard.

Tramps seldom achieve anything. Are you a tramp? Have you a spiritual home or have you no fixed place of abode? Are you a detached Christian? Is your spiritual pilgrimage one of carefree enjoyment without responsibility? Tramps not only seldom do anything, they seldom have anything—not anything to spare for anyone else! Are you a tramp? Isn't it time you had a home?

Expectancy

I count not myself to have apprehended: but this one thing I do, forgetting those things which are behind, and reaching forth unto those things which are before, I press toward the mark for the prize of the high calling of God in Christ Jesus

Tuesday

Philippians 3:13, 14

Some Christians seem to have little expectancy in their hearts of anything new happening, or of making any further spiritual progress. In the heart of Paul this expectancy was a very real thing. In his life there was always a beyond, there was always something new awaiting him; and that was one reason why he was always rejoicing.

In this expectancy three things had their part. In the first place there was the *voice that calls*. Paul calls it (as Bishop Handley Moule translates it), "The summons from the heights, the voice of God." That was the thing that mattered in the heart of this man. Neither the voices of his Christian friends nor even the voice of his own heart mattered; the voice that counted was "the summons from the heights," "the high calling of God." The heights speak of climbing, of effort. "Does the road wind uphill all the way? Yes, to the very end."

Also in his expectancy there was the *vision that counts*. Paul says, "I follow after, if that I may apprehend that for which also I am apprehended of Christ Jesus." The thing that mattered in Paul's life was to fulfill the destiny planned for him by Christ. Every father and mother have a dream for their child, and Christ had a dream for Paul. Paul said, "I want to fulfill the dream. I was apprehended by Christ for a special purpose, for a special task, and I am going to go on and on until that dream is realized."

And then the third contributing factor to the expectancy in the heart of Paul was the *verdict that crowns*. For what prize did Paul strive? It was not a material prize. What was this final thing to which Paul looked forward as his great reward? What will be our reward? Surely it will be the Master's, "Well done." This is the verdict that crowns the servant who has pursued so long, traveled so far and fought so well!

What is the Devil?

Resist the devil, and he will flee from you

James 4:7b

James, like all other early Christians and like our Lord Himself, has no doubts about the reality of the devil. He says we are to resist the devil, and behind this exhortation lies the assumption that we will be attacked by him. Know your enemy is a wise bit of counsel in warfare; it is a wise bit of counsel in spiritual warfare.

What is the devil? What is he like? He is described in three ways, and in each of these ways we can understand something of his strategy. He is called "the deceiver" (Rev. 12:9), and right from the very beginning this has been his practice—to trick and deceive us into thinking that his way is right, that sin will bring happiness, that God's way is wrong, and that God is unkind, ungracious, and restrictive.

He is also called "the accuser" (Rev. 12:10). He delights to bring the remembrance of our failures and our sins before our minds, and to tell us again and again that we are not fit to be Christians and that God will have nothing more to do with us. We need to meet him with the witness and testimony of the blood of Christ. That is something to which there is no answer when he accuses us of our failure.

He is also called "the destroyer" (1 Peter 5:8), under the analogy of the lion, the devourer. He is out to destroy our usefulness, our testimony, our witness. We must expect this attack. There are, of course, the clever people who would like to make us believe that there is no such person as the devil. But nobody can read the New Testament without knowing that whatever men may think or say, as far as Christ Himself was concerned, the forces of evil were a tremendous reality.

I love that story about the small boy who heard somebody saying, "There is no devil," to which the boy replied, "Then I would like to know who is doing all his dirty work."

The Sphere of our Victory

In all these things

Romans 8:37

There are two challenging little words here: the first is the word "*in*," the second is the word "*all*." What do these words teach us? They teach us that the sphere of our victory covers the experience from which *no escape is provided.*

Paul speaks about being more than conquerors *in* all these things, in circumstances from which no escape is provided. There are times when a way of escape is promised. 1 Corinthians 10:13 tells us of this. But how often for us the place of defeat is that place to which we are tied by circumstances that have remained unchanged for years and promise to remain as they are for years to come. It is in those circumstances that there is a breakdown of our Christian witness and profession. The circumstance may be in our home, where we work, the church where we are a member, or the mission station to which we must return. But God has included in the sphere of our victory that very place. It is *in* all these things, not out of them.

But it is in *all* these things; and so the sphere of our victory includes that sphere in which *no exception is permitted.* Our attitude may not be that which longs to escape but it may be that which makes exceptions. We excuse ourselves in one way or another. We say, "It doesn't matter," "It is quite impossible." But the verse we are considering tells us that the sphere of our victory is to be inclusive of every circumstance, every temptation. *In . . . all*"—what a challenge this is!

Diverted

Nor to occupy themselves with myths and endless
genealogies which promote speculations rather than the
divine training that is in faith (RSV)

Friday   1 Timothy 1:4

Paul is concerned with the way in which people can become obsessed with error and at the same time unmindful of the truth. These are people who have, to quote J. B. Phillips, "lost themselves in endless words," or who, as Dr. J. E. Scott puts it, are "like travelers who leave the highway for a path that leads nowhere, a byway of empty argument or vain chatter." Instead of the life and energy of the church being integrated in spiritual effort and impact, it is dissipated in mere talk and discussion. People have been diverted from the highways of the truth of God, the will of God, the mind of God, and the glory of God into the byways of mere discussion, tradition or downright error.

I have never forgotten words of wisdom spoken by the late Brother Edward, "If the devil cannot keep a Christian back from the truth, he will try then to push that Christian past the truth into an unbalanced view of it." Highways can be so easily deserted and the byways can so easily become crowded.

In Judges 5:6 there is a remarkable verse, "In the days of Shamgar . . . the highways were unoccupied, and the travelers walked through byways." How far is this true in the life of the Church today, in the local congregation and in the individual Christian? It is possible that much time may be given to things of no real importance; much discussion takes place about things that are valueless; much energy is spent on trivialities that are a sheer waste of time.

The details of the danger that concerned Paul may not be our concern but the danger most emphatically is.

Born in Sin?

David says, Behold, I was shapen in iniquity, and in sin did my mother conceive me

Saturday

Psalm 51:5

The Christian Gospel states that man is "born in sin." Not that it means by this that there is anything sinful about the fact of man's birth, but rather that there is something inherently sinful about the nature of man at birth. Christianity would trace this back to the time when man first sinned. Whether or not we believe that the form in which the story of Genesis 3 is told is literal and historical fact, as I myself do, we must believe the fact for which it stands—namely, that there was a time when man first sinned.

Years ago when I was a student at Edinburgh University I had the privilege of studying under the late Professor A. E. Taylor, professor of Moral Philosophy, regarded in those days as having one of the most acute minds in Europe. I well remember in the midst of one of his lectures how he paused and, looking at the students in front of him, said, "Ladies and gentlemen, please remember this, there must have been an Adam." In other words, there must have been an occasion when man sinned for the first time; and from that day to this, through heredity, the whole personality of man in the physical, mental and spiritual realms of life, bears the traces of the heredity of sin.

Surely it was this profound truth that lay behind the words of a little girl in one of my churches who said to her mother when being put to bed one night, "Mummy, why is it that there is something inside me that likes being naughty?" This may not have been the language of the schools but it was the truth of the Gospel. Man needs to be saved because of man's own sinfulness.

The Final Briefing

Ye shall receive power . . . ye shall be witnesses unto Me
Acts 1:8

Sunday

Here we face the implications of the final commission spoken by our Lord to His Church, a word that is surely still binding upon all those who name His name.

There was a *program which challenged them*—to be witnesses to Christ. And that witness would be borne by what they were able to say of Christ with their lips and what they were able to show of Christ in their lives. It was challenging also in where they were asked to go, literally to the ends of the earth. They were to go everywhere and to everybody. This program has never been withdrawn and is binding still upon the Church. We are all called to carry it out. How we carry out our share of it will be made known to us.

There was a *program which changed them.* The natural reaction to the program was to cry out, "Impossible," but they were promised "power after the Holy Ghost is come upon you." Whom God sends He enables; whom God calls He equips. A study of the Acts and of the Epistles reveals two things about this Divine presence. In the first case, a diversity of gifts was bestowed by Him. These were gifts of differing abilities and capacities which were interrelated and inter-dependent. These gifts the Holy Spirit would bestow in His own sovereign way and will. It was not for any Christian to demand any specific gift. In addition, however, there were ministries of grace the Holy Spirit would want to exercise and fulfill in every Christian; things that He, the Spirit of God, had been given to do in every Christian. Possibly the most important thing for any Christian is to find out what these ministries are and to see that the Holy Spirit is being allowed to fulfill them.

The *prospect which cheered them* was, of course, the return of their Lord. "This same Jesus . . . shall so come in like manner as ye have seen Him go" (verse 11). This lent an urgency to their work. He had said that no man could know the time of His return and the early Christians therefore saw to it that the work was being done, lest He should come and find it undone. It also gave a quality to their lives. "Every man that hath this hope in him," wrote John, "purifieth himself—even as He is pure." "Let your loins be girded about, and your lights burning; and ye yourselves like unto men that wait for their Lord," said Jesus Christ Himself.

One of the students at my theological college had a little plaque standing on the desk in his study. On it were just two words, "Perhaps today!" If He did come "today," would the work be done that He has given us to do, and would our lives be pleasing in His sight?

Afraid of Men

The fear of man bringeth a snare

Proverbs 29:25

Monday

How many people do we know—it may be that you are one of them yourself—whose lives are fettered by fear? How many people are living lives on a standard well below that of their own ideals and intentions simply because they are afraid of what others would say! The set they move in might comment; that friend might raise an eyebrow; that fellow might smile; that girl laugh. And so the good thing, the right thing, the decent thing is left undone and the person finds that he is living a life fettered by fear.

If there is anything more common than this way of life what is it? I am convinced that the vast majority of those who boast in their freedom, and glory in doing as they like are, at the same time, the most degraded of all slaves. Like the captives of old they are being dragged along beneath the chariot wheels of the forces and opinions to which they have surrendered themselves. Is this freedom? Are we afraid of men?

Meekness

I am meek and lowly in heart

Matthew 11:29

Tuesday

If this testimony of our Lord to Himself is to be believed, then this quality of character is one about which every Christian should be deeply concerned. Again and again meekness is set forth as that quality of mind which is receptive to the saving grace of God. James 1:21 says, "Receive with meekness the engrafted word, which is able to save your souls." Meekness is receptive, while pride is resentful. The reason why some folk never become Christians is simply that they are too proud. To experience conversion, to be the recipients of the grace of God is beneath their dignity. Why should they need to receive this gift? Spiritually and intellectually they feel they are adequate in themselves.

I often recall the words of the servants of Naaman recorded in 2 Kings 5. How angry Naaman was when the prophet of God told him to go and wash in the waters of the river Jordan seven times, and then his flesh would become like that of a little child. Naaman protested and in a rage turned away, his pride offended. But he had good and faithful servants who halted him as he turned his back upon the only possibility of a cure. They reproached him, "My father, if the prophet had bid thee do some great thing, wouldest thou not have done it?" They confronted him with the fact that he would have responded if the prophet of God had flattered his pride.

But why should the pride of a man who was a leper need to be flattered? And why should modern man—who is at the same time as truly a sinner as ancient man—need to be proud? The Old Testament, in the prophetic voice of Isaiah 61:1 describes the preaching of the Gospel as the preaching of "good tidings to the meek." Yes, it is indeed good news to those who are humble enough and honest enough to recognize that they need to be helped by God!

Testing Needs Wisdom

If any of you lack wisdom, let him ask of God

James 1:5

Wednesday

J. B. Phillips translates verse 5, "If, in the process, any of you does not know how to meet any particular problem, he has only to ask God (what for? the ending of the trial? No! escape from the pressure? No.) and he may be quite sure that the necessary wisdom will be given him." We need discernment when we are undergoing trial; we need wisdom and insight to discover what lessons God is trying to teach us. If we lack this wisdom we are to ask for it, and there is here a delightful touch that encourages us to ask of God. He is described as one "that giveth to all men liberally, and upbraideth not." There is not only a lavishness but a kindliness about God's giving. With some people it is not so. If they give help they do so reluctantly and reproachfully.

James inserts two thoughts here that throw light upon the manner of our asking. Although God will not fail us in His response we can fail God in our request, so James throws in a note of caution in verse 6, "Let him ask in faith, nothing wavering, with no doubting," RSV. J. B. Phillips puts it, "Without secret doubts as to whether he really wants God's help or not." When we are asking God for discernment and wisdom we are to be completely sincere. We are not to approach God with two minds about the matter. We must really want to know God's way; we must really want to experience God's grace.

Then James goes on to speak of the kind of trial that may have been particularly familiar to the Christians to whom he was writing—variations in their material welfare. In verses 9-11 he shows how wise people would react, whether rich or poor. The poor man has discernment to see that he is wealthy, not in material things but in spiritual things, and therefore his material lot is a matter of comparative indifference to him. The rich man has discernment to see how worthless his so-called wealth really is. This is not the foundation of his living, and if it should be taken from him, his true wealth still remains.

Breaking a Habit

. . . free indeed

Thursday

John 8:36

Christian experience is not just the hope of "pie in the sky," nor is it only forgiveness of sins. It is the offer of a new life, the very life of Christ Himself, who comes to dwell in our lives. This new life is the answer to the problem of habits formed which are difficult to break. We do not have to rely on our own unaided strength to break them, but on the new strength which God gives us through the life of Christ indwelling us by His Spirit. It is just as if a living hand were inserted into a lifeless glove.

But there are two things to note about this strength. The first is that it must be accepted. Christ must be welcomed and invited into our lives just as we would welcome a friend into our home. The life must be received, and then having been received it must be renewed and nourished day by day with Bible study and prayer. Then we shall begin to know something of what it means to be "free indeed"!

With You

Lo, I am with you alway, even unto the end of the world
Matthew 28:20

Many years ago I hear Dr. W. Y. Fullarton saying at Keswick that if the Greek were translated literally it would read, "I—with you—am." What a lovely picture—ourselves surrounded by the Lord and His love!

I remember reading many, many years ago of a man riding through a dark forest where the trees overhead shut out the very light of the sun. But as he rode along a shady path he came at last to a clearing. Here the sunshine was brilliant! At the farther side of the clearing was an old tumbledown shack and in the garden an old black woman with snowy white hair. As the rider drew near he called out a cheery greeting. "Hello, auntie, living here all alone?" The old woman straightened her back, lifted her wrinkled face to see who the caller was, and then replied with a great smile lighting up her face, "Yes, jes me and Jesus, Massa."

With Him because He is with us!

Preaching the Unfulfilled

Ye lade men with burdens grievous to be borne, and ye yourselves touch not the burdens with one of your fingers
Luke 11:46

Here surely is the thought of an obligation laid upon the hearer and of an obedience withheld by the preacher. Christ is speaking of the sin of asking others to do what we are not attempting ourselves. This comes home especially to those of us who are engaged in Christian work in Sunday School, Bible Class or the taking of church services.

Some of us do not hesitate to preach on prayer, but we do little to practice a prayer life. Thus we are guilty of laying a burden upon others which we are not trying to carry ourselves. But this has a wider application. The Church condemns the outsider for not obeying the truth of the Gospel, while all the time the Church itself knows very little of a life of obedience to the will of God from day to day. This is the attitude that our Lord is exposing and condemning.

I do not say that we are never to preach truth that is beyond our experience, for we are to preach Christ; but we must at least make sure that it is within the realm of our aspiration and endeavor.

What Should a Sermon Do?

When they heard this, they were pricked in their heart, and said What shall we do?

Acts 2:37-47

Sunday

So many of us go to church and listen to sermons—good, bad and indifferent. I wonder how many of us ask ourselves what we expect a good sermon to do? I suppose that one of the greatest sermons ever preached was preached by Peter on the day of Pentecost. What did that sermon do?

I think we ought to expect a sermon in which the Word of God is preached to *disturb*. The reason for this is quite simple. The Bible says, "The entrance of Thy words giveth light," and light can be disturbing. The light of God's truth can disturb our thinking, the light of God's holiness can disturb our living. The important thing is the response we make to the breaking in of this light. So often we forget that what really disturbs us is the need to act. "What shall we do?" the people who heard Peter cried out. So many of us don't want to do anything. We are quite content with ourselves as we are. But the coming of the light brings with it the challenge to action. Elsewhere in the Bible we are warned against being hearers of the word and not doers also.

The preaching of the Word of God should also *direct!* Once these people knew that they must do something and asked what their action should be, they were directed. "Then said Peter unto them, 'Repent . . . Receive.'" It is worth noting the clarity with which he spoke. Nobody was left with any doubt at all about what they were to do. Some sermons that are called deep are really simply muddy. I can sense, too, the certainty with which Peter spoke. There was no "possibly" or "maybe." Instead there was a ringing, "Ye shall." There ought to be that ringing note of absolute certainty when we are dealing with the truth of God and the promises of God. It is not presumptuous to believe what God has said.

We should not be surprised that the preaching of the Word of God also *divides*. The crowd that heard Peter that day were divided by the time he had finished preaching. The response of some was rejection. Peter calls them, "This untoward generation." The word means a turning off, a turning aside from the truth of God.

177

There are always people like that. They don't know what they are missing. There were also those whose response was reception. "They that gladly received His word." And when it is good news surely that is the way to receive it.

Good Soil—Good Harvest

And the fruit of righteousness is sown in peace of them that make peace

James 3:18

Monday

The fruit or harvest of righteousness is sown in peace. That is to say, the soil in which spiritual work will come to full fruition is one of true fellowship among Christians where there is no discord or disharmony. Peace is the atmosphere in which we may expect the good seed to ripen. Let us remember that discord always damages God's work. Work that is full of promise can be blighted by quarreling, self-seeking, and self-promotion.

This verse is tremendous. It suggests a bountiful harvest, not just a few stalks here and there, with a few ears of corn hanging from them, but a field of grain bent low with the weight of the corn. How few churches experience this kind of harvest, and yet this is what we are meant to have.

One of our modern scholars commenting on this says, "The seed which brings the rich harvest can never flourish in any other atmosphere than one of right relationships between man and man." Right relationships are the soil in which the reward of righteousness alone can grow. The man who disturbs personal relationships and is responsible for strife and bitterness cuts himself off from the reward which God gives to those who live the Christian life in harmony and fellowship with other believers.

Won

Won by the conversation of the wives

1 Peter 3:1

Tuesday

Peter is here obviously speaking of a divided home in which there is a converted wife with an unconverted husband, and he stresses the opportunity of winning the unbelieving husband to faith in Christ. In verse 1 we have the tremendously challenging statement that our whole concern should be "that they may be won without the word, by the behavior of their wives." What they see will win them, not what we say. He is speaking of an attractiveness due to an inner beauty. There will be a serenity, a gentleness, a peace, a radiance in the life of a converted woman that will provide irrefutable evidence for the reality of the grace of God that will convince her husband.

Here is an important point that we should all note. Those closest to us are most likely to be won not by what we say, but by what we are. Of course Peter is not speaking here of a home where a converted woman has married an unconverted man, something forbidden in God's Word, but a home in which a woman has been brought to faith in Christ after her marriage and then finds herself facing both the challenge and the opportunity of witnessing to and winning her husband to a like faith.

Unselfish Concern and Unstinted Service

. . . who will naturally care for your state

Philippians 2:20

. . . he was nigh unto death

Philippians 2:30

Wednesday

Paul had some wonderful Christians about him with great qualities of character. In Timothy he found an *unselfish concern for others.* "The kind of man who will genuinely care for your affairs" (Philippians 2:20). Are you the kind of Christian in the fellowship of your church who genuinely cares for the affairs of others? You should be there not just to be invited to sit in a group, or to be thanked by the minister, or to be put on a committee. You should be there because you are genuinely concerned about others.

In Epaphroditus he found an *unstinted service for Christ.* "He nearly died for the work of Christ, hazarding his very life" (Philippians 2:30). The physical effort and exhaustion, the illness that dogged his footsteps as he worked himself to the limit in serving the Philippians and in serving Paul, brought his very life into danger. Even today there are places in the world where danger is part of the price of devotion.

I remember helping somebody put on her coat on a streaming wet Sunday night at my church in Troon, and saying as I did so, "I think you deserve a medal for coming out on a night like this!" The rain was thundering on the roof and the congregation had not been large. She turned to me and said, "I won't get a medal when I go to work tomorrow morning, even if it's as wet as it is tonight." The thing that absolutely shocks and shames me is that on a wet day the average age of a congregation leaps up. You get the old folk out on

179

a wet night. They are the ones who, if they wanted an excuse, could say they had no business to be out because of their rheumatism. The people that stay in because it is wet are the lazy folk!

Selfless concern for others, unstinted service for Jesus Christ—we need folk with these characteristics in our fellowships today.

A Clay Pot

We have this treasure in earthen vessels, that the
excellency of the power may be of God, and not of us

Thursday
2 Corinthians 4:7

Paul describes himself here as a common clay pot. What comfort there is in this, and also what caution. The mistake so many of us make is thinking that the only people God uses in His service are those who think highly of themselves, and that unless we think we are wonderful Christians God can't use us, while all the time the very reverse is the case. Christians who are greatly used do not think they are wonderful. They realize and know that they are worthless and useless, that they are of no value at all—just "common clay pots."

Someone has pointed out that although Paul knew he was a "chosen vessel" (Acts 9:15), he also knew that he was "an earthen vessel." All this is in keeping with the whole trend of scripture. In 1 Corinthians 1:27, Paul writes, "God chose what is foolish in the world to shame the wise, God chose what is weak in the world to shame the strong" RSV. If we want God to use us, we must remember that He is looking for clay pots—and clean ones too!

A Crazy War

And the three companies blew the trumpets, and brake
the pitchers, and held the lamps in their left hands, . . .
and they cried, The sword of the Lord, and of Gideon.

Friday
Judges 7:20

It was a crazy way to fight, wasn't it? First of all to cut the numbers down from over thirty thousand to three hundred, and then to stand in a very thin line around the great host of the Midianites. We talk about the "thin red line," but this was barely a line; there must have been huge gaps in it. Just to spread three hundred men right around the sleeping host and then take torches and trumpets and pitchers and wake up the crowd down below—what a ridiculous way to fight!

But it was God's way. It was the strategy laid down by God, so Gideon followed it and the enemy was routed and the people of God were delivered. We are told that the country was in quietness for forty years in the days of Gideon, so long did the influence of this man live on.

God always has a strategy for the spiritual warfare in which we are involved. We are wise men indeed if we learn it and follow it.

At the Door

Behold, I stand at the door

Saturday

Revelation 3:20

The first thing many people need to learn about Jesus Christ is the nearness of His presence. In today's verse we read Christ's words, "Behold I stand *at the door.*" That is not far away! For many of us He seems to be so very far away, either in the far distance of history, the Christ of our Bible story books with their pictures, or He seems to be far away in heaven, wherever that may be! This is possibly a relic of our childhood with its hymns, "There's a Friend for little children above the bright blue sky." That childish figure has never really faded from our minds and so Jesus Christ has always seemed to be far away and unreal.

But when we turn to the New Testament the picture is so very different. To men of all ages and at all times, Jesus Christ presents Himself as being "at the door" of our hearts and lives and our personalities. This means that for you too, at this very moment, He is as close as that—"at the door." Think out quietly what this could mean to you. If He is as near as that, He is near enough to hear you! What would you want to say to Him? What is He doing at the door—what is He waiting for you to do?

Unpaid Debts

When thou vowest a vow unto God, defer not to pay it; . . . pay that which thou hast vowed

Sunday

Ecclesiastes 5:2-5

Here we see God's attitude to the vows we make so glibly and so readily to Him. First of all there is *God's plea for restraint:* "When thou goest to the house of God, . . . be not rash with thy mouth, . . . to utter any thing before God" (5:1, 2). One of the characteristics of the ministry of Christ was the restraint He was always imposing upon the would-be disciples. What were the reasons for this? Sometimes the reason may have had to do with the circumstances under which vows were made. So often we vow to God when we are in trouble, but trouble can pass and with the passing of the trouble passes the desire to fulfill the vow. The results of such restraint on the part of Christ can be seen in the quality of discipleship He secured. Christ picked only twelve men but look at the work they did.

We have also in these verses what I have called *God's preference for refusal*. "Better is it that thou shouldest not vow, than that thou shouldest vow, and not pay." There is the thought first of the tragedy that God would avert—"that thou shouldest not vow." What greater tragedy can there be in the spiritual experience of a man or woman than that their life should be marked by no response whatever to the voice of God. But there is also a travesty that God would avoid—"Better it is that thou shouldest not vow, than that thou shouldest vow, and not pay." This travesty of Christianity that God would do anything to avoid is a lip religion that contents itself with words and not deeds.

But we find also *God's passion for reality*. "When thou vowest a vow, defer not to pay it." First God makes an assumption here. He does not say *if* you vow, but *when* you vow. The assumption is that all of us at one time or another do make vows to God. But there is also the action God wants—"Defer not to pay it." Apparently postponement has been permitted but God says, "Cut it out." The vow has been made but the payment has been deferred. When did you make your vow to God? How long have you been in putting off the payment of it?

Plain Speaking by Christ

Son, thy sins be forgiven thee

Monday

Mark 2:5

Very few of us relish being spoken to plainly and bluntly. This is one of the features of Christ's dealing with men. He so often mentions matters that they would far rather He did not. "Son, thy sins be forgiven thee." Such direct speaking was both a challenge and a difficulty. It was a challenge to the man to be honest, but at the same time a difficulty in his finding the deliverance that Christ was prepared to give him.

Christ saw that this man's need was deeper than his friends realized. He not only had a sick body but also a sick soul and the sickness there was due to sin. His first step was to get the man to face this deeper need. What did Christ see in this man's life? One wonders too what the man called the things that Christ saw? What are the names that you and I give to things that Christ would call our "sins." Do we call them "pleasures" or "weaknesses"?

One of the first steps towards spiritual health is to be honest with God. Christ spoke of "sin" and placed the guilt where it belonged and said, "Thy sins." The man could have been evasive, angry, resentful, bitter—instead he was honest and found not only forgiveness but also health. Are we honest about our sins?

The Constant Judgment of Love

He that judgeth me is the Lord

Tuesday

1 Corinthians 4:4

It is told of a preacher that there came a time in his life when he withdrew himself from his work for a period of three months. When he was asked why he had done so, he replied, "I'm going to have my judgment day right now while I can do something about it." I like that, don't you?

And linked in with this incident is a text that has been very much on my mind, the words of Peter—"The time has come that judgment must begin at the house of God." You see, it is not enough to be converted nor is it enough to be an evangelical. Some of the most difficult people to get on with, and some of those who bring most discredit on the name of Jesus Christ where they work, are supposedly Christians.

Here we have a man, Paul, living under the constant judgment of God and the love of God. Paul says, "He that is judging me continually is the Lord." In the light of the truth apprehended by us, in the light of the task assigned to us, and in the light of the time available for us, judgment must begin at the house of God.

I have on my bookshelves an incisive book called *What's wrong with the Church?* When that kind of question is posed, most of us think of what is wrong with other churches, with the liberals, or with the high churches. We do not stop to ask what is wrong with our church or with ourselves as members of it. May we realize that in these urgent days when the Church is fighting for her very life, the paramount need for committed Christians is that we should start living where Paul lived, under the constant judgment of love.

He . . . would not go in

And he was angry, and would not go in

Luke 15:28

Wednesday

I believe it was Ruskin who said, "I am not surprised at what men suffer, but I am surprised at what they miss." There is something terribly sad about people who stay outside all that God's love has provided when God is asking them to come inside. This is what happened to the elder brother. We often forget about him in considering the parable of the Prodigal Son. There was feast going on inside, everybody was in jovial mood, except the elder brother who was staying outside. We are told, "He was angry and would not go in."

What a pathetic figure he is, staying outside when he could have been inside! I don't know anything sadder than the person who either is not a Christian or is staying away from the fellowship to which they belong. That person is missing so much. When our Lord told another parable about an invitation to a wedding feast you remember that those who were invited made excuses. And their excuses were accepted. They were excused. It wasn't that God turned them down, it is just that they asked to be excused and God said, "All right, I will excuse you"—and they never came!

There is nothing clearer from the Word of God than this. If a man has made up his mind that he is not going to accept Christ, then he is not going to have Him. This is true even though the love of God has done everything to make it possible and will do everything possible to make us accept Christ. It is said of Jesus, "Behold, I stand at the door." He stands at the door but He doesn't force it open. Christ will never force His way into our lives without our consent. Are you refusing to let Him in?

The Bride Acclaimed

How fair and how pleasant art thou

Song of Solomon 7:6

Thursday

The opening verses of this chapter are spoken, in all probability, by the daughters of Jerusalem, and later on, the words are spoken by the bridegroom. The testimony was evoked by the sheer loveliness of her life and it was spoken by others. We often talk about giving a testimony or of having a testimony to give, and by that we mean something that we have to say about Christ, about what Christ has done for us. But here is a testimony that is different: it has to do with what others are compelled to say about us, and what the Lord Himself has to say about us.

We might do well to pause and ask ourselves, "What kind of a testimony do you and I have along these lines?" Do you remember from Hebrews 11:5 that Enoch had this testimony, that he pleased God? I wonder how many of us have this testimony, that we give pleasure to God. This ties in with what the bridegroom has to say in verse 6, "How fair and pleasant you are, O loved one, delectable maiden!" RSV. So attractive was the life and appearance of the bride that the daughters of Jerusalem think of her as captivating. In verse 5 they say, "flowing locks . . . a king is held captive in the tresses" RSV.

We might pause to ask ourselves, "Are we that kind of Christian? Are we so attractive that the tongues of other Christians speak well of us and of our Savior?" This testimony was evoked by the quality of her life. But it is of course important to note that this testimony was spoken when she was seen in the company of her lord, in fellowship and in communion with her beloved. I wonder if this is perhaps the secret of it all: that it is only when we are in close touch with our blessed Lord and Savior and walking in very real fellowship with Him that others will speak well of us, and of Him.

Not a New Convert

Not a novice, lest being lifted up with pride he fall into the condemnation of the devil

Friday   1 Timothy 3:6

Paul rules out the wisdom of a new or young convert being given heavy responsibilities because in such a case there has been no time to test the man's worth. Paul reveals his reasoning "lest the unproved man being lifted up with pride falls into condemnation of the devil." It was pride that led to the fall of Lucifer recorded in Isaiah chapter 14—a passage which some consider as referring indirectly to the fall of Satan.

One thing is clear, pride is something God will not tolerate in His work. The proud, conceited man is the kind of man that God just will not use. The Bible states it clearly, "God resisteth the proud, but giveth grace to the humble." It was this danger that unconsciously threatened Paul himself and that was why there was given to him the thorn in the flesh "lest I should be exalted above measure."

The proud man is always looking for the praise of men but the Bible says that God will not give His glory to another. Jeremiah 45:5 has a piece of advice, "Seekest thou great things for thyself? Seek them not." We can seek great things for God but we are never to seek them for ourselves. There is always the danger that a new or a young unproved convert will be snared with the wrong kind of spiritual ambition.

To Whom do we Belong?

I have redeemed thee . . . thou art Mine

Saturday

Isaiah 43:1

When I purchase something it belongs to me. The rights on which the lordship of Christ is based are not simply creator rights but redeemer rights. Nothing that you have is yours, and nothing that I have is mine. What a profound truth there is in that well-worn story for children of the wee boy who lost the boat that he had made. Only eternity will reveal how many versions of that story have been produced. With each version the size of the boat, its length, the details of its manufacture, the price paid for it and all the rest vary! But there is a profound truth in the story all the same.

The little boy lost the boat he had made and then saw it later on in the window of a shop. But the owner made him buy it back, and as he went away with his small boat in his hands he was heard to say, "You're my own wee boat twice ower. I wrocht ye and I bocht ye!" "I made you and I bought you!" The rights upon which Christ's claim is based are the same and these rights are undisputed.

The Restfulness of Faith

Truly my soul waiteth upon God

Sunday

Psalm 62:1

In another more modern version of the Bible these words have been translated, "Leave it all quietly to God, my soul." This sentence sparkles like a diamond.

I read here of the *wholeness with which my faith is asked to trust.* "Leave it all," and how significant that little word "all" can be. There are so often exceptions which I am prone to make. I am prepared to trust God with many things, with many people, many problems, but not with all. But these instructions I do well to heed. "Leave it *all* . . ." How wise we are if we trust everything to God our Father!

I read here of the *stillness in which my faith is asked to rest.* "Leave it all quietly . . ." Of course there is often a turbulence through which my faith must pass and in that turbulence of mind and heart my faith will be tested and tried. But after and beyond that there must be a confidence to which my faith comes. In the final analysis there is a restfulness about faith. When a babe is safe in the mother's arms that baby will be at rest.

I read here of the *fullness on which my faith is asked to count.* "Leave it all quietly to God, my soul." What wonderful words these are—"All . . . quietly . . . God." Think of the Person He is—the Creator and Father God—possessing limitless resources of perfect wisdom, perfect love and perfect power. Think of the people we are—His children, if we have been born again into the family of God. Christ gave us this truth as the grounds for our freedom from anxiety. "Your Father knoweth." In that knowledge our faith can rest.

What is God's Will?

Not willing that any should perish

Monday

2 Peter 3:9

The will of God is not just an abstract ethical standard. It includes an ethical standard but it is more than that. The will of God is active and redemptive—it is action in redemption. "The Lord is not willing that any should perish." "God so loved the world that He

187

gave His only begotten Son." For Christ, the will of God meant bearing the sins of the world in a unique way in His own body on the tree, on the Cross. For us, too, surrender to the will of God has as its ultimate expression and purpose the identifying of ourselves with that redemptive will. Our surrender to the will of God means that upon us too, in a very real though different sense, the sins of the world will be laid. We will accept this burden in our prayer life. We will face it in our giving, in our living. This business of surrendering to the will of God is not the singing of a hymn, not the emotion of a moment. It is the sacrifice of a life.

The Costliness of Love's Giving

Neither will I offer burnt offerings unto the Lord my
God of that which doth cost me nothing

2 Samuel 24:24

Tuesday

It was the cheapness of the way that was offered to him that revolved the mind of David. To offer to the Lord his God that which cost him nothing was utterly abhorrent to him. Love is not only willing to pay a price but love insists that there should be a price to pay. How many of us have wanted to buy a present for someone we loved and found ourselves looking for the gift, not among the cheap things that we could easily afford but among the expensive things that we knew we ought not really to purchase!

Is it not true that the Christian Church needs today to rediscover this mark of real and true devotion to Christ? So much of our church and Christian work is determined by our convenience or comfort. If the weather is reasonable we go. If we have nothing more important to do we will attend. When it comes to giving money we give to God and His Church what we would hesitate to give for a tip and far less than a man would give for a packet of cigarettes. Then we think we have done our bit, while all the time the truth of the matter is that we have given to the Lord our God that which has cost us nothing.

Free from the Law

Free from the law

Romans 8:2

Wednesday

This is a common cry among those of us who glory in our evangelical faith. But sometimes that cry carries with it a failure to realize that freedom from the law in the New Testament sense is freedom from the law as the grounds of our acceptance before a righteous God together with a freedom from the ceremonial Jewish law. But it is not freedom from the moral law as a way of life and as a requirement of God.

"Except your righteousness shall exceed the righteousness of the scribes and Pharisees, ye shall in no case enter into the kingdom of heaven." So spake the Master! Paul adds that the consummation of all God's dealings with His own people is "that the righteousness of the law might be fulfilled in us."

We find inherent in these words a tremendously exacting standard of holiness and righteousness that we neglect at our own peril and to the grave dishonor of our Lord and Master.

The Grounds of Love's Confidence

We love Him, because He first loved us

1 John 4:19

Thursday

The reality upon which our love for Christ and for God rests is the certainty of His love for us. Where do we have the guarantee, the assurance, the reality upon which our love can rest? Listen! "He that spared not His own Son but delivered Him up for us all, how shall He not with Him also freely give us all things?" The reality of the love of God is seen in the Cross of His Son. That is the reality upon which my love can rest.

There is the story of a little girl who used to shrink when her mother touched her, for her mother's hands were badly scarred. How hurt the mother was to see that little child of hers shrink away almost with abhorrence. One day when she could not bear it any longer she took the little one into her arms and told her about those ugly scarred hands. She told the child that when she had been a little baby her cot had caught fire. Her mother's hands had gone into that flaming cot and had lifted the little one out. As a result, the hands were scarred. That little girl was never afraid of those hands again!

I like to think that the Master's hands are scarred hands, and if we are ever tempted to doubt His love, then let us look at His scars.

I can't Speak

And Moses said unto the Lord, O my Lord, I am not
eloquent, neither heretofore, nor since Thou hast
spoken unto Thy servant: but I am slow of speech, and
of a slow tongue

Friday

Exodus 4:10

It is incredible the way Moses protested and made excuses when
God wanted to send him out on a great task. Incredible, that is,
until we listen to ourselves making protests and excuses that are
very similar. When we see some outstanding Christians who seem
to speak readily and witness gladly and happily to Christ, we tend
to say, "It is all right for them," but when God asks us to do the
same thing we say, "Well, I can't speak."

Yet we do speak about so many other things. Housewives share
recipes. Some good lady has a friend to tea and she brings out her
best baking—cheese scones or something like that. She doesn't find
it difficult to share the recipe for that with a friend. But how many
of us have shared Christ? I wonder how many of us have ever
spoken to anybody else about our faith. Not that we are to speak
intrusively or rudely. I don't think God normally means us to but-
ton-hole complete strangers and ask them intimate questions like,
"Are you saved?" But once we have earned the right to share with
somebody on the deeper level, it is another matter.

How many folk have you shared your faith with, if you have a
faith to share? When God wanted Moses to go and speak in His
name, the reply was, "I can't speak." Moses said, "They will not
believe me, they will not listen." It is what we say—"It is no good
talking." Finally Moses insulted God by saying, "Please send somebody else." One of the great tragedies of Christian fellowships is
that so many of us are content to leave the witnessing to others.

We can speak, of course we can. We do it every day. The only
trouble is we are reluctant to speak about Christ. Why?

The Impartiality of Divine Love

My brethren, have not the faith of our Lord Jesus
Christ, the Lord of glory, with respect of persons

Saturday

James 2:1

James is aware that we may assess people differently while God
would evaluate them as being of equal importance to Him. We may
be impressed by some people because of their outward appearance
or their material or social status, and this might well affect our

attitude to them. We might welcome some and treat them as being important, or turn a cold shoulder to others and treat them as insignificant. What a strange and distorted picture of the grace of God we would then present, for this God who so loved "the world" loves each one of us equally. So James deals with a kind of snobbery that can creep in even to Christian fellowship.

We want to be careful of course that we do not think of snobbery only in one way, that which treats the wealthy as being of special importance; for there is a kind of inverted snobbery which can treat the wealthy as being of no importance! There is always a danger that we fail to recognize the true worth of every individual, and James tells us in verse 5 of this chapter that to act thus is to forget that God acted otherwise. The poor and rich are all within the scope and circle of God's love.

The words of our Lord to His disciples come to us with a sense of tremendous challenge, "As My Father has sent Me, even so send I you" (John 20:21). The Father sent the Son to redeem mankind, and also to reveal to mankind the nature of God. Part of that revelation was that the love of God evaluated people as people, all of equal importance to Him. And because of this and because of their need, the love of God has acted in Christ, through His cross and resurrection, to redeem and save the individual.

Examination

That which . . . our hands have handled, of the Word of life

Sunday   1 John 1:1

We are familiar with what we call tangible means of communication, when samples are given by firms anxious to convince us that their wares are worth buying. They don't just write to us, they don't just call, they don't just send a picture. They actually hand us a sample across the door or send it through the mail. They want us to test it and see that it is better than others, and so we take it and try it out. The firm is anxious to get their product actually into our hands and are convinced that if once it is there then their case is won.

This was the final piece of evidence that brought John to faith in Christ. Let us note *how close the examination he made*. In John 1:14 we read, "The Word was made flesh and dwelt among us." For three years John lived as close to Jesus as any man could live to another. He had seen Him under every conceivable circumstance;

he was able to examine Him and handle Him. Of course this is the kind of close contact the world has with us where we work and live.

How clear the conclusion he reached. "And we beheld his glory, the glory as of the only begotten of the Father, full of grace and truth." Here was a life so arrestingly different that it was obviously divine, a life that could only be explained in terms of divinity. We ought to be living such a quality of life that it can only be explained in terms of Jesus Christ. Someone has said rather cynically that the better you get to know most Christians the less respect you have for them. How tragic! Is it true of many of us that "distance lends enchantment to the view," or do people reach the conclusion that John had reached about the life of Jesus Christ, that the quality of His life could only be explained in terms of Deity?

There is a third thought—*how complete the analogy we must face.* If it was true that the Word was made flesh in Jesus Christ, then it is surely still true that the Word is made flesh in us. The same life of the same Christ is dwelling in you and me. I wonder if people conclude when they have met us that they too have "seen the glory."

So Natural

The natural man receiveth not the things of the Spirit of God

1 Corinthians 2:14

Monday

When we use the word "natural," we very often take it to mean something complimentary. For example, we say, "She is so perfectly natural." But in the New Testament the word is used to describe the condition of people, apart from the grace of God, as they are by nature when they are born. The note of tragedy and need creeps in, for they are described as being spiritually blind. It is always a tragedy if a person is physically blind. It is a greater tragedy when a person is spiritually blind, and this is the condition in which every human being is born.

Like puppies, we are born blind! People like this cannot see why they should go to church, they cannot see what there is in the Bible, they cannot see what's wrong with this, they cannot see what Jesus Christ has to do with them. In all these matters they cannot see. Of course they cannot, because they are blind. The reason for their blindness, however, goes deeper than we think. The reason why they have no spiritual sight is that they have no spiritual life.

Our Lord said, "Except a man be born again, (or from above) he cannot see the kingdom of God." Our first need is spiritual life. When we have that we will find that we have received spiritual sight as well.

The Mocking of a King

Hail, King of the Jews!

Tuesday

Mark 15:16-20

What depths of humiliation the Son of God plumbed when, after being named as king by Pilate, others named Him thus but only in jest or hate! The ignorance of the soldiers named Him King. He had been sent to them for scourging, for the carrying out of a punishment. The nature of the basic charge had somehow filtered out of the courtroom and while the leather thongs lashed the bare back of the Son of God, bound to a pillar until the blood flowed in streams to the ground, they passed word from mouth to mouth. "He says He is a King—the King of the Jews." An exquisite jest.

Professor Gossip has suggested that some clever creature surpassed himself that day—a faded tunic that will serve for royal purple; and for a scepter, here is a reed, fit symbol for so unstable a power; and now for a crown, these thorns will do. And with that the investiture was complete, and the room was all a roar of merriment. Down on your knees, men. Don't you see the King! The King! The King! They spat in His face; they smote Him on the head, and they plucked His beard.

And so He stood with the blood from the thorn wounds mingling with the spittle of ignorant fools, for whom later His prayer would be, "Father, forgive them; for they know not what they do." But while He stands, the taunts are flung at Him from every quarter. Somehow the taunts seem to merge into truth and the sheer sovereignty of the King breaks through the insults, the ignominy, and the shame and humiliation. "The King," they said, and the King He is.

Cleansing the Depths

Thy word have I hid in mine heart, that I might not sin
against thee

Psalm 119:11

I remember many years ago hearing a Christian psychologist say
that if these words were written in our modern language the quotation would read, "Thy word have I hid in the subconscious depths
of my personality and mind, that I might not sin against thee." The
thought is that the Word of God can somehow penetrate right
down into the realm of the subconscious and there exercise a
beneficent ministry.

There is another verse from the New Testament that seems to be
linked with this. In Ephesians 5:26 we are told that Christ's purpose
for the Church was, "That he might sanctify and cleanse it with the
washing of water by the word." These two scriptures seem to say
there is a power of cleansing in the Word. Let us allow it to operate
in the place where it is needed. Let us take time to read it and
meditate upon it so that it sinks slowly and deeply into our very
soul.

Sometimes when we have read the Word of God we may not
always be able to remember or recall it, but we shall be clean for all
that. For the power that the Word claims is the power to cleanse. It
cleanses the depths of the personality.

I remember hearing of a minister who called on a member of his
congregation on a Monday when she was busy with the washing.
He insisted that she continue the work, and while they were talking
with the washing going on, she said she had been greatly helped by
a recent sermon of his. When he asked what the sermon had been
about she said, "I can't remember." This seemed disappointing to
him and sensing his disappointment she turned to the tub where the
clothes were and said, "Do you see these clothes?" He said, "Yes."
"Well," she said, "they don't know how many times they have been
rinsed in water but they are clean for all that." That is just what the
Word of God can do in the subconscious depths of our mind. We
shall find that we are "clean for all that."

Why have we been Saved?

Elect according to the foreknowledge of God the Father
. . . unto obedience . . .

1 Peter 1:2

You and I may sometimes ask, "Why has God saved us?" The answer is that God has saved us in order that we may be obedient to Him. This is clearly stated in our verse for today. I have heard so many people discuss the problem of election but very few show any concern about its purpose. The whole purpose of God could be summed up in this one word—obedience.

Obedience means first of all an acceptance of God's way of redemption. We are elect "unto obedience and sprinkling of the blood of Jesus Christ," Have we obeyed God and accepted His way of reconciliation in the cross? Or are we relying upon our church membership, our goodness, our family, our upbringing? None of these avails. There is only way—through Christ and Him crucified. So the first obedience that God asks is that we accept the way of redemption that He has provided. Beyond that initial step is our continued allegiance to Christ and our acceptance of God's will in our lives. The mark of a Christian is that he or she will do what God wants.

A Ministry to Other Christians

Many of the brethren . . .

Philippians 1:14

Have we realized that there is a ministry we are to exercise toward other Christians? Many keen Christians are well aware of the fact that they have a ministry to the unsaved. They are quite prepared to recognize their responsibility toward those who never come to church. But they are not aware of their responsibility to minister to other Christians.

A ministry to other Christians? Not a ministry of the Gospel but a ministry of the grace of God—of the adequacy of it, the sufficiency of it, the glory of it, the wonder of it, the victory of it. We are in our present situation not just for the unconverted we may reach, but also for the Christians we may help.

But how are we going to exercise that kind of ministry unless first of all we ourselves have been tried and tested?

Even Paul did not realize all that was at stake. Paul was thinking of the brethren in Rome. But God was thinking of something infinitely greater. This ministry achieved in the Church by which many brethren were waxing confident and were being blessed and becoming active, this ministry has not ended yet! For if Paul had not been in prison, the prison epistles would never have been written and a great part of our New Testament would never have come into existence. Paul was put into prison not in order that he might preach but that he might write. And that ministry by Paul has gone right on and on and will never end until the Church is in glory.

Does God want us to exercise a ministry to others? In the New Testament we read of being able to comfort others with the comfort with which we ourselves were comforted. God puts us into a situation not just so that we can reach people with the Gospel but in order that, out of that situation, we may minister to other Christians.

Evidence Required

Except I shall see . . . I will not believe

Saturday

John 20:25

Thomas was willing to believe but only upon the production of certain evidence. It is of course true that Thomas had no right to dictate the terms on which he would believe. But when we examine the nature of the terms, they are not altogether unreasonable, and in their application to us today they are not incompatible with the terms of our commission to be witnesses to Christ. Thomas demanded evidence that would be visible—"Except I shall see." The other disciples had seen and he, too, wanted to see for himself and so make sure that this was the same Christ he had known before the crucifixion. The identification that would make the evidence irrefutable would be the marks of His suffering—the wounds in His hands and side. By these marks he would know that the Lord was risen indeed.

Is this not in keeping with the terms of Christ's commission to us? Has He not said, "As My Father hath sent Me, even so send I you?" Not only had He been sent to redeem but also to reveal and to renew.

When John in his First Epistle recalls the ministry of his Lord he writes not only of what he had heard but of what he had seen. Is it not true that the unbelieving world today is still saying," Except I shall see"? The Church is called "the Body of Christ"—visible instrument through which the hidden unseen life is expressed. Thomas demanded evidence that would be visible and this evidence would then be credible. Thomas did not say he would never believe, but if he could see he would.

Is the world today waiting to see something of the suffering Christ in us, of that sacrificial, caring, costly love that reaches out to man in his need? Paul was able to say, "I bear in my body the marks of the Lord Jesus," and those marks were the marks of suffering. Perhaps the world does not believe because it does not see such marks in us.

What Has Happened?

The things which happened unto me have fallen out rather unto the furtherance of the Gospel

Sunday   Philippians 1:12

In our verse for today we find Paul speaking of the things that "had happened to him." We often ask when we meet someone, "What's happened?" Maybe we can learn how to handle the happenings of life as we read what Paul has to say about his "happenings."

The pattern of his life had been destroyed. That sometimes happens to us as well. Two things in his life had been drastically affected. *The work that he loved had come to an end.* That work was preaching. This may be very different from the work that we love, but the one thing we have in common is that we both love our work. *The way that he lived had come to an end.* His way of life had kept him constantly on the move; on land or by sea, he was never still. Yet here we see him confined in one room with no congregation of any size to preach to.

I find myself wondering about him and as I read these verses I can see how the pressures on his faith can be discerned. There must have been the basic *temptation to think his present life was useless.* He might have been tempted to think that because he had lived one way profitably, there could be no useful alternative.

And what of the *temptation to think his Lord faithless?* He had been in prison before, but prayer had been answered and he had been released. This time it seemed as if nothing was happening.

We can certainly meet such pressure in our own lives and as we watch how the purposes of his Lord were disclosed to Paul we can learn much. In the first place there were the other people he was able to reach. Through his guards he was reaching right into the very heart of the Roman military power. There were also the people he reached through his writings. Most of what he preached has long been forgotten but not what he wrote. So it will be for us. We must never forget the "other people." There was also the value to his own spiritual character—the better person he would be. The finest flowers are often found growing in the soil of sorrows. The things that happened were turning to his salvation (verse 19).

The Importance of Strategy

The three companies blew the trumpets, and brake the pitchers

Judges 7:20

Monday

The issue was settled not with swords but with trumpets, torches and shouts! It is so still. "The weapons of our warfare are not carnal." When will the Christian Church learn to accept the Divine strategy? Strange weapons God wants us to use—the weapon of prayer; the wielding of the sword of the Spirit which is the Word of God; the power and ministry of the Holy Spirit; the testimony of the believer!

In one night the vast might of a powerful army that had for years pillaged and robbed an enslaved nation was shattered! How powerful seem the forces arrayed against the Church today. But cannot the omnipotent God deliver His people today as He did yesterday? The question for us to ask ourselves is this, is the Church today following the Divine strategy? God's work must be done in God's way to have God's blessing!

Bound by Habit

Whosoever committeth sin is the servant of sin

John 8:34

Tuesday

How many people are held by habits? How about that fellow, and that girl, who so glibly talk about being free to live as they like, only to find that they are not free to change their course of action. Are you held by habit? It may be in the realm of thought, desire, or action. But there it is, something that you cannot get victory over, something of which in your better moments you are ashamed, and in your worst moments you laugh at. But you know that this thing is your master. If you are thus held, how can you in honesty talk about freedom when you don't know it in your own life? What a tragedy this is!

You know the story of the snake charmer who used to enthrall great theater crowds all over the world. On one occasion during his act, his body was swathed in the coils of a mighty snake, from his feet to his neck. He had done it a thousand times before, but this time it was different. Suddenly the nature of the snake asserted itself and before the horrified gaze of the crowd the snake charmer's life was crushed out of him. The plaything had become the master.

So often it is thus with sin; we think we are free and all the time we are fettered. How perfectly the Bible describes some people as those who talk about freedom while all the time they themselves are slaves. May God save us from falling into that hypocrisy and that inconsistency.

Fire!

Behold, how great a matter a little fire kindleth

James 3:5

Wednesday

I remember in my young days going for a holiday to Speyside and seeing great areas of the Rothiemurchus Forest just one great mass of ash. What had previously been a scene of beautiful heather, bracken, silver birch and pine had been reduced to death and blackness, dust and ashes. How did it happen? Perhaps someone driving through the forest had tossed a cigarette out of a car window, and as a result acres of beauty were destroyed. Of course it was unintentional. The person never even realized that he was responsible for it.

And how destructive our tongues can be. That may be accidental too. When we lose our temper we don't know but that we may have destroyed something precious. The person working alongside us who knows we are Christian may have been watching us and beginning to consider whether the secret that we have might be what he or she needs. Our lost temper has ruined our testimony and destroyed the hope that was being born in that colleague's heart. Their reaction was probably, "Well, what's the use! They are no different from me after all," and they lost interest. From the accidental spark a life was blasted. We never meant it but we did it!

Ministers, nowadays, are more and more facing the problem of people who have been divorced wanting to remarry. One question that always crops up is whether the person wishing to be married again is the innocent or guilty party in the previous divorce. The law often pronounces one to be innocent and the other guilty. But from my experience of life I wonder time and time again if the law is right, because with the tongue a home can be destroyed. Whether it be the husband or whether it be the wife, their words can make a home into a hell and drive the other one out. If it drives them into sin, then the law will pronounce that one guilty and the person who has driven the other out as "innocent." Yet all the time the one whose tongue had destroyed was the guilty person.

How little do we dream of what the end of just a flash of temper is going to be. Remember, the tongue is a fire and remember how great a matter a little fire can kindle.

Have We Robbed God?

Will a man rob God?

Malachi 3:8-10

Thursday

The prophet Malachi accuses God's people of having robbed God and indicates that when they stop doing that and bring the whole tithe to the storehouse, then God will bless them. I used to interpret that text with a spiritual implication, but has it not the material and financial aspect too? So often Christians have said, "If God blesses the work we will find the money." But I suggest this verse implies that if we give the money, then God will bless the work!

A most grievous sin possible in the Church today lies in the Christian's attitude to money. Our buildings, which we call "Houses of God," are unattractive; our equipment is out of date; our manpower is reduced; our workers are harried by anxiety; our work is being curtailed and even closed down; and why? Because the Christian is so often robbing God and God has something against us. There is failure all round. Do we give a tenth of our income to God?

I think the thing which is breaking the heart of God today is that the work of the Church of Christ is crippled because God has something against us. If I called you a thief you would say I was insulting you, but God called His people robbers because they were not giving a tenth of their income to Him. The giving of a tenth was taught in the Old Testament and assumed in the New. Do we give a tenth of our income to God and His work?

The Publicity of a Transformed Life

They were all amazed . . . saying, We never saw it on this fashion

Friday

Mark 2:12

How varied were the problems the Master met, and how transformed the people He left behind! When John the Baptist sent his own disciples to ask if Jesus was indeed the Christ, He pointed them to the transformed lives He left behind Him wherever He had been. "The blind see, the lame walk, the lepers are cleansed, . . . and the dead are raised . . ."

This is the underlying challenge beneath the words of Christ when questioned by the Pharisees as to His right to forgive sins. He said to them, "Whether is it easier to say to the sick of the palsy, Thy sins be forgiven thee; or to say, Arise . . . and walk?" Of course it is always easier to speak words than to demonstrate power.

The greatest challenge facing the Church today is, by the power of Christ, to produce lives the quality of which can only be explained in terms of divine miracle. When our Lord was on earth there was no publicity to compare with this! Where lives were changed, the crowds came.

Knowing the Will of God

That ye might be filled with the knowledge of His will in all wisdom and spiritual understanding

Saturday

Colossians 1:9

If we are going to do the will of God we must be able to discern it. This has always been true in the case of God's servants. Again and again we are told in Old Testament times that "the word of the Lord came to . . ." and when the servant of God acted in obedience, it was in conscious knowledge of what the will of God was. He was obviously not necessarily acting in accordance with his own will, and certainly not in accordance with the will of the society in which he was placed. But it was the will of God for him made known to him through the Word of God. We must then be able to discern the will of God if we are to do it.

So it is that Paul in one of the great prayers for the Christians at Colosse prays, "That ye might be filled with the knowledge of His will in all wisdom and spiritual understanding." But if we are to know the will of God we must want the will of God. Our Lord Himself made that plain. He says, "If any man will do His will, he shall know." So let us realize that if we are going to do the will of God we must take the trouble to find out what that will of God is, and be willing to obey it.

When Trials Come

Sunday

Count it all joy when ye fall into divers temptations
James 1:2

It is worth noting that James does not say "if" but "when." It is assumed that trials are part and parcel of the life of every Christian. We are all certain to meet these. These will come from three directions.

First of all there will be trials that are part of the lot of fallen humanity. There is no indication anywhere in the New Testament that by becoming Christians we are insured against the kinds of trials that affect the human race. Our Christian faith is not an insurance policy against trial; it is not a way of escape.

Secondly, there are trials which are part of the divine plan. God deals with us as children. The New Testament speaks of the chastening of the Lord. Hebrews 12:9-11 is full of this aspect of divine discipline by the Father of His children, and speaks of submission to such discipline that "yieldeth the peaceable fruit of righteousness unto them which are exercised thereby."

And there are, thirdly, trials that are part of the satanic war. 1 Peter 5:8 speaks of "your adversary the devil." The whole atmosphere of the Christian life is one of conflict with the forces of evil, and the Christian is right in the thick of it.

So James speaks of "manifold trials" and the word translated here "manifold," or "divers" in the Authorized Version, literally means "many-colored." Some of the trials are lit up with the love of God, others are shadowed by the hatred of the enemy of our souls. Constantly and differently we shall inevitably be tried, but James says, "Count it all joy." J. B. Phillips translates this even more suggestively, "Don't resent them as intruders, but welcome them as friends!" The New English Bible translates, "Count yourselves supremely happy."

This is quite remarkable. Why are we to count ourselves happy? Surely because of the evidence the trials become. I am sure that the truth of the New Testament is that we are tried because we matter.

We matter to God and we matter to the devil. J. B. Phillips' translation of Hebrews 12:8 reads like this, "If you had no experience of the correction which all sons have to bear you might well doubt the legitimacy of your sonship."

The Disappointment that Words can be to Others

Fountain . . . Fig tree . . .

Monday

James 3:11,12

What do people look for when they go to a fountain? Surely, water that is sweet to drink. What do people expect to find on a fig tree? Surely, figs. The suggestion that James is making is that so often, so tragically often, the words of Christians do not correspond to the profession of a Christian. The world expects more from the Christian than the Christian realizes.

And so does God expect certain things from those who are His born-again children. He longs to hear the voice of prayer. The world expects to hear the voice of testimony and of witness. But what do they find? Is there not the same sense of disappointment that a person would experience if they found that the water was not sweet but bitter—if they discovered that instead of figs the fruit was olive berries? How often the world is let down by the Christian! How often the Father is disappointed with His child!

Faith Seeking

He went unto Him

Tuesday

John 4:47

It is worth nothing that God does not encourage laziness, for here we find that faith must strive to relate the ability of Christ to its own poverty. Think of the demands of the search. Capernaum was some little distance from Cana, and Christ was continually on the move. I wonder if the weather was really hot! I wonder how many false trails this man followed! Christ had been here or there, so he was told, but by the time the nobleman got there the scene was cold and Christ was gone. But through it all he pushed on, determined to find Christ at all costs. Let us not think then that God gives to those who do not ask; that those find who never seek; that doors open without our knocking.

But the search was not just demanding; it was also long. Did it take one day, or two, or a week to find the Master? The return journey took one whole day, the Bible tells us that. How quickly we want our problems resolved; how easily we want the answer found! Perhaps the duration of the search did something to this man's faith. Did the time spent in the search underscore the desperateness of the situation? Did it focus his faith and trust more and more vividly in Christ? Did the conviction now grip the father that Christ alone must be the answer? And when finally he found Him, was it not as a desperate man that he flung himself at His feet?

Is there a lesson here for us? Is there a quality that can be given to faith which time alone can give, a measure of desperation? Too often we want to dance lightly and easily along and almost flippantly tap the resources of the power of Christ. But again and again in God's dealings with us, the time element plays a vital and decisive part. I make no pretense to be an expert in the culinary art but I do know that in cooking the time element is vital. Take a thing out too soon, or leave it in too long, and in both ways it is spoiled. There is a right time for cooking and there is a right time for believing.

Faith Hearing

He heard

Wednesday

John 4:47

This man heard that Jesus had come to Galilee, and what he heard he believed. In this simple statement we can learn two things about faith. The *background to this man's faith* in Christ was that he had lost faith in everything else. The illness of his son had tested his faith in the doctors' ability to heal his son, and in the sufficiency of his own resources to save him. The son he dearly loved was at the point of death and he was at the end of his resources. It was the bankruptcy of his own resources that paved the way for faith in Christ. This man would never have experienced the power of Christ unless he had first experienced the poverty of his own soul.

But also we can see the *basis of this man's faith*. It was, very simply, the person of Christ. We need to remember that we cannot talk about "faith" in the abstract but about faith in someone, in something. Reports reaching this man brought to him the picture— inadequate and incomplete, but enough—of One who, he felt, could meet the need of his life. He heard, and what he heard, he believed. This is what Scripture tells us about faith: faith is always a response to knowledge gained. Romans 10:17, "Faith cometh by hearing, and hearing by the word of God." To us the Person of Christ is revealed not simply in the chance reports of men but through the written Word of God in which is unveiled the living Word. Knowledge is therefore the basis of faith. And only as we come to know Him can we ever be prepared to trust Him.

Faith Resting

Jesus saith unto him, Go thy way; thy son liveth. And the man believed the word that Jesus had spoken unto him, and he went his way

John 4:50

Thursday

There is a time when we must stop praying a certain kind of prayer. Look at the faith of this man in his desperate need. The simple words of Christ have been heard. His need had been met completely. "Thy son liveth." Gradually we can see the tense look going from his face; his hands unclench; his body relaxes; his head drops; then he rises quietly and goes his way with nothing more than the statement of the Master. The statement, not the promise, "Thy son liveth." Praying has become believing. Faith pleading has become faith resting. He stopped praying!

Sometimes our praying becomes little more than an exercise in unbelief. Like the Israelites we march round and round our Jerichos not seven times but seventy times seven. And the longer we march the closer we get to the walls of our problems, until they seem to tower above us shutting out the very light of the sky. Is there someone reading these words whose soul, too, is on the march around some Jericho of a problem that is towering above them?

Surely there comes a time when we must stop marching, indeed stop praying, if we are praying in unbelief, and start believing. And so this man believed the word that Jesus spake and went his way— with nothing more than the word of Christ, and yet did he need anything more than that? For as he traveled, we are told, he met the servants and then he knew that Christ's word was to be trusted. There is not tension in faith, there is simply trust. How many of us love and know the words of the hymn

> Jesus, I am resting, resting
> In the joy of what Thou art;
> I am finding out the greatness
> Of Thy loving heart
>
> Keep me ever trusting, resting;
> Fill me with Thy grace.

Discouragement and Disparagement

If the foot shall say, . . . the eye cannot say . . .

Friday   1 Corinthians 12:15

Paul sees something a little bit ridiculous in the way some Christians talk. He has used the analogy of the body with its different members to describe the Christian Church with its various members, each with its own function and gift. But there are some Christians who talk in a very stupid way and he puts it into words like this (verse 15), "If thy foot shall say, because I am not the hand, I am not of the body; . . ."

Paul is dealing with the absurd way in which people suggest that just because they do not possess certain gifts they are not really important and so become discouraged.

The absurdity lies in their discouragement. It usually arises because other Christians make them feel inadequate and they assume God cannot use them. Paul says, in effect, "Don't be so absurd: don't be so stupid," and he deals with this in verses 15-20. "Because I can't speak like so-and-so I am no use." This is the absurd situation that can arise when misguided and uninstructed Christians say to others that if they don't have one particular gift then there is something lacking.

Others talk equally stupidly from a background not of discouragement but of disparagement; the disparagement of Christians who, in their judgment, are less spiritual, less gifted. Paul says again, "Don't be so silly," In verse 21 he says, "The eye cannot say unto the hand, I have no need of thee: nor again the head to the feet, I have no need of you." Here are two exceedingly stupid ways of talking: one by Christians who have been made to think that because they don't have a particular gift they are of no use, so they might just as well not be Christians: and the other is to speak about these very people as if what they said was true. Discouragement and disparagement show themselves in the way some Christians talk about others. Don't let us fall into this stupid way of talking.

Time to Go

The time of my departure is at hand

Saturday   2 Timothy 4:6

Is there a hint here of the time of his departure being God's time, a time ordained, a time that is the right time, a time that was fixed not just by the authority of Rome but by the wisdom and love of God? In Psalm 31:15, the Psalmist records his faith in God's ever-ruling providence in the words, "My times are in thy hand." There seemed to be for the Psalmist a realization that the will of God was ultimately in control of the circumstances of his life. He was not just the object of chance, tossed about like a cork on the stream of the circumstances of life.

This sense of God's controlling hand was most vividly seen in the experience of our Lord Himself. We meet it on more than one occasion in John's gospel. The first time is in chapter 7 verse 30, "No man laid hands on Him because His hour was not yet come." What a difference this makes to our whole thinking about life and death when we remember that there is a controlling hand, which is the hand of the Savior! What comfort this brings to the life that is sorely tried! Paul's conviction was that this controlling hand was about to set him free and this controlling hand will take charge in our lives and will call us when it is our time to go.

Restoration

Take it up to thee . . .

Sunday

2 Kings 6:1-7

The miracles of the Old Testament like those of the New Testament are but parables in action. This miracle has a message of hope for those who have lost the spiritual effectiveness they once had.

Think of the *leadership in the work of God that was thrilling!* There was first of all the presence of the prophet Elisha in their midst. How much depends upon the kind of leadership we have known in our lives, the kind of minister, parents, Bible class leader. But the presence of the prophet meant something else; the prospect of progress in their minds. "The place is too strait for us," they said. The talk, the thought was all of progress, of expansion and development. Have some of us not known something of this in our lives, when we were in the thick of it all? Those were exciting days!

But there was also a *loss in the work of God that was tragic.* "As one was felling a beam, the axe head fell into the water" (verse 5). This man had lost that which made his contribution effective. The shaft of the axe was useless without the head and its keen cutting edge. We can say about the loss of the axe head that it was a conscious loss. The man knew what had happened, and so did those

207

who were working alongside him. It was also a confessed loss. In reply to the question, "Where fell it?" we are told that the man showed Elisha the place. The Christian usually has a pretty good idea where he, too, has lost his keen cutting edge!

The story however ends happily when we see a *life in the work of God that was taken up again.* In spite of the seeming impossibility of recovery, the axe head was brought within sight and within reach. The prophet used a piece of wood that became wet with the waters of the Jordan. Today the servant of God needs a bigger piece of wood than that, a cross that is wet with the blood of Jesus! The swift immediacy of the man's response to the word, "Take it up to thee," brought back to him what he had lost, And just as swiftly can God give back to us through the forgiveness of our sins all that we thought we had lost and lost for ever.

Love Serving

All manner of pleasant fruits, new and old, which I have
laid up for thee, O my beloved

Monday   Song of Solomon 7:13

Here the thought is not only that of serving with a person but of caring for that person. The person of her beloved is looming up more and more in the mind of the bride and in verse 9 she interjects that what she is and what she has is "for her beloved." In verse 13 she indicates that all she does is "for thee, O my beloved." Then in chapter 8 verse 1 she speaks of a longing for the opportunity of caring for him, of serving him—away from all the big occasions of life. She longs to serve him in the little ways that an older sister would care for the needs of a small brother—meeting the personal needs, the intimate needs, the little needs. The tiny little acts of thoughtfulness and consideration are born out of the insight of love which studies the more personal and intimate needs. She longs for the opportunity not simply of serving with her beloved but also of serving her beloved.

How true this is of human love! It creates a great longing to enjoy not only the big and important issues in life but the small and seemingly insignificant details of the commonplace things that take up so much of living and of loving. Someone has said that saints are those that deal with God in little things. In the total identification of the bride with the bridegroom, this sharing of the little things is exactly what she longs for. It is an attitude that he welcomes. There will be much that he will want to say to her and that will be said within the enfolding arms of his love, with her head resting on his shoulder (8:3).

A Divine Intolerance

Thou hast loved righteousness, and hated iniquity
Hebrews 1:9

Tuesday

We live in an age when tolerance is exalted to a place it doesn't deserve and certainly doesn't have in the mind of God. We have almost reached the stage of tolerating anything and everything. God's Word draws a very different picture. In Hebrews 1:9 we read, "Thou hast loved righteousness and hated iniquity." There is an intolerance in the very character of God. He loves the sinner but He hates the sin. Someone has put it this way—"It is possible to value tolerance so much that clear-cut distinction between right and wrong may become impossible," and I think we might add, between truth and error.

And so when Paul finds that forces and people are at work to destroy the Church of Jesus Christ, he is fearless and merciless in what he says, and we need to remember that this is exactly what our Lord did. When He had something to say about the sins of the Scribes and Pharisees He said it bluntly! Maybe it is time for more plain speaking by more Christians!

Fuel for Prayer

Ceasing to pray . . .

Wednesday

1 Samuel 12:23

The first of prayer can burn low through dullness, through monotony, or through ignorance. One of the great needs for maintained intercession is information. This applies to both personal and corporate prayer. If I am going to pray about a a person's problem, I need to be informed about it so that I can pray intelligently. In the case of my personal prayer life, it is my responsibility to secure that information. In the case of a prayer meeting it will be the responsibility of the leader to obtain it and then to pass it on. I must take careful note of all such information.

There needs to be a backward look so that I may continue to pray for matters not yet "prayed through" and answered, or so that praise may be offered for answers given. There must be a forward look to anything that needs to be prepared for prayer, whether in my own life, in the life of my church, or in the lives of that circle of contacts for which I feel God has given me a sense of responsibility.

Obviously the personal responsibilities in prayer will vary with the individual. While there may be some responsibilities I share with others, there will be some that are specially my own. But I must know the facts so that I can pray with understanding. This is one reason why it is so vital to maintain correspondence with missionaries, and for them to maintain correspondence with me. If I know what is happening and what is needed, my prayers will be more meaningful than a simple, "God bless him today."

Are Men Cowards?

The fear of man . . .

Thursday

Proverbs 29:25

I have never been able to understand the mentality of those who look on being a Christian as something "soft." Some men I know, are prone to pride themselves upon their so-called "manliness" and leave religion and church-going to the wife or the children. Yet I remember once calling on a lady whose husband never came to church. She told me that she was convinced that the only reason he never came was that he hadn't the courage to do so. What would his friends say if they heard that he had been to church?

Having knocked around quite a bit, and having met a great number of all kinds of people, I have come to the conclusion that cowardice is possibly the most common reason why many people today are not committed Christians. The one thing most of us find most difficult to stand is being laughed at, being different. And the coward in us takes control and keeps us back from taking the step we know to be right and which deep down we really want to take. The Bible says, "The fear of man bringeth a snare." How true that is!

Where?

Where be all His miracles which our fathers told us of?
Judges 6:13

Gideon was a man who just could not reconcile things as they were with what he knew of the God of his fathers—the God who had brought His people up out of the land of Egypt. Surely that same God could handle this situation! The taunt of the heathen touched him to the quick when they said, "Where is now their God?" It is no wonder that today we have people saying, "God is dead." What evidence is there in your church that He is alive? Apart from the platitudes which are sung and preached every Sunday, what evidence is there that there is a God who saves?

Have you heard the story of the evangelist who preached so long that at least one of his congregation fell asleep sitting in the gallery? The man woke up when the evangelist was making his appeal, and noticed that the person sitting next to him had his hand up, so he put up his hand too. As he looked around the church and saw that there weren't many hands up, he whispered to his neighbor, "I don't know what we are voting for but I think we have lost." Do you feel you are voting for a lost cause when you look at your church, at your own heart, at God's people, and search for evidences of God's power? You are compelled to say, "Where?" "Where are all the miracles which our fathers told us of?"

On Being Hurt to be Honest

The hollow of Jacob's thigh was out of joint
Genesis 32:25

God hurt Jacob deliberately by dislocating his thigh. How often God still wounds those He is waiting to bless! Sometimes He allows us to hurt ourselves in our struggle against His love. Have we ever been hurt by God? Have we the traces of such a wound? Is there still even now a sensitiveness about the place in our memory?

What a change has come over the attitude of Jacob now! At the beginning of this encounter with God he was wrestling with Him but now he is clinging to Him. "I will not let Thee go except Thou bless me." "What is thy name?" asks the heavenly Visitant. "Jacob," he confesses. The man's name stands for his character, "I am Jacob, the cheat—the rotter." The first step into real blessing with

211

God is taken when we are really honest about ourselves and our sins. The tragedy is that so often we have to be hurt before we will be honest.

Sufficient

My grace is sufficient for thee

Sunday

2 Corinthians 12:9

These four verses (7-10) form one of the most wonderful and intimate passages in the writings of Paul. How often we think that life must be easy for really great Christians, but for this man it certainly was not.

There was *difficulty* in his life which took two forms. In the first instance Paul takes note of a presence that seemed unhelpful for he writes of a "thorn in the flesh, the messenger of Satan to buffet me." Something, we know not what, made the going very tough indeed and seemed to make him aware of the reality of the old nature, the flesh, within him. Second, his prayer seemed unheard. Paul says, "For this thing I besought the Lord thrice, that it might depart from me." But in spite of the prayers of the good man nothing seemed to happen. The thorn remained. Paul was convinced that this thing had to go, but it didn't. Have we known pressures like that? Have we offered prayers like that?

Then Paul made a *discovery*. First he prayed, but then he stopped and started listening to what the Lord said to him. What a wise thing that was to do! As he listened he made two discoveries. One was God's unrecognized purpose. Twice he mentions it, "Lest I should be exalted above measure." God could not afford to run any risks with this man who was so important for His purposes. He had been so greatly used that the temptation to pride which would have spoiled him for God's service had to be watched. This thorn was designed to keep him humble. The other discovery was the unrestricted plenitude of grace. "My grace is sufficient for thee" was the Word of God. There was no need for the thorn to be removed since God's grace was sufficient for Paul to endure it.

The experience brought *doxology* into his life. "Most gladly therefore will I rather glory in my infirmities, that the power of Christ may rest upon me." Paul's attitude was changed. Now he would rather the thorn remained. His acceptance was complete. "I take pleasure in infirmities . . . when I am weak then am I strong." Paul is praising while the thorn remains. Difficulty had led to discovery and that had led to doxology!

Born Again . . . By the Word

Being born again, not of corruptible seed, but of incorruptible, by the word

1 Peter 1:23

The Word of God plays an indispensable part in the work of regeneration. Many years ago I spoke to the late Rev. J. R. S. Wilson whom I met quite casually in the street. I was beginning my Christian work and he was speaking out of a vast experience. He reminded me never to forget that the seed of the Word that I was sowing was an incorruptible seed. The result of its worth might not be seen immediately. It might lie dormant in the heart and mind of the hearer for many years. But the seed was "incorruptible" and would be the instrument in the hand of God for the creation of the new life within the soul.

How essential that in our sermons, our Sunday School lessons and our personal witness, we should be sowing this seed. We should not be content with achieving a reputation for popularity or cleverness, not content simply that we have held the attention of the children with interesting stories. We should know that we have sown the seed of the Word of God in the minds of the hearers.

Perhaps the reason why a good deal of the preaching of today is lacking in spiritual results is because men and teachers have felt it more important to proclaim what they think than what God has said. If we want to witness the birth of new life it is absolutely essential that the "incorruptible seed" should be planted in the hearts and minds of those to whom we minister. Here we face the fact that the Bible is absolutely indispensable in our witness.

That Will Be the Day

Every man's work shall be made manifest: for the day shall declare it

1 Corinthians 3:13

The Bible makes it plain that there is a judgment day awaiting the Christian—not a judgment concerning his sins but concerning his service. The quality of our service is to be tested. In the previous verse, Paul has indicated that we can build with what is perishable and worthless such as wood, hay and stubble, or with what is of permanent value such as gold, silver and precious stones. But this will be revealed and tested at the day of judgment for the Christian. Not only will quality be tested but the secrecy will be terminated.

In chapter 4:5 Paul writes, "Judge nothing before the time, until the Lord come, who both will bring to light the hidden things of darkness, and will make manifest the counsels of the hearts: and then shall every man have praise of God." It is foolish and wrong to try to evaluate the service of Christians when we really know so little. There are many hidden mysteries of prayer, of giving, of caring, and these of course are an essential part of Christian service. You will recall that in Matthew 6 our Lord spoke of what is done in secret being rewarded openly. So often we think that preaching is important because it is public and that praying is unimportant because it is private, but which in the sight of God is more important? Which achieves more—preaching or praying?

Not only will the hidden mysteries be revealed but also the hidden motives. Even in Christian service motives need to be examined, and when the motives are wrong God's judgment will take due account. When it comes to that day of disclosure, there are certain to be strange and unexpected re-assessments which will exalt some who have been disregarded, and humble others who have been exalted. That will be the day indeed, the day when the whole truth will be finally and fully known.

"Far Ben" with God

That I may know Him . . .

Wednesday

Philippians 3:10

The whole atmosphere of Paul's wonderful testimony (Philippians 3) is intimacy of communion with Christ. The key verse is verse 10, "That I may know Him, and the power of His resurrection, and the fellowship of His sufferings, being made conformable unto His death." that word translated "know" is not the "know" of the intellect; it is the "know" of intimacy. The Scots have a delightful way of describing friendship which is on such terms of rare intimacy. It is the phrase "far ben," which is based on the old country set-up where a cottage would have two rooms, a but and a ben. The but was the room that everybody went into; the ben was the room into which you took only those you wished peculiarly to honor! Then the term was transferred from ordinary life to the sphere of friendship. If you were on privileged terms of friendship with someone who rejoiced in your friendship, you were described as being "far ben" with such a person.

If anybody remembers the books of Ian Maclaren, (. . . stories of the Drumtochty folk: *The Days of Auld Lang Syne, Beside the Bon-*

nie Briar Bush and others), he may recall how Maclaren describes the village folk gossiping around the walls of the kirkyard, talking about one and another as country folk do! When almost everybody had been discussed, somebody mentioned the name of one man who was quite outstanding for his Christian worth and character.

"What do you think of Burnbrae?"

At the mention of the name silence fell; it was not easy to do justice to such a man.

"Well, there is only one thing you can say about Burnbrae and that is that he is 'far ben'."

Burnbrae was "far ben" with God, and that is what Paul wanted to be with Jesus Christ. "That I may know Him, and the power of His resurrection, and the fellowship of His sufferings."

Watch Your Tongue

Slow to speak

Thursday

James 1:19

How easily and willingly some people will talk the language of Zion. It flows from their lips so glibly. They know their Bibles, they understand the Gospel, but their tongues run away with them, and the language on their lips goes far beyond the experience of their lives. They become heated in their talk to the point of anger and will argue fiercely for the faith. They will dispute some point of difference in doctrine or interpretation until the blood mounts in their faces, and their tongues lash those who disagree with them.

James wants us to be cautious about all this, "Be swift to hear," he says, and "slow to speak." In other words, remember that you have two ears to one mouth so keep that proportion in your living. Listen twice as much as you talk. Listen more to others than you talk to them or of them. Listen more to God than you speak to Him. Not that the Christian will not take upon his lips aspirations or truths beyond his experience: we are not to limit our preaching or witness to the truth of God to our experience of it. But to talk without any intention or desire, to talk as if we knew it all is quite wrong.

It is this easy talk that James is condemning. He is thinking of the person who talks as if he was concerned about the spread of the Gospel but doesn't get down to doing anything about it—the kind of Christian who talks with apparent concern about the well-being of the Church but is seldom present at the services. This kind of chatter without a corresponding experience or desire in the heart is something that the Bible has no time for.

Being in Earnest

Israel doth not know, My people doth not consider
Isaiah 1:3

Friday

I believe that the root of many problems today in the Church at large is a basic ignorance about Jesus Christ. Recently a leading personality of the Roman Church in Holland visited Edinburgh. The Roman Church in Holland is in a state of ferment and change, and this particular churchman is playing a leading part.

Interviewed by a Presbyterian minister, he was asked what he thought was needed to produce the same kind of upsurge of spiritual life in Scotland. His reply was significant. He said, "It will happen when you begin to take Jesus Christ seriously."

Let us face the fact that most Christians don't take Jesus Christ seriously at all. "My people are destroyed for lack of knowledge" was God's charge in the days of Isaiah. And the Church today desperately needs to learn what Christ has said, what He claims to be able to do, what He wants us to do, and how He wants us to live. "Faith cometh by hearing, and hearing by the word of God."

God has no time for ignorance. Faith is not a feeling but a response to truth learned. Faith and hope will begin to kindle in our hearts when we hear and know of Jesus Christ and are obedient to Him. That means getting down to our Bibles in our own homes and in our own rooms. It means being in our places in church twice on Sunday. It means getting to a Bible Study if there is one. If there isn't, then it could mean starting one in your own home.

There is no substitute for this kind of basic knowledge of Jesus Christ. And if we are going to take Him seriously, we must get down to the business of getting to know Him.

Full Surrender

Present your bodies a living sacrifice, holy, acceptable unto God
Romans 12:1

Saturday

Professor Henry Drummond used to say that while the entrance fee to the Kingdom of God is nothing at all, the annual subscription is all we've got, and that's what so many of us are afraid of. If Jesus Christ was just a Savior, if the Gospel was just forgiveness, we would take Him as Savior and we would take His forgiveness. But we know deep down that this one who is the Savior is the Son of God. And although there is forgiveness to be found in Him through His death on the cross, there is infinitely more involved.

We know that He is not simply a Savior. He is also a Sovereign and a Lord, and we just don't want to hand over the control of our lives to Him or to anybody else. That is where the rub comes. That is why we pretend and why we make our excuses. The real reason why you are not a Christian, if you are not, is that you don't want to become one because you don't want Christ to take over the running of your life. You want to run it yourself.

C. S. Lewis says somewhere that when he was a boy and had a toothache, he knew that all he had to do to ease the pain was ask his mother for an aspirin. But he never did so because he also knew that if he asked her for an aspirin, she would give it to him but she would also phone the dentist. And the dentist wouldn't give him an aspirin; he would take the tooth out and Lewis didn't want that!

Some of us might like to take any aspirins that Jesus Christ would give us but are not so keen for Him to look around our lives and see what really needs to be done. Dr. Leslie Weatherhead said that in all the times he had interviewed people who were trying to evade the challenge of Jesus Christ, producing all sorts of intellectual problems and difficulties, nine times out of ten the real problem was not intellectual but moral. It wasn't that they couldn't believe, it was simply they didn't want to—and they wouldn't.

The Tactics of the Tempter

The serpent was more subtle than any beast of the field
Genesis 3:1

Sunday

There were three elements in the devil's tactics when he tempted our first parents in the garden of Eden; and just in case there may be some readers who doubt the existence of this enemy of the souls of men, may I remind you of the boy who when he was told there was no devil, met the statement with the words, "Then who is doing all his dirty work?"

The devil raised *doubts* in the mind of Eve, by asking, "Hath God said?" as if to suggest that whatever He had said might well be questioned. He cast doubts upon the goodness of God. "Not to eat of every tree!" Surely that was hard. God was unkind to say that! God of course had said nothing of the kind. The prohibition covered but one tree. How the devil delights to misquote the word of God. He cast doubts too upon the guilt of sin. "Hath God said ye shall not?" Surely He never said that. God would not be so unreasonable. It will be all right, go on, go ahead and do it and enjoy yourself.

His words contained an explicit *denial*. "Hath God said? . . . Ye shall not surely die!" This was a blatant contradiction to the word of God, and the devil does not hesitate to deny the word of God. The tragedy arose because a denial was believed. Is it not tragic when we find ourselves prepared to believe the devil's lie rather than God's truth? It doesn't matter. It won't hurt. Nobody will ever know. So the lies are poured into our ears, and we are foolish if we believe the devil's lie sooner than God's truth.

The third element was sheer *deceit*. "Ye shall be as gods" was the promise the devil made. How attractive sin is made to seem! One of the Puritans, speaking of this attraction, describes faith as the ability to see "sin, before its finery be on and it be dressed for the stage, to be but a brat from hell and bringing hell with it." How deceptive sin is proved to be. Someone put it vividly like this: "When sin long held in alluring expectation is actually done, how swift the alteration in its aspect. It passes from anticipation through committal into memory and will never be beautiful again." "As gods"—were they? I think not!

The Discernment of Love

Let her alone; against the day of my burying hath she kept this

Monday   John 12:7

Love always sees further than others see. Love is strangely sensitive to the moods of those it loves. A mother can very often tell a child's thoughts without the child ever speaking. I remember in my own childhood on one occasion sitting by the fire in the drawing room at home. My mother was busy doing the mending sitting in a chair opposite. I had a raging toothache but I was trying to bear it because I knew that if I told my mother it would mean a visit to the dentist and I didn't relish the thought of that. So I sat gazing pensively into the fire, and then my mother spoke. She said, "George, have you got toothache?" She knew, and she knew because she loved.

And so Mary's eyes were watching her Lord that night and she knew that His heart was heavy with the thought of the cross which was so near. As Mary looked up into the eyes of her Lord she saw there the gathering darkness. And I think that Christ was glad that she knew.

God's Unfaithfulness?

I therein do rejoice . . . and will rejoice!

Philippians 1:18

Tuesday

Resentment, jealousy, doubt. These reactions are not specifically stated here, but surely they must have been in the mind of Paul the prisoner! They must have been among the weapons that the enemy of souls used to try to cripple this great warrior. "What about unanswered prayer, Paul? Two years in jail, back there in Palestine, the long sea voyage as a prisoner, and now, for two years, in bonds again. This is something that has gone on a long time. You have been in prison before, but not as long as this. You have prayed about it, and others have prayed, but God hasn't done a thing!"

Not only was his prayer unanswered, but his potential seemed unused. Who was this man, so long confined? He was a great preacher, but he was silenced. He was a man with preaching in his very blood and his very bones, a man called to preach—and he couldn't preach! He was a pioneer, a great strategist of the church; yet he was confined and couldn't get out! The only marching Paul ever knew now was the tramp of feet as they passed by outside; he was anchored and fettered, restricted to one room! This man couldn't move—this man who had journeyed everywhere for Christ and had founded churches here, there and everywhere. Satan would point to the seeming unfaithfulness of Paul's Lord. What was God's purpose in all this? Paul had been called to be an apostle, not to be a prisoner. He had been called to preach and he couldn't preach.

This writer, then, is no theorist. this man who says, "I therein do rejoice, yea, and will rejoice," is a man talking out of circumstances a thousand times more difficult than ours. No matter what our situation is, it is not more difficult than Paul's.

A Burning Bush

The bush burned with fire, and the bush was not consumed

Exodus 3:2

What was the meaning of this sign that God gave to Moses? It may have been that God wanted to remind Moses of the sufferings of His people and the burning bush was a picture of that. The fires of persecution and suffering were burning fiercely in Egypt but the people were not destroyed. But they were still suffering, they were still in desperate need. And here was Moses, miles away from it all, quite content to live his life as a shepherd while his people were in the fires of affliction. "I have surely seen the affliction of my people," said the Lord, "I have heard their cry . . . I know their sorrow." The need for action, for deliverance, was as real at that moment as it had been forty long years before when Moses had been a prince in Egypt. Nothing had changed.

The burning bush may have been a picture of Moses' people, but it may also have been a picture of himself. It was just an ordinary bush and he was just an ordinary man, a shepherd. But the bush was ablaze with the fire of God's presence. His ordinary life could become a miracle life if possessed utterly by God's Spirit. I wonder sometimes whether God brings across your path and mine such a life—a bush ablaze and burning—so that we face the challenge of what God can do with a life that is completely possessed by Him. Was this the challenge to Moses—that he, an obscure shepherd, was wanted by God?

What are you? What am I? Just ordinary people. Nobody perhaps would stop and look twice at us, but we are the very people that God wants. And He doesn't want just one or two, He wants all of us. And His word to us is, "Come now and I will send you." Through the ministry of the Holy Spirit, through the effectiveness of our praying, through the generosity of our giving, through the reality of our witness and our testimony, it is possible for us to find that there is no limit to what God can do. It may be that God wants to turn you into a bush that burns with fire.

This shall turn to my Salvation

For I know that this shall turn to my salvation through
your prayer, and the supply of the Spirit of Jesus Christ

Thursday
Philippians 1:19

There are various interpretations of the meaning of the word "salvation" and its connotation in this particular verse. Perhaps the best interpretation is that Paul realized even in this difficult place that an opportunity was being granted to reach the unsaved, a ministry was being achieved to strengthen the Church, but also a quality and purpose of grace was being fulfilled in his own soul. He was in prison not only for the sake of the Imperial Guard and the church at Rome but for his own sake.

"This shall turn to my salvation (to my full spiritual health) through your prayer, and the supply of the Spirit." A quality of life was going to be secured in Paul that could not be secured in any other way—a completeness, a maturity, a Christlikeness . . .

"This shall turn to my salvation." There may be qualities lacking in your life as a Christian that God can only secure if He puts you in a place that is utterly difficult, where it is desperately lonely, where doubt beats in upon your soul, where jealousy is tending to thrust up its angry and ugly head, where resentment fires are liable to burst into flame. Such a place is going to turn to your salvation. God is going to do something to you that is going to make you sweet and gracious and lovely. He can't do it anywhere else except in the fire, so He puts you right there!

Looking Ahead

Henceforth . . .

Friday
2 Timothy 4:8

Paul is looking beyond the horizon that we call death and in that beyond, the most exciting for him would be the appearance by his Lord and the assessment of all his service. Already he had been standing at the bar of Roman justice (so-called), perhaps tried by the Emperor Nero himself. The verdict he was already anticipating. He knew it would be one of condemnation, but on that day it would be the Lord, the righteous Judge who would try his case and who would bestow on him the crown of righteousness. So he was excited and expectant as he anticipated the appraisal of his life by the Lord he loved and who loved him. This thought of appraisal and approval just filled and thrilled his soul.

Some of us have no doubt watched ice-skating championships on television. We marvel at the skill and effort that the skaters put into the competition, but the important thing for each of them is the final assessment of their performance. We have watched them on the ice and when their program ends as they look expectantly towards the scoreboard that would reveal the appraisal of their judges. How eagerly they wait, how expectantly they watch as the verdicts are made known.

What a day it will be for us and for every Christian when divine appraisal is made of our use of the opportunities and resources that have been ours in Christ. It is a judgment that will be based upon perfect knowledge. Again and again in the assessment passed by the risen Lord on the churches in the Book of the Revelation there come the words, "I know thy works." The righteous Judge knows what we have done and also why we have done it. He knows not only when we have failed but also how near we came to success.

So, in the mind of this great Christian warrior, there is a looking ahead, but the very realization that the end is so near brings home to him the fact that all the opportunities that his life on earth have provided are now nearly over. We do not know how much time we have left. All we know is that one day the time of opportunity will end. The time of appraisal and, we trust, approval will be on us.

Love in a Hurry

The voice of my beloved! behold, he cometh leaping
upon the mountains, skipping upon the hills. My
beloved is like a roe or a young hart

Song of Solomon 2:8,9

Love is always in a hurry whether it is to open a letter, answer the telephone, or keep an appointment. Love knows nothing of sluggish and dragging feet. If, by any chance, some of you are dating and you find that the one you love and that you think loves you is always late for the appointment, I think you should be justified in questioning the reality and the sincerity of that love. Love is always in a hurry.

As her beloved comes to her, leaping upon the mountains, skipping upon the hills, there is expectancy in his heart. But what is the bridegroom expecting? Surely he is expecting a glad welcome! Surely he is looking for a light in her eyes, arms outstretched in welcome, the warmth of a joyous and a glad smile! One of the pictures we have of Christ in the New Testament describes Him in this very attitude of expectancy. In Hebrews 10:13 we read of Him as seated on the right hand of God "from henceforth expecting till His enemies be made His footstool." Have we ever stopped to ask ourselves if Christ finds in us that which He expects to find, and has a right to find in the lives of those who profess so much and have received so much? He comes then with expectancy.

The effort involved and the time taken mean nothing to love so he comes over the mountains skipping upon the hills. Does this speak of the difficulties love has to surmount? Our heavenly Bridegroom had to go to endless pain and trouble, but He perseveres in His dealings with us. To love, all this effort and expenditure of time, thought and strength mean nothing. Love is concerned only with the happiness and the response from the one loved.

A Boldness that can Sing

. . . as always, so now also

Sunday   Philippians 1:20

Some of us sing as long as the sun shines, but the moment the clouds arrive we cease to sing and begin to complain. Paul is a brave man, a courageous man. I think we should remember that courage has its place in Christian experience. Be brave! "My earnest expectation and my hope, that in nothing I shall be ashamed, but that with all boldness, as always, so now also Christ shall be magnified in my body" (Philippians 1:20).

Two things went into this boldness:

His Concern for God's Glory—That "now also Christ shall be magnified in my body." Paul's aim was that Christ should be made great. Utterly forgetful of himself, Paul's one concern was for Another, his Lord. He longed that Christ should be made visible, apparent, obvious. He was not concerned that Paul should be heard, but that Christ should be seen; not that Paul should be free, but that Christ should be found. His aim was not that he should be responsible for a great work, but that men should be reached in a mighty blessing. His concern was that Christ should be magnified.

Paul knew that in his contempt for his own comfort the place he was in was not only difficult but dangerous. The very threat of uncertainty hung over the whole situation. Life was a possibility, but so was death, and Paul was ready for either.

His Confidence in God's Control—He said, "I am in a strait betwixt two" (verse 23). "I am in a situation where I am quite helpless.

I am hemmed in. I'd love to go, I'd love to die. I know the alternative is to live. But even if I am helpless in this situation, it is under control." Then, because he had this confidence, he said, "I know that I shall abide and continue with you all for your furtherance and joy of faith" (verse 25). He had assessed his circumstances and he realized that Christ was in control. Although his situation was not easy he felt sure that the thing that was more needful—not the thing that was most comfortable—was the thing that would happen.

A difficult place? Yes, perhaps. It wasn't the first time, though, that Paul had sung praises in prison! Christian, in a difficult place, learn to sing with Paul!

An Abiding Sense of Wonder

Unto me, who am less than the least of all saints, is this grace given, that I should preach among the Gentiles the unsearchable riches of Christ

Monday

Ephesians 3:8

There would seem to have been in the heart of Paul an abiding sense of wonder that God should ever have chosen him, and a complete abasement in the light of the knowledge of what God had done through him. When Paul speaks of himself, it is with a sense of utter amazement that such a priceless message conveying such a priceless truth had not been entrusted to somebody very special to proclaim to men, rather than to an ordinary person like himself.

Surely God requires someone much worthier—but no, God wants to use ordinary people. If this be so, then there is hope for us. We know that we are just ordinary Christians. Yet we can remember that ordinary people are the very people that God wants to use. What a tremendous comfort that is! But is there not also a word of caution here for those who think they are rather extra special? God doesn't want to use such people. In fact, He seldom does. But if, like Paul, we feel that we are "less than the least of all saints," then, as there was hope for him, there is hope for us.

A Dangerous Assumption

If any man have not the Spirit of Christ, he is none of His

Tuesday

Romans 8:9

The assumption that many church folk make, and many ministers too—although they ought to know better—is that everybody in the Church has already received the gift of the Holy Spirit, that everybody has already been born again! This is not what the scripture teaches. Romans 8:9 says quite clearly that it is possible for a person not to have the Spirit.

Acts 19:2 is another verse which, if misunderstood, can add to the confusion. Paul is speaking to that little group at Ephesus whose instruction had been incomplete, and in whose lives Paul could see that there was something missing. He discovered that their teaching was based upon the expectations aroused by the message of John the Baptist concerning Christ, but not upon an experience of the new birth.

Paul's question was not as the Authorized Version translates it, "Have ye received the Holy Ghost since ye believed?" but "Did you receive the Holy Spirit when you believed?" (RSV). They replied, "No, we have never even heard that there is a Holy Spirit." Obviously these people were religious but not regenerate! They were living in the pre-Calvary, pre-Pentecost knowledge that had apparently preceded Paul and had reached as far as Ephesus.

It is perfectly possible to be a member of a church without being a member of Christ, and without having understood enough to have repented of sins and to have received the new life in Christ by the Spirit. Such people expect the fruit of the Spirit without possessing the life of the Spirit. They are trying to live the Christian life and they don't have it. God does not ask us to live the Christian life until we possess it—or rather until we possess Him.

The Trustworthiness of Christ's Love

Through Him that loved us

Romans 8:37

Wednesday

How trustworthy is the love of Christ! Paul has just spoken of it in verse 32. "He that spared not His own Son, but delivered Him up for us all, how shall He not with Him also freely give us all things?"

So much of our trouble lies, does it not, in the fact that we do not trust God? We will not trust Him to shape our lives as His perfect wisdom sees best. We are continually arguing with Him and saying, "Lord, I do not want this in my life." But God in His wisdom says, "It is best for you." We will not trust His love. Probably one of the most difficult lessons to learn in Christian living is that God's

225

love is trustworthy. The circumstances of your life and mine are the very best for us. Do you find that difficult to believe? We tend to cry out in the darkness and loneliness of our night as our Lord cried out in the garden of Gethsemane, "If it be possible, let this cup pass from me," and your sweat too has been as it were great drops of blood. You may have cried like that to God for years, but the answer has come back, "No, my child, it cannot pass."

Perhaps you know the story of the little boy who went to bed and for some reason or another he was sharing a room with his father. When his father got into bed and had put out the light the little fellow called out in the dark, "Daddy, can I sing?" The father gave his consent. The singing however was of such a lusty nature that it precluded sleep, so after a while the father said, "Sonny, I think now that you had better stop." Silence fell in the room and then after a while the little chap, in the darkness, called out, "Daddy, is your face turned this way?"

God's love is trustworthy and His face is always turned our way.

Are You a Spiritual Cripple?

Borne of four

Thursday

Mark 2:3

Here was a man who possessed life, but lacked health. We Christians may possess spiritual life, but do we enjoy spiritual health? Are we "well" Christians or spiritual cripples?

Two things marked the life of this cripple. He suffered from a disability that was seen by others. Everybody knew that he was a sick man. I wonder what others see when they look at your life and mine. Do they see things in us that are certainly not the marks of a fully developed and healthy Christian experience? Oh yes, they know what we *believe*, but what do they *see*? That is the question. Members of the family see a lot. So do our colleagues, our employer or employees, all those with whom you come into contact. What do they see?

This man was also marked by a consciousness of his dependence on other people. If he was to go anywhere, he had to be carried—he was "borne of four." How dependent are we upon the prayers of others, the keenness of others, the service of others, the fellowship of others? Are we "carried" by our church? If we were deprived of all that "others" mean to us in Christian things, would we be able to stand alone? Or are we spiritual cripples with disabilities seen by others, and a dependence upon others known to ourselves?

Stressing the Unimportant

Ye tithe mint and rue and all manner of herbs . . .

Friday

Luke 11:42

Here is an example of the sin of stressing the unimportant to the exclusion of the important. Our Lord is not saying that details do not matter. He is very careful to say, "These ought ye to have done." But they ought not to matter to the exclusion of the larger issues.

We would cite an example set against the background of the evangelical tradition of Great Britain. In this country it has long been regarded as undesirable that a lady should over-do her make-up. But the Christian who gets indignant about the presence of paint on the lips and does not get worked up about the absence of prayer on the lips is in danger of falling into the self-same sin that our Lord was dealing with in the lives of the religious leaders of His day.

Which is more important, paint on, or prayer off? The detail may be in conduct, or it may be in creed, but if it is only a detail let it remain a detail. Don't turn a molehill into a mountain. I remember a lady saying to me concerning someone, "He did not drink and he did not smoke, but he had other sins!" Are we Pharisees in this matter?

Given

The Lord said unto Joshua, See, I have given into thine hand Jericho

Saturday

Joshua 6:2

The phrase that sticks out is, "I have given into thine hand Jericho." And the truth that breaks through like a sudden shaft of light is this—what was a problem to Joshua was no problem to the Lord. Can we grasp that? Can we let the wonder of that really startle and awaken us? "I have given you Jericho." The intention of the Lord was victory and triumph and that victory was to be received as a gift.

This ties in with words that seemed to light up with new meaning the other day when I was reading 1 Corinthians 15:57, "Thanks be to God, which giveth us the victory through our Lord Jesus Christ." The Lord says, "I have given you Jericho"; Paul says, "Thanks be to God which giveth us the victory through our Lord Jesus Christ." I wonder if there is a line of truth here that we need to explore. We tend to think of victory as a goal, whereas the Word of God speaks of it as a gift, and that is quite different. It is not a goal away up there; it is a gift which we have here and now in Jesus Christ.

A Spirit of Expectancy

From henceforth expecting . . .

Sunday   Hebrews 10:13

These three words sum up the atmosphere of heaven, the spirit in the mind of the exalted Christ. Surely there should be a corresponding atmosphere in the Church on earth in which His Spirit is found. But so often it is otherwise; despondency rather than expectancy is the normal thing. We might well ask ourselves some questions so that we can be precise.

What should the members of a church expect from their minister? What do they expect of him as a preacher? Surely that he will proclaim the Word of God in its purity and in its authority, in its relevancy to every situation in life. They don't expect to hear what he, the minister, thinks, but what God has said, and it is his job to find out what that is and then to tell them. And as a pastor? Surely that in his life and work among them, he will portray the love of God, that caring love which recognizes the worth of every individual no matter what the world thinks of that person.

What should the minister expect from his members? The first thing surely would be their presence. In Galatians 4:26 the Church is called "the Mother of us all." If part at least of the mother's work is to see that good meals are provided for her children, surely there is nothing more maddening for a mother than to prepare a meal and the children not to be there. Surely the minister, too, has a right to expect his members' prayers. We live in a day when prayer is going out of fashion. Christians don't pray very much, and churches have long since given up prayer meetings. What a tragedy this is! "Ye have not, because ye ask not," warns the Bible.

What does the Master expect from ministers and members? He expects a worship that enthrones Him. Worship means giving worth to a person. What worth does Jesus Christ have in our lives?

228

He should surely have the pre-eminence. Does He? He expects, too, a witness that exalts Him. "Ye shall be witnesses unto Me" was His final word and this involves proclaiming Him with our lips and portraying Him in our lives. Expectancy! Is this the mood in which we come together?

The Sorrow Love Knows

Turn, my beloved

Monday

Song of Solomon 2:17

In the parable before us the physical presence of the bridegroom is withdrawn. In its spiritual application it is the sense of Christ's presence that is withdrawn. We can hear the words of dismissal spoken so carelessly. What does she mean when she says, "Turn, my beloved?" Some commentators suggest that she is saying, "Turn to me"; but the context which follows suggests that she is saying, "Turn from me," that she is dismissing him; that she is saying in effect, "It is too hot just now. "It would be too exhausting for me to reply and respond. I would rather wait. Please go back to the mountains from which you came. It is not convenient. You are mine, and of course I am yours, and I know where you work, but please go away just now."

How often it happens still. If we don't tell Christ to go we turn away from Him. Could any words be more hurtful than those words of dismissal for one who has come expectantly? Yet, how often Christ comes to us, expecting so much, expecting an eager response and we turn away, we dismiss Him. We neglect to read our Bibles, to have our time of prayer, or to respond to the call to serve and witness. Instead of an eager and glad response, the bridegroom is dismissed. Incredible it must have seemed to him, but dismissed he was and he turned and went. And if we dismiss Christ He will turn and go too—to our own irreparable loss.

What do we want in Prayer?

That ye may stand perfect and complete in all the will of God

Tuesday

Colossians 4:12

Here is what Epaphras wanted from God for his friends. This is where he wanted them to be and this is how he wanted them to live—"In all the will of God." That will of God which affects our character, our conduct and our careers. This, of course, is something basic that leads to Christian living which is marked by stability and maturity.

The word "perfect" could be translated "complete" and has various shades of meaning. It can mean "carried out fully," it can mean "fully convinced," or it can mean "fully satisfied." The sense is that of fullness and completeness. They were not to be partially, but completely, identified in every area of their lives with every aspect of God's will.

What a prayer to pray and how wise and right to pray it. We are to be content with nothing less than complete conformity to the will of God. We need to remind ourselves that in that will there will be a negative side, things that God will not want to see in our lives. There will also be the positive side, things that God will want to see in our lives. Our Christian living has to be marked by this stability and maturity.

Sowing and Reaping

Be not deceived; God is not mocked: for whatsoever a man soweth that shall he also reap

Galatians 6:7

Wednesday

How often people's lives are caught up and entangled in the consequences of deeds they have done and words they have said. One of the most solemn verses in the Bible is today's verse, warning us that "whatsoever a man soweth, that shall he also reap."

Years ago as children we frequently went for holidays to the Highlands of Scotland. The Spey valley was one of our favorite haunts and many a wonderful bicycle ride was taken through the moors, the forests and the hills. Often when we were cycling along a forest track we would come across a stretch of water cradled on the face of the moor, a lochan we would call it. On a fine summer's day we could see reflected on the still surface all the loveliness of the purple heather, the light and shade of the birch tree and pine, the bracken, the mighty shoulders of some great mountain, the blue of the sky and the white of the cloud.

Boy-like, I would reach for a stone to throw and away it would go, to fall with a splash in the very center of the lochan. In a moment the picture was broken, and from the center, in ever-widening circles, the ripples would spread until the whole surface was a-quiver. It might be possible to get the stone out again but nothing could stop the ripples spreading.

Life is like that. We may have forgiveness for a single act but nothing we do can stop the consequences spreading from day to day, from life to life. One of the grimmest discoveries that we can ever make in life is that we are reaping what we ourselves have sown. The tragedy is that often those we love most have to share in the reaping. The lesson we learn of course is this—be careful what seeds we sow. The consequences of some deeds and words are lovely—the consequences of others are frightening.

Memories!

. . . every remembrance of you

Thursday   Philippians 1:3

Note how constantly love thinks of those loved. "I thank my God upon every remembrance of you." Paul could never calculate how often he thought of and prayed for the Philippian Christians. When a mother and father go away from home for a vacation and leave a child behind, can you imagine their not thinking of their child, not wondering how their child is getting on? When a husband must go on a trip and leave his wife, if he loves her, he thinks of her often. If you have a loved one in a hospital, you think of that one all the time.

Do you, in the fellowship of your church, think like that of one another? "I thank my God upon *every* remembrance of you." How constantly and how intimately love thinks of those loved. Paul says, "I have you in my heart." Everywhere I go, I carry you around with me, as I think of you, your needs, your successes, your work. What a wonderful love was this!

Perhaps I can illustrate such love in this way: when a man is engaged to be married, he thinks often of the girl he loves and he always carries a photograph of her in his wallet. And even after he is married, a man will carry with him a photograph of his wife even though it may have been taken many years ago and you would hardly recognize her as the woman who is now his wife. But he carries her picture in his wallet and memories of her in his heart.

"I have you in my heart." If only we could get this kind of warmth of fellowship into the Church today, what a difference it would make! "I have you in my heart . . . every remembrance of you." What a warmth of affection and love there was in this wonderful group—between Paul and themselves and between them-

231

selves and Paul. Such a love should characterize the fellowship we have with one another.

Ashamed

Be not thou therefore ashamed of the testimony of our Lord, nor of me his prisoner: but be thou partaker of the afflictions of the gospel

Friday

2 Timothy 1:8

Paul is writing strongly because he was afraid Timothy might be tempted to be ashamed of the Savior and of the message that was centered in that Savior. He was also afraid Timothy might be tempted to be ashamed of the servant, Paul himself. When Paul was the successful preacher, Timothy had been proud to be known as his friend, a close and intimate friend indeed. But now Paul was a prisoner, a man on whom a social stigma would rest. Would Timothy be ashamed of him now?

How often Christians are tempted to be ashamed of the Lord's person. To be ashamed of the Gospel is just as real a danger today as in Paul's day because there is so much about it that men find offensive. The condemnation it passes upon the sin that either pleases men or pays them is not acceptable and so it is resented. Man's pride is offended by the preaching of the cross.

Then there is the capitulation that the Gospel asks—the surrenders of man's freedom and submission to the Person of Christ. All this breeds antagonism. Paul reminds Timothy that he himself had known this. Indeed, it was because of the Gospel and the antagonism to it that he was in prison. Nevertheless, Paul says, "I am not ashamed." Later he points out that Onesiphorus was not ashamed either. He was saying, "Timothy, don't you be ashamed."

Destruction and Construction

I have set you this day over nations and over kingdoms, to pluck up and to break down, to destroy and to overthrow, to build and to plant (RSV)

Saturday

Jeremiah 1:10

In every work we seek to do in the service of God and in all our witness there will be both a destructive and a constructive aspect. The truth of the Gospel of the glory of the blessed God destroys man's pride and conceit; it shatters man's ideas and conclusions. This was brought out clearly in the call that came to Jeremiah, for

232

God said that he would have to "root out, to pull down, to destroy, and to throw down," before he ever could begin "to build and plant."

We have seen all over our great cities destructive work going on. Houses by the hundreds have had to be pulled down, sites have been cleared, in order that constructive work might then be undertaken. Similarly, there is no good in planting seeds in a bed full of weeds; the ground and the soil must first be clean if the seed is to grow.

Was there ever a time when this destructive aspect of the truth of God was needed more than today? But we must not stop there. We must be positive. When the old buildings have been pulled down the new buildings can go up: when the weeds have been rooted out then the seed can be sown.

The Near Tragedy of a Partial Obedience

And Lot went with him

Sunday

Genesis 12:4

The story of the early stages of the life of Abraham tells us how nearly Abraham never succeeded.

Think of the *revelation* he had known. It was a twofold one for there had been a revelation of the person and purpose of God. In Acts 7:2, Stephen in his defense tells how "the God of glory appeared unto our father Abraham," so although he went out not knowing where he went, he went out knowing well with Whom he went. The conditions of God's purpose were made clear, and the consequent blessing would be certain. He had to leave the place where he lived and the people there and go out alone.

But Abraham made an important *reservation*. In verse 4 we are told, "So Abraham departed, . . . and Lot went with him." The reservation was deliberate because the terms had been clear. He was to forsake "his country, his kindred and his father's house." What was he doing, taking Lot then? How often we are tempted to do exactly this. The reservation was disastrous. The early stages of the career of Abraham were marked by muddle and misery. "The way of transgressors is hard," says the Bible. The way is made deliberately hard to turn us from it. We see that God seems to have less and less to say to Abraham when he builds his altars, until he seems to have nothing to say at all. Instead of blessing he ran into trouble with a famine on his hands and so went on to Egypt.

233

Praise God, though, that he found *restoration*. We have to read on to the next chapter and there we see that another chance was given to him. There was trouble between Abraham's herdsmen and Lot's. God seems to have ordered the circumstances to give Abraham the chance to do what he should have done long before. It was really not practical or possible for things to go on the way they were. In his choice we see the saving of the whole purpose of God for this man and through the man for the whole world.

I wonder if God held His breath as He waited to see if Abraham would take the chance given to him. Abraham did take it and the words were spoken at last, words that God had waited to hear for so long. In Genesis 13:9 they are recorded. "Separate thyself, I pray thee, from me." Lot goes his way and Abraham goes God's way. Immediately communion with God is restored and in verses 14-18 we have the story of what God now can say to his obedient servant. Is there something that God has been waiting a long time to hear us say?

Where Temptation Leads

And sin, when it is finished, bringeth forth death

James 1:15

Monday

In these verses James is dealing with temptation. There are three things that are obvious regarding the nature of temptation.

First, it is *deceptive*: that bait contains a hook; that lure will lead to a trap. Temptation is never as simple as it seems, and so James writes here, "Sin, when it is finished, bringeth forth death." The end product of the whole process of temptation is death itself. It may not be quite clear what is in the mind of James here. He may be thinking of death in the sense of separation. For example, when we say a person has died, we do not mean they have ceased to live but that they are now living in a realm in which they are separated from us.

So it is also important to note how *divisive* temptation is. Sin will separate us from God in the sense of broken fellowship; sin will also separate us from God's people and the experience and enjoyment of their fellowship. We all know something of this.

How *destructive* temptation is too! It may be that James is thinking, when he uses the word "death," of the destruction that is involved in death. For while it is true that the person who has died continues to live, yet there is so much that has been brought to an end. The body itself is destroyed and returns earth to earth, ashes to ashes, dust to dust.

And so when we yield to temptation and go the way of disobedience there is a great deal that can be destroyed in our lives as Christians—our peace can be destroyed, our testimony can go, even our usefulness in God's service will be brought to an end.

Dr. Fosdick of America, speaking of temptation, describes the transformation when "it passes from anticipation, through committal, into memory" and adds the comment, "Then it will never be beautiful again." How true! How tragic!

The Song of Love

The song of songs, which is Solomon's

Tuesday   Song of Solomon 1:1

This is unquestionably a difficult book but Dr. Martyn Lloyd-Jones describes it as "a mine of spiritual treasure and one of the most exquisite expositions of the relationship between the believer and his Lord to be found anywhere in Scripture." Hudson Taylor writes that behind the imagery of bridal love is set forth "the deep truths of the believer's personal union with the Lord." Dr. Stuart Holden says that it is a "fenced portion of God's Word," while Matthew Henry makes the quaint comment, "There are shallows here in which a lamb may wade and there are depths here in which an elephant may swim."

The relationship of bridegroom to bride which is set out in the Song of Solomon is one which is used to describe, both in the Old Testament and in the New Testament, the relationship between God and His people, and more specifically between Christ and His Church.

The title of this book—"The Song of Solomon" or "The Song of Songs"—reminds us that love is a joyous thing. In Galatians 5:22 we are told that the fruit of the Spirit is love, and many scholars would ask us to pause at that word and understand the list of attributes that follow as a list of the characteristics of this love. If this be so then the first thing about love is the sheer joy of it. The fruit of the Spirit is love—joy.

When folk grow old they very often look back to the happiness of their childhood days. What is the secret of that happiness? Surely it is that when we were children most of us were surrounded by love. All the happiest memories of life are found in this context of love, whether human or divine. When we experience the love of God in Christ for the first time we know what the psalmist meant in the opening verses of Psalm 40. He speaks not only of being lifted up out of the miry clay but he adds, "He hath put a new song in my mouth." Every revival in the history of the Church has been characterized by a revival of praise and song.

Dangerous Influence

Not many of you should become teachers NEB

James 3:1

James issues a warning not to covet lightly the position of influence held by those called teachers. The work of teaching is referred to in many places in the New Testament. In 1 Corinthians 12:28 teaching is given a high place among the gifts of the Spirit. In Ephesians 4:11 this activity of the Holy Spirit and gift of the Spirit is mentioned again. In 2 Timothy 1:11, Paul calls himself, "a preacher, and an apostle, and a teacher."

It may well be that something of the status of the Jewish Rabbi had been passed on to those who fulfilled a similar function in the Christian Church, particularly in that section of the Christian Church which was still influenced strongly by Jewish tradition. The Jewish Rabbi was held in the very highest esteem, and in that way his position, no doubt, was coveted by others.

So the NEB translated James 3:1, "My brothers, not many of you should become teachers." Apparently James had sensed an ambition among the Christians to exercise this kind of influence. Consequently, he speaks of the danger that can go with such a responsibility, pointing out that a much stricter judgment will be applied to those who hold such positions. This leads into a much wider consideration which includes teachers but does not exclude other Christians, and stresses the importance of the influence of our words and speech in daily life. We need to be careful about being ambitious for position and influence. So often we want it, not for the glory of God but for the glory of ourselves!

Jesus and our Sins

Thou shalt call His name Jesus: for He shall save His
people from their sins

Matthews 1:21

Thursday

In some way, far beyond our understanding, when Jesus Christ
died upon the cross He was bearing the penalty for our sin and
paying the price of it. The price was what one of our great theologians has called "the infinite worth of the Son of God." There was a
price because there was a penalty to be borne. But there is a further
cost to be borne because salvation is more than forgiveness—we
are not only guilty, we are sinful. We need more than forgiveness.
What good is forgiveness to me if I am going to go on sinning? I
need more than pardon, I need power.

Every great city has its areas of poverty and degradation and
every responsible city authority and government is doing its utmost
to wipe out these areas of housing where conditions are not fit for
human beings to live. Everything is against those living in those
conditions. If we have known what it is to live in a lovely home,
would we find it easy to go and live in a slum?

Do you think then it is easy for Jesus Christ to come and live in
our hearts; those slum-like hearts of ours? How costly it was to
Christ and is to Christ, to save us from our sins. A life was laid
down so that the penalty would be met. A life is lived out in our
hearts so that a remedy may be found. This is no cheap tawdry
salvation that God gives. It is a wonderful gift, a costly gift, a royal
gift, a divine gift.

Vigilance

Watch unto prayer

Friday

Peter tells the Christians that they are to watch unto prayer in
1 Peter 4:7, and in 5:8 they are told why. They are to "be vigilant;
because your adversary the devil, as a roaring lion, walketh about,
seeking whom he may devour." There are two areas in which we
are to be on our guard as Christians as we seek to live and serve
within the fellowship of the Church of Jesus Christ.

We are to be on our guard concerning the *power that may attack*—the power of the devil which was very real to the mind of
Christ Himself and in the life of the early Church. How easily we

forget the very existence of the devil, and how seldom we are on our guard against his strategies as he seeks to destroy the fellowship, and therefore the usefulness, of the Christian Church and its witness.

The phrase, "as a roaring lion," suggests the speed of the attack. The lion doesn't walk about roaring all the time; he roars at the moment he is about to spring, and the purpose of the roar is to petrify the victim. It is this thought of the swift unexpected leap that Peter has in mind here. Coupled with the speed of the attack is the strength of the attacker. He is a lion, a powerful animal. Look out for him, resist him, don't give way, don't give in. This defamer of the brethren, this deceiver of the heart, this destroyer of the Church is everywhere active.

We must also be vigilant in another area and that is concerning the *prayer that will avail*, and so we are told "to watch unto prayer." Guard this part of your life with extreme care. In your personal life as an individual Christian, guard it; in your corporate life as a member of a praying fellowship, guard it. The New Testament speaks of both kinds of praying, praying alone and praying with others. Yet tragically this is the most neglected part of our Christian lives although prayer carries more promises than any other activity that God asks of us who are His born-again children.

Vigilance: on our guard against the attacks of the enemy. Vigilance: on our guard to secure that prevailing prayer that is the privilege of every child of God.

I Can do all Things Through Christ

I can do all things through Christ which strengtheneth me

Saturday

Philippians 4:13

May I illustrate what I think Paul has in mind by recalling an experience in my own life. I have always found it necessary to run a car for my work but sometimes it has been very difficult to afford one. When I was in Edinburgh I found myself not only running a car but running a family, and eventually I had to choose between giving up the car or the family! I just could not afford both.

Just before I left the parish, where I had, of course, sacrificed the car, I had a very heavy burden of work to do. I wanted to visit every home, and a member of the congregation in extraordinary kindness offered me one of her beautiful cars. I thanked her warmly as she said, "If ever you want my car let me know," but I never did let her know. It happened to be a very big car and I was thinking of the fuel it would consume. I have no doubt that she wondered at my silence, and then one day she telephoned and said, "Mr. Duncan, I do want you to use my car. I want you to run it at no expense whatever to yourself. Every account is to come in to me."

Well, for a few weeks out of all the years that I have been running cars, I ran one with no anxiety. I was running that car on somebody else's resources, and while the lady concerned was not a multi-millionaire her resources were so infinitely greater than mine that I had no anxiety at all. Before that I had been afraid that if anything happened to the car a big bill might come in that I couldn't meet, but if any bill came in now it would not be my worry. I was running it not on my inadequate resources but on her adequate ones.

What a tremendous truth this is. Paul does not say boastfully, "I can do all things," but he does say, "I can do all things through Christ who strengthens me," or as somebody has translated, "I am master of every situation through Christ who makes me strong."

The Gladness of Giving

It is more blessed to give than to receive

Sunday   Acts 20:35

Many will be familiar with this saying of Jesus recorded not in the gospels but in the Acts. The NEB translates it a little more accurately, "Happiness lies more in giving than in receiving." We very badly need to face the solid truth of this statement in a day when society seems more concerned with getting than giving.

Think of the *delight that love finds in giving!* Think of the pleasure we give, when we give to others! What family at Christmas or birthday time has not ample evidence to support this. But think, too, of the pleasure we gain. When the mother sees the happiness of her child, her own happiness is increased. When the sweetheart sees the smile in the face of the girl he loves as she accepts his gift, his own happiness is multiplied. Yes, there is a delight that love finds in giving.

Think, too, of the *demand that love makes in giving!* there are two factors which combine here. The gift of love is usually a costly gift. Love abhors anything cheap! It was with scorn that David turned down a cheap opportunity to give something to his Lord with the words, "Neither will I offer unto the Lord my God that which doth cost me nothing" (2 Samuel 24:24). And think, too, how worthy the gift of love must be. When choosing a gift we always have the person who is to receive the gift in mind. It must be worthy of such a recipient.

Consider finally the *delay love hates in giving.* Delays are sometimes inevitable. Which of us has not had to wait sometimes to save enough money to buy the gift, or it could be that the gift we have ordered has not arrived. Delays are always unbearable. The delay seems to add fuel to the fire of love's desire to give. How we long for the moment when the gift is actually given and received. The givers are the happy people in this world, not the getters and the grabbers. If you doubt the truth of Christ's words why not put them to the test and prove for yourself the gladness of giving.

Why are we Tempted?

Then was Jesus led up of the Spirit into the wilderness to be tempted of the devil

Monday   Matthew 4:1

I want us to grasp this—Jesus was tempted! Not because He was bad but because He was important. And you will be tempted too, not because you are bad but because you, too, are important. You matter; you are someone to be reckoned with; you are someone of whom the devil must now take account. After the heaven opened, after the voice of approval, and after the experience of the Spirit of God, Christ went straight into battle.

And you and I will very often find that battle follows immediately after blessing. The devil doesn't waste his time. If some of us have known what it is to experience God's goodness and then to speak of it and bear testimony to it, we can be quite certain the devil will react at once. The moment we bear testimony to any act of God in our lives, any response that we have made, the devil says, "Fine, now we will just get to work to destroy that testimony," and that is exactly what he does.

Remember then, Jesus was tempted, not because He was bad but because He was important. So there is nothing to worry about in being tempted; the time to worry is when we are not being tempted.

Witness Through Unity

That they all be one . . . that the world may believe . . .

John 17:21

Our Lord prays "that the world may believe," Unity between Christian people is apparently bound up in the mind of our Lord with a recognition by the world of the authenticity of His own claims. What lies behind this? I would submit that disunity is part of the problem of mankind and part of the problem of man's sin. In Isaiah 59:2 we read, "Your iniquities have separated between you and your God."

Sin is always divisive. Sin separates not only between man and God, but between man and man, between husband and wife, between employer and employee, between nation and nation. If Christ claims to be the Savior from sin then He must be able to save not simply from sin but also from its divisive effects. Let Him then prove the authenticity of His claims by bringing unity and harmony where there is, through sin, disunity and discord. If Christ cannot do this, then, argues the world, we have the right to doubt the validity of His claims to be Savior.

While we must recognize the logic and rightness behind this kind of reasoning, let us not be deceived by an overstressing of the argument by unbelievers who make this merely an excuse to reject the whole content of the Christian faith. The divisions between Christian churches are not necessarily an argument against the validity of Christianity. I don't discard the grocery trade because there are several different firms with their own branches in my town. I don't refuse to eat ice cream because there are different firms marketing their own brand in my neighborhood.

There is an element of insincerity in the kind of argument that rejects the Gospel because of the divisions within the church. There can be a scandal in division if this is accompanied by bitter enmity, but there need be no scandal in division if it simply secures a diversity and variety that enriches the sum total of what is offered to the world by the Christian Church.

Is Our Religion a Position or a Passion?

When He had so said, He showed unto them His hands and His side

John 20:20

We sometimes think of our religion as involving the holding of a position in a church or congregation. Christ, in His life, was not concerned with the holding of a position but the acceptance of a passion. If the significance of this was not at first clear to His disciples, the day was to come when they were to gaze upon the marks of that passion, those scars of His redemptive work for men upon the Cross, and cry out as they bowed in adoration before Him, "My Lord and my God."

Professor Gossip, in one of his flaming sermons, ends with words that burn almost at white heat. He recalls the doubts of Thomas as he faced the rest of the disciples who were now convinced that the Lord was risen indeed.

Thomas expressed those doubts in the words, "Except I shall see in His hands the print of the nails . . . I will not believe." Professor Gossip suggests that the world of today, still largely unbelieving, confronts the Christian Church demanding the same evidence concerning the fact of the risen Christ. "Except I see in *your* hands the print of the nails, I will not believe."

What marks of the passion of Christ can be seen in us?

The Discipline Love Needs

By night on my bed I sought him whom my soul loveth: I sought him, but I found him not

Song of Solomon 3:1

The Lord says in effect, "If you don't want Me then you needn't have Me." So we read (8:1) of the bride's discovery that the bridegroom had taken her at her word and was no longer there. "By night on my bed I sought him whom my soul loveth: I sought him, but I found him not." In Hosea 4:17 we read again of this discipline of withdrawal, as we might call it. God says, "Ephraim is joined to idols: let him alone."

Many years ago I heard Mr. R. Hudson Pope make this comment on those words: "What we will not learn by precept, we must learn by experience." We see here how bitter that discipline of withdrawal can be. It is bitter for the bride and bitter for the bridegroom too. The bride is restless and unhappy, stirring uneasily upon her bed. Her beloved had done what she had bade him do— he had turned and gone. Only now that he has gone does she realize that she cannot do without him. At first her search is only half-hearted. We read, "By night on my bed I sought him whom my soul loveth." Matthew A. Henry comments, "She searches for him but it was by night and upon her bed. It was late and lazy seeking."

But it is so often when the darkness falls that we realize after all how much the love of the heavenly Bridegroom had meant to us. At last she is thoroughly roused, and in an agony of mind she searches until she finds the one who is always so ready to be found by the seeking soul. Having found him she speaks, "I held him, and would not let him go." And with a passion of longing and posses-sion she brings him home. Life had proved to be unbearable and unthinkable without him. She had sought for him and found him.

Not at Home

To the strangers

Friday

1 Peter 1:1

This world is not home to the Christian. Paul says in Philippians 3:10, "Our citizenship is in heaven" NASB. Here we are strangers, exiles. We are traveling home but this world is not home. In He-brews 13:14 the writer says, "Here have we no continuing city, but we seek one to come." This in practical terms means that there is a basic alienation in mind, thought, and spirit, between the Christian and the worldly man, the unbelieving man. The Christian thinks differently; his values and his standards are different, his interests and ambitions are different.

The world, in which he thus feels ill at ease, is not the physical world. But what is meant by "the world" in the New Testament, is that whole structure of society from which God has been excluded by man. It is that whole way of life which has nothing in common with the mind or will of God, who is both light and love.

This is exactly what Jesus was talking about in John 15:18 and 19. He said, "If the world hate you, ye know that it hated me before it hated you. If ye were of the world, the world would love his own but because ye are not of the world, but I have chosen you out of the world, therefore the world hateth you." And again in John 17:14-16, "The world hath hated them, because they are not of the world, even as I am not of the world. I pray not that thou shouldest take them out of the world, but that thou shouldest keep them from the evil. They are not of the world, even as I am not of the world." The Christian is "not of the world." He may be in the world but he doesn't belong to it. He has no real kinship with it.

When you have traveled in other lands you realize something of what it is to be a stranger. I have traveled in many countries; I have many friends in these countries, but their way of life is different from ours, their language is sometimes different, many things about their customs and habits are different. And sometimes one feels conscious of being an alien and longs for a bit of home. In addition, the Christian has recognized that the things valued by the world are not the things valued by the Christian. The Christian is not at home in the world.

Charged with Lying

If we say that we have fellowship with Him, and walk in darkness, we lie, and do not the truth

Saturday

1 John 1:6

The charge that John makes here is quite simply the charge of lying. He says that we cannot persistently, deliberately and continually walk in darkness and at the same time claim we are enjoying fellowship with God. The Word of God is absolutely clear on this point, that sin spoils fellowship. In the Old Testament this note is struck, "Your iniquities have separated between you and your God, that He will not hear." In the New Testament the same note is struck, "What communion hath light with darkness?"

Do you remember the tremendous words of our Lord in the Sermon on the Mount when He said, "If ye forgive not men their trespasses neither will your Father forgive your trespasses"? It is obvious that what our Lord is referring to is not the forgiveness that constitutes salvation but the forgiveness that conditions fellowship! The claim that men can enjoy fellowship with God and simultaneously live in rebellion against Him is quite untrue. And if we take the attitude that sin no longer matters in the life of a Christian, then we are facing the charge John makes here of lying, whether with our lips or in our lives.

What is Man?

What is man, that Thou art mindful of him?

Sunday   Psalm 8:4

A great philosopher who had fallen asleep on a seat in a park was awakened by the park warden when the time came to close the gates at night. The philosopher was dressed rather untidily and the official addressed him somewhat roughly with the words, "Who do you think you are?" to which the philosopher replied, "I wish to God that I knew!" What is man? One thing is certain, man is his own greatest problem. What view does man take of man?

There are optimists who believe that man is naturally good, given a chance. They admit that things are far from well but on their basic assumption they offer two remedies in which they trust. The first is educational; they believe that man will do what is right provided he is taught what is right. But our own experience knows this to be untrue.

The other remedy is environmental. If a man has decent housing and good wages, he will get on well. If this were true, then all the finest people would be living in the biggest houses with the biggest incomes. This again is untrue. The realities through which they fail are so obvious as scarcely to need mentioning. My problem is that I usually know what is right but don't want to do it! Education and environment may each have a part to play in the lives of men but neither is the answer to man's problems with himself.

There are the pessimists who don't accept that man is naturally good. The form their thinking tends to take varies between totalitarianism and determinism. Totalitarianism means simply that the state does not trust man to do what it says is right. So the state has sanctions that it will not hesitate to apply usually by appealing to fear, thus insuring that man does what the state thinks is right. Determinism means that man's conduct is predetermined by man's individual make-up. He really has no choice and in a sense is not the captain but the victim of his own fate. This is something that most of us just cannot accept. Surely there is ultimately a freedom of choice for which we must accept responsibility.

There are the realists who are of course the Christians. Think what Christianity affirms. It acknowledges that there is some validity behind all the previously mentioned approaches, but states categorically that man is a sinner. He is born one! Think too how Christianity answers! The sinner can become the saint. A new relationship with God has been made possible through the death of

245

Christ. New resources are available in Christ, received and released in the life of the sinner, making him or her "a new creature in Christ."

The Obligation to Love

Beloved, if God so loved us, we ought also to love one another

Monday   1 John 4:11

This is the obligation that is laid upon us. We owe it to the Lord, to God Himself. Since He has made it possible for us to love one another, we ought therefore to make it actual and visible. We bear His name, we are members of His family, born again of the Spirit of God, so we owe it to the Father to behave in a way that is commendable to Him. We owe it to the world.

God still loves the world. And though Christ no longer walks the earth in bodily form as He did long ago, showing the love of God, He still walks the earth in the lives of those in whom His Spirit has come to dwell. His love must be made manifest through the lives of His own. Anything less is a failure to fulfill at least part of His intention for us and through us, where we live, where we work or where we worship.

Of course we also owe it to the Church. We owe it to other Christians that we should meet this obligation. One of the tremendous stresses of this epistle of John is that the love Christians have one to another is one of the great marks of the family of God. This is part of the testimony, and also part of the privilege and thrill of being a Christian.

Spiritual Babies

Babes in Christ

Tuesday   1 Corinthians 3:1

There is nothing so like a miracle as a newborn baby. But a baby that does not grow up is not a source of wonder, but of worry and grief. This is not only what can happen but what does happen and indeed has happened in the spiritual lives of thousands upon thousands of Christians. They are born again but they are still babies; they have never grown up; they have never developed.

Paul was very conscious of this having happened in the church at

246

Corinth and he called the Christians there "babes in Christ" as a term of rebuke. What are the marks of a spiritual baby? Paul describes them here as being "not able," and this inability was found in certain departments of their lives.

First of all, supremely and obviously, it was found in their spiritual feeding. They were quite unable to take anything more than the simplest elementary aspects of spiritual truth. Was this what was in the back of the mind of John when he writes in 1 John 2:12 to those whom he calls "little children," adding to the description about them, "Your sins are forgiven"? The spiritual baby is at ease and at home in what he delights to call, "The Gospel." The baby loves the Gospel! He is found in the kind of church were every evening service is attended by the babies, where the Gospel and only the Gospel is preached and those who come never hear anything else, never learn anything else. And it would seem as if they don't want to learn very much more.

Paul writes here, "I have fed you with milk, and not with meat." What a limited diet they had! I believe our churches have far too many Christians who are converted people but cannot assimilate anything more than the Gospel message. Perhaps we ought not to have pews in our churches but prams and in many of the prams a great big fat, bouncing, spiritual baby. What a tragedy!

Self Deceived

If we say that we have no sin, we deceive ourselves, and the truth is not in us

Wednesday

1 John 1:8

John is speaking about the possibility of deceiving ourselves in the area of holiness. God's Word refutes the claim that we are without sin. If we make this claim then we are walking in the darkness of error and ignorance. John does not say that we deceive anybody else, but we do deceive ourselves and to be deceived is always dangerous. It means that we can expose ourselves to peril when we are not aware of it and this can lead to disaster.

Occasionally one meets Christians who make this precise claim. It is spoken of sometimes as "sinless perfection," that God by some strange work of grace has eradicated the old nature from within. I always feel when I meet such a person that all I need is just five minutes with that person's wife, or husband, or child, or maybe even their cat or dog, and I will soon discover the truth.

God's truth is that "all have sinned" and our Lord Himself has told us that it is "from within, out of the heart of men" that all evil proceeds. To claim that sin no longer exists or continues within our own nature and to deny the corruption of sin within our own personality is to deceive ourselves and to have abandoned the truth of God.

Kindling the Fire of Prayer

Is there any word from the Lord?

Jeremiah 37:17

Thursday

We are all only too familiar with prayer—either personal or corporate—which is cold, formal and lifeless. One certain remedy for this is to make sure that before we speak to God in prayer we place ourselves before Him and His Word so that *He* may speak to *us*. I am sure that the most helpful way to start praying is not to pray at all but rather to listen! This applies to a prayer meeting just as much as to personal and private prayer. Allow the living Word to speak to us through the written Word.

I believe it was Robert Murray McCheyne who said, "Turn the Bible into prayer." Nothing so kindles the spirit of prayer anew in us as making our prayer in the first instance a response to God's voice coming to us through His Word.

In private prayer this practice insures that there will always be a note of freshness in our praying. In a prayer meeting it throws a special responsibility upon the leader of any such meeting. He should bring a living word to those who are there, taken from the written Word. It throws a responsibility, too, upon those at such a meeting. The Word as it comes must find a response, and that response must find expression. If this happens, then the spirit of prayer will burn brightly and strongly as our hearts respond to whatever God has to say to us.

Sensing an Authority in the Words We Say

He taught them as one having authority, and not as the scribes

Matthew 7:29

Friday

We read these words concerning our Lord's spoken ministry. We should then remember the one factor in our witnessing and in our preaching which must never be taken for granted, namely the working of the Holy Spirit. If others are to sense authority in our spoken word, we must look to Him and His working in and through us. This is His work—"When He is come, *He* will convict."

But the Holy Spirit will not work automatically. He must have the right conditions in which and through which to work. His ability to work will depend both upon the content of the message and the condition of the messenger.

As evangelicals we glory in the Person of the indwelling Spirit of Christ. But let us be careful lest even while we are glorying in His Presence, we are, at the very same time, grieving His Person. "Grieve not the Holy Spirit" is a Pauline injunction which the Church today would do well to heed. We grieve the Holy Spirit when we fail to allow Him to do and to be in us that for which He was given.

A Tragic Possibility

If I wash thee not, thou hast no part with Me

Saturday   John 13:8

When Peter heard the Master say these words it was quite unbearable. To have no part with his Lord when he had had such a part, to be shut out while others were shut in, to know nothing of the unfolding of the heart of Christ as he had known it in the days of the past, was unendurable. To have no part with Christ! He just could not stand the thought of the future days and months and years and have no part with Christ in His work and in the fellowship of His Spirit. It broke him!

Can you stand the thought of having no part with Christ in that quiet, deep, strong eternal work of redemption? If you can, I question whether you are a Christian at all. If you cannot bear it, then may God make that truth break your pride now, because if Christ does not cleanse you from your sin, if you maintain your refusal, He will maintain His rejection. Not so far as salvation is concerned, for that is settled, but as far as fellowship and usefulness are concerned you shall find that you have no part with Him.

As you go on in the days ahead, is the record of these coming weeks and months to be "no part with me"? You will still be busy, you may be very complacent, you may feel very important, you may maintain your part. But as far as Christ is concerned, you may have no part with Him. A tragic possibility indeed!

Who is There?

This verse inspired one of the best known religious paintings in the world—Holman Hunt's, "The Light of the World." One of the two originals hangs in St. Paul's Cathedral in London.

This is a *picture that is arresting.* I am arrested when I read of the presence of Christ at the door. If I found certain people at the door of my home I would not find their presence arresting at all, but if I found the Queen standing there I would be both amazed and arrested. When I am told of the presence of Christ at the door of my heart, I find that arresting in very truth. I am also arrested when I read of the patience of Christ at the door. "Behold, I stand." How patiently, how long he stands—though not for ever!

Here, too, is a *promise that is assuring.* The word for which Christ waits is our word of welcome, "If any man hear my voice and open the door." As simply as we invite a friend into our homes, we can welcome Christ into our hearts, but we must welcome Him. Also here is the word on which faith rests. "I will come in." How do I know that Christ enters? I know because He said He would.

Again, there is the reminder of a *presence that is abiding.* Think of the difference His presence will make. Christ comes with all the immeasurable resources of His wisdom, grace, love and power. What a change this will make as all these replace our own inadequacies. Think, too, of the permanence His presence will have. The words of Christ speak only of coming in, not of going out. The children's chorus responds in these words:

Into my heart, into my heart
Come into my heart, Lord Jesus
Come in today, come in to stay
Come into my heart, Lord Jesus.

A Church in a House

It is clear that this man lived in nearby Laodicia, some twelve miles distant from Colosse and that the Christians there were accustomed

250

to meeting in his home. Of course, the Christian Church in those days had no special buildings set apart for churches as we have today. Christians were dependent upon the hospitality of those whose homes were possibly rather larger than the rest. We know that Philemon had a church in his house and that Aquilla and Priscilla opened their homes when they lived in Rome and later in Ephesus. This shows that wonderful diversity which always marks the service that Christians are able to give to the cause of Christ and His Church.

Nymphas was a man who recognized that he was not his own but had been bought with a price. He recognized, too, that everything that apparently belonged to him was not his either—that even his home belonged to Christ. Some Christians have grasped this in a wonderful way. Why do not more of us consider this possibility? It seems sad that we are ready to use our homes for ourselves alone, or for ourselves and our close friends but never for our Lord. It is not necessarily God's will that everyone should devote their houses in the same way to the service of the Lord, but surely in some way everyone should.

Praying about Everything

In every thing by prayer and supplication with thanksgiving let your requests be made known unto God

Tuesday   Philippians 4:6

There is more to prayer than just "saying our prayers." It is not just something we do by our bedside in the morning or at night when the door is closed and our eyes are shut. Of course prayer is something that we do then, but prayer is also talking to the Lord at any time and about any problem. "The Lord *is* at hand," Paul has just said. And somebody has translated that, "The Lord is near: the Lord is at your elbow." Well, talk to Him then! Don't just talk about the big matters but about *any* matter.

If you lose your car key in the morning, don't start shouting. Don't get the whole house in a ferment because you can't find it. Don't rush about getting increasingly irritated saying, "Where did I put it? Where did I put it?" until the whole family is upset and everybody is looking for it. If you find you have mislaid your car key say to yourself, "Now, Lord, where did I put that key?" And then start looking for it with the Lord.

Ladies, when your husband brings someone home for a meal unexpectedly, don't go off to the kitchen in a temper saying, "He

251

might have told me he was going to bring so-and-so home today! Doesn't he know I wasn't expecting anybody? What does *he* think he is doing?" Why not go off to the kitchen saying, "Now, Lord, I am in a predicament. What are we going to do about it? There is one thing, Lord, I would do that I am afraid I have not done this time. I could see that I always have something in reserve for just such an occasion. Sorry, I haven't got it today, Lord, but I will try to remember to keep something always by me for an emergency." So you talk it all over with the Lord, and that is prayer.

I believe it was C. T. Studd, the great cricketer, who once said in his room at Cambridge to the surprise of his hearers, "You know, when I play cricket I don't think I play fair." They asked, "Why?" He replied, "When I play, I pray." For C. T. Studd the Lord was at his elbow when he was playing cricket.

Concealing the Unworthy

Ye are as graves which appear not . . .

Wednesday   Luke 11:44

Here we have the sin of concealing the unworthy, and I think that at the back of our Lord's mind was the thought not only of concealment but also of condonement. This is a condition that has been allowed to go on and on and on. On the surface there is nothing, but underneath there is the vilest corruption. The fact of condonement must be stressed, because every one of us is aware as Paul himself was that in our flesh, that is ourselves apart from Christ, there "dwelleth no good thing." May God save us from ever thinking we are anything.

But that is not what our Lord is thinking here. He is dealing with a condition that is allowed to go on. This is peculiarly a danger for those who hold high positions of leadership as did the Pharisees. A position of leadership carries with it the temptation to think that we can get away with anything provided it never becomes known. "Is this really possible?" our hearts would exclaim! Well, the only reply is that our Lord said that it is possible.

And if we look a little closer into our hearts we may understand why He did say so. Am I a Pharisee?

252

How to Prove our Love

He that hath My commandments, and keepeth them, he
it is that loveth Me

Thursday   John 14:21

How do we prove our love and devotion to our Lord? It is through
our obedience to His will. This is made abundantly plain in the
Bible. In John 15:14 we read, "Ye are My friends, *if* ye do whatsoever I command you." Many are the substitutes that we try to find
for obedience. We may judge our devotion as Christians by the
place we occupy in the life of the church, the position we hold. We
may say, "I am a deacon, an usher, a choir member, a Sunday
School teacher, an elder, even a minister." But none of these offices
proves any devotion to Christ. The proof of our devotion lies in the
measure of our obedience.

You remember the searching words of the prophet to King Saul,
"Hath the Lord as great delight in burnt offerings and sacrifices, as
in obeying the voice of the Lord? Behold, to obey is better than
sacrifice." Can you imagine the transformation that would happen
in the life of our church fellowships if every professing Christian
was able to prove his devotion to God through a life of simple, true
and complete obedience? Mary said to the servants at the wedding
feast in Cana of Galilee, "Whatsoever He saith unto you, do it." In
our obedience to God lies the proof of our love for Him. If we do
not obey, we do not love.

Every Christian a Gifted
Christian

But all these worketh that one and the selfsame Spirit,
dividing to every man severally as He will

Friday   1 Corinthians 12:11

The gifts of the Holy Spirit refer to gifts of abilities and capacities
that the Christian will, and does receive, from the Holy Spirit. It is
worth noting that the Bible tells us these are gifts in which *every*
Christian has a share. It is not that every Christian will have every
gift, but that every Christian will have at least one gift. No Christian will be giftless; every Christian will be gifted. Twice over in
this passage Paul uses the phrase, "To every man" (verses 7 and
11).

This teaching makes nonsense of a phrase that has become popular in our day. Some people talk about a charismatic movement or
a charismatic Christian, as if these words described some Christians

but not all. The word "charismatic" is derived from the Greek word "charisma" meaning "gift" or "free gift," and every born-again believer has been given one gift or another. Every Christian therefore is a charismatic Christian, that is to say a gifted Christian.

To use the word "charismatic" as it is being used today creates a sense of division within the Church which is the last thing the Holy Spirit intends to do. Such usage creates the idea of two kinds of Christians—some gifted, some not gifted—whereas the Bible teaches the opposite. Those who use the word in this narrow sense really mean that some Christians have experienced one particular gift of the Holy Spirit. Such Christians, they imply, are in some strange way different. It may even be thought that such people are better or more mature than other Christians who have received one of the different gifts. How unbiblical such thinking is!

Forgiven but Unforgiving

And his fellowservant fell down at his feet, and
besought him, saying, Have patience with me, and I will
pay thee all. And he would not

Saturday   Matthew 18:29, 30

Our Lord once told a parable about two servants. One servant was forgiven a vast sum of money that he could never hope to repay. Then, having been forgiven such a vast sum, he went straight to another servant who owed him a paltry sum and refused to forgive him! I once preached a sermon on that entitled, "Forgiven but Unforgiving."

Is that true of you? Although you have been forgiven so much, have you been unforgiving? Is there someone with whom you are not on speaking terms? You haven't forgiven them for something they did or something they said? Our Lord has this to say on the subject: "If ye forgive not men their trespasses, neither will your Father forgive your trespasses" (Matthew 6:15). Christ was not talking about salvation, He was talking about fellowship. If we don't forgive someone who has wronged us, not only do we lose fellowship with them but we lose fellowship with God.

No wonder the song dies. If I am out of fellowship with another believer, and out of fellowship with my divine Lord, how can I sing? How can I rejoice? How can I praise?

"I'll forgive her, but I don't want to have any more to do with her." Have we ever spoken like that? We thought we were being generous; we thought we were being Christian; we thought we were quite outstanding. Listen for a moment to the Savior's words:

"Forgive us our debts as we forgive our debtors." *"As we forgive."* "O God, I am so sorry I did that—please forgive me." Suppose a voice from Heaven should say, "I'll forgive you, but *I don't want* any more to do with you!" That would not be forgiveness at all!

Declaration

That which we have heard

Sunday   1 John 1:1

There must be an audible and vocal communication of the Gospel. This is what had sparked off John's experience. He listened to what Jesus Christ had to say, was arrested by it, and finally was convinced by it. In the experience of John on his way to faith there is a primacy given to the spoken word.

But if people are to hear the spoken word, we must *find an audience for the message.* So much of our speaking and preaching never reaches those for whom it is destined. People who need to hear the Gospel are usually outside the church, so either they must be brought into the church, or the church must go to the people where they are. The responsibility for this rests upon the whole church, not just the minister; therefore, the opportunity must be given to the whole church. We have opportunities in daily life but if we are to bring people, special opportunities must be given within the structure of our normal worship.

We must *stress the accuracy of the message.* In 2 Corinthians 5:20, Paul says, "We are ambassadors for Christ." We are not to invent the message; we are to proclaim it. This means that the truths of God have to be learned; otherwise the Spirit of God, who is Himself the Spirit of truth, will not own or bless the message that we speak. Not only must we learn the truths of God, we must use a tone of voice in keeping with the character of God. Sometimes we can misrepresent the Gospel of the grace and love of God just as badly by the way we speak as by the content of what we say.

Finally, the *authority in the message must be sensed.* We read of the Lord, "He taught them as one having authority, and not as the scribes" (Matt. 7:29). Here we are thrown upon the Person and ministry of the Holy Spirit. We dare not and must not take Him for granted. Ultimately, He alone is the one who can bring anyone to faith in Christ, and He must have a life that He is able to use. There is a monopoly here that the Christian must respect. The work of conviction and of conversion is something we are not asked to do.

It is something, however, that we are told the Holy Spirit of God will do when He comes, and He wants to do it through us.

If there is a monopoly we must respect, there is a ministry that we can restrict. We have to face the fact that the Holy Spirit can be grieved. Paul warns us in Ephesians 4:30, "Grieve not the Holy Spirit," and if we grieve the Holy Spirit, He obviously cannot work through us. The Gospel must be declared but it makes these three demands upon us—the audience must be secured; the accuracy must be stressed; and the authority must be sensed.

Your Own Salvation

Work out your own salvation with fear and trembling
Philippians 2:12

The thought here is not so much, "Work out from within," but work out to completion, work out to the end. Work out your own salvation. Don't be halted in your Christian development and growth. Work it out until the whole job is done.

There is something absolutely unique about the experience of God's grace which God is wanting to work in *you*. Your experience of Christ, your contribution to the Church, is quite different from anybody else's. You have something to offer that nobody else can give. If you don't offer it, if you have stopped progressing and your growth and development have become arrested, the Church is going to be so much the poorer. Work out your own salvation—work it out to the end. If your growth becomes stunted, you will be robbing the Church. Remember, too, that salvation is God's work. God is working in you, both initiating and seeking to fulfill. So Paul said, "Do it with fear and trembling." You and I should be terribly afraid. Afraid of what? Afraid of disappointing God.

Work out your own salvation. Work it out to the end, to its fullness, to its completion. Don't be halted. Don't be brought to a standstill because something has gone wrong.

Meditate

Thou shalt meditate therein day and night
Joshua 1:8

The art of meditation is one that is almost forgotten, but God told

Joshua that it was an essential requirement for true success. If we are really going to tackle this matter seriously then there will be three parts to it. First, there must be the *gathering of the tools.* We must have a good Bible and a quiet place, and maybe we need pen and ink in order to do the job properly.

There will also have to be the *giving of our time.* Most people suffer from the speed at which we live and this can particularly affect the time of communion with God. In our friendships we don't reveal the depths of our thoughts to the casual stranger who chats to us for a few minutes. Neither does God reveal the deep things of the Spirit to the casual Christian.

Then will come the *gleaning of God's truth.* Every Christian should be learning the truth of God daily and steadily from the Word itself. Yet so many Christians seem to learn so little this way. They depend almost entirely on sermons they hear rather than on what they have found for themselves in the Word of God.

Just as God included the task of meditation in His commission to Joshua, so through the centuries you will find that wherever true and deep success has marked any Christian life, hidden away in the secret place has been faithfulness in meditation.

The Will of God Concerned with the Whole Man

And the very God of peace sanctify you wholly; and I pray God your whole spirit and soul and body be preserved blameless unto the coming of our Lord Jesus Christ

1 Thessalonians 5:23

Let us remember that the will of God is concerned with the whole man. There is no conflict between the social Gospel and the true Gospel. The social Gospel, if the true Gospel be left out, is missing the heart of it all; but if the true Gospel leaves out the social Gospel, it is presenting a parody of the grace of God. Mark that—for the will of God is concerned with the whole man. Paul writing to the Thessalonians says, "The very God of peace sanctify you wholly; and I *pray* God your whole spirit and soul and body be preserved blameless." The love of God is concerned with every detail of life. Christ said, "The very hairs of your head are all numbered."

It takes a caring church to present and proclaim a caring God. If we do not care—as so often we do not—how can the world see, how can others know, how will they believe? All we give to the world is condemnation and criticism instead of compassion. Such care is possible because the love of God has been shed abroad in our hearts by the Holy Spirit which has been given to us. The love of Christ constraineth us. With the new life that comes in conversion there comes the new love. The obligation is not only, "Thou shalt love the Lord thy God," but also, "Thou shalt love thy neighbor as thyself."

A caring church will be a communicating church. A church like this and only one like this will represent the God we seek to serve in the world He longs to save. How long have you been a Christian? How many people have you "cared into the Kingdom" during that time?

Holiness in Ordinary Things

When Paul had gathered a bundle of sticks, and laid them on the fire, there came a viper out of the heat, and fastened on his hand

Thursday

Acts 28:3

Here is danger to Paul's life coming out of a fire at which he and others were warming themselves. Doesn't this warn us that the simplest and most ordinary things can, at times, suddenly become a source of danger? How far are we able to cope with the sudden thrust of temptation that arises out of the ordinary things of life—when the saucepan boils over, when a child drops a dish, or when someone leaves the iron on and a dress is burnt through? How do we react when the serpent strikes out at us from the ordinary things? It is said that home is where we are treated the best and where we behave the worst.

This viper that endangered Paul's life fastened on him as it came out of the fire. If there was a *peril endangering his life*, there was also a *power that exalted his Lord* for we are told that Paul shook the viper off. Christ had promised His earlier disciples that if they were bitten by serpents they would not die. It was part of the initial promise made by Christ to them and here it was being fulfilled.

What the Christian Church needs today more and more is not the kind of power that is demonstrated in a great crusade but in the ordinary things of life, so that when the serpent leaps out of the ordinary things we can shake it off unharmed. It is not so much the witness of conversion, but the witness of what the Bible would call sanctification; not the theoretical truth that Jesus saves us from our sins by His death on the cross, but the practical demonstration of the fact that He does save us day by day, moment by moment, and hour by hour from the sins that assail in the ordinary affairs of our daily life.

The Wisdom of Forgetting

This one thing I do, forgetting those things which are behind, and reaching forth unto those things which are before

Philippians 3:13, 14

Friday

If we reexamine these words of Paul we may find part of the secret of that happiness which has so far eluded us. These words speak to us of the way in which the past can cripple. Paul, like anybody else, had a past with elements in it that could have ruined his usefulness and fettered his spirit, and he knew that there was much he must forget.

But there is more to forget than is immediately apparent. The Christian needs to forget not only his failures but his spiritual progress and growth lest he becomes fettered by complacency. What a record of spiritual growth and achievement lay behind Paul! But in the very record there was a risk of his becoming smug, slack and undisciplined. That record had not been achieved by accident, for spiritual progress and power are never accidental. Yet Paul deliberately turned his back upon his past spiritual growth, knowing that he had much further to go.

A Christian ought also to forget his personal grievances lest he be crippled by complaining. He may have a grievance against God because of some bereavement, illness, or hardship through which the spirit is bogged down in self-pity. He may have a grievance against himself because of some failure or against some other person, and an unforgiving spirit is fostering that grievance. Let us remember there is wisdom in forgetting. There may have been sin, but if it has been confessed it has been forgiven and forgotten by God. We do well ourselves to forget what God has forgotten and to press on.

The Motive of Love

The love of Christ constraineth us

2 Corinthians 5:14

Saturday

J. B. Phillips translates this verse, "The very spring of our actions is the love of Christ," and the Amplified New Testament says, "The love of Christ controls and urges and impels us." So love becomes the motive of our service. It is significant that one of the first evidences of the new life is a new love, showing itself in a concern for others and a desire to do something.

We glimpse such a reaction on the Damascus road when Saul of Tarsus found his Lord. He said immediately, "Lord, what wilt thou have me to do?" He wanted to do something for the Lord. We read of Andrew first finding his own brother, Simon, and bringing him to Jesus. We cannot possess this love of Christ without caring, as God cares, for the world for which Christ died. And when we stop to think, we realize that love is seldom idle and is never happy to be idle.

When I see a mother who is expecting her first baby I am always intrigued to notice that the knitting needles are scarcely ever out of her hands. Her hands are busy hands, because already she is loving that little life that God is giving. She wants everything to be ready, everything to be perfect. Love always wants to serve. At a recent memorial service for a preacher, his most intimate friend said of him that he loved preaching. "Preaching was his life and when he ceased to preach he ceased to live." "The love of Christ constraineth us." Here is the divine urge, compelling us so that we can be neither idle nor indifferent. We must pray! We must give! We must care! We must act! Such service is no burden but a delight.

Do you remember the story of Dr. Guthrie—that great lover of children? Meeting a small girl carrying her big baby brother he said, "That's a big burden you are carrying, my dear." But all that happened was a reproachful look and the reply, "It's no a burden, it's ma wee brither." How often we say, "It's no trouble, I love doing it." And it really is no trouble, if we love doing it.

Don't Be Afraid

Sunday

And the angel said unto them, Fear not

Luke 2:10

Since the whole atmosphere of Christmas is one of fun and gaiety, it is strange that the message at the first Christmas produced an atmosphere of fear. The shepherds were afraid, Mary was afraid, Joseph was afraid. Think for a moment of the spiritual world upon which the shepherds stumbled that night. How startlingly and unexpectedly things happened, so that we read, "They were sore afraid."

What were the reasons for their fear? They found themselves in an *atmosphere which was alien* to them, alien to that in which they normally moved; they found themselves facing an *authority which was absolute*. The shepherds that night knew they were listening to the voice of the living God and men are still afraid when they hear Him. The response the shepherds gave, however, was a wonderful one. They came with haste and found Him.

What about Mary? Think of the personal experience into which Mary entered at that Christmas time. Mary's moment of fear had come nine months earlier. God was asking of her a most wonderful relationship, the most holy and sacred one that God could have asked of any woman—that she should bear the Holy Child and be the mother of His Son. Yet how similar the relationship is to that which God still asks of men—that Christ should dwell in our hearts by faith. How blessed if we can give the same response that Mary gave, "Be it unto me according to thy word."

The ground for Joseph's fear lay in the social complications to which he was exposed. His moment of fear, like Mary's, had come earlier. Think how cruel tongues would talk. Recall how Christ must have been born with that shadow hanging over Him—conceived out of wedlock. We are so afraid of what men will say. No wonder that God said to Joseph, "Fear not." What courage Joseph had when in obedience to God's word he took Mary to be his wife!

"Don't be afraid" is the message that comes to us at Christmas, for "Love came down at Christmas, Love all lovely, Love divine." Do we need to be afraid of perfect love like that?

Are You Ready?

Let your loins be girded about, and your lights burning; and ye yourselves like unto men that wait for their lord, when he will return from the wedding

Monday   Luke 12:35, 36

The motto of the Boy Scout Association is, "Be Prepared." I went to a school where the school motto was, "Ready, Aye Ready." The Church has always believed that Christ would come again in majesty and power, and Christ Himself said He would. Again and again He made it plain that He would come back to this earth, and this is His word of counsel—that we are to be ready.

Some years ago at Keswick, morning prayers were taken in the Speakers House each morning by the late Mr. R. Hudson Pope. It was, I believe, under his ministry that I came to know Christ as my Savior as a schoolboy of twelve years of age. On this occasion at

Keswick, many years later, Mr. Hudson Pope (or R.H.P. as we called him) gave me some words that he had found in his mother's Bible after she died. This is how the verses run:

> My work for the day is almost through,
> Was it all as in His sight?
> Would Jesus be able to say, "Well done"
> Supposing He came tonight?
> There's a tiny sin on my soul today
> And I can't make my face look bright.
> Would Jesus ask, "Aren't you glad I've come?"
> Supposing He came tonight.
> Lord Jesus, I want more grace each day
> To help me to walk aright,
> So that my heart may welcome You
> Supposing You came tonight.

Supposing He did come today. Would we be ready and would our hearts welcome Him?

The Empty Place

Come . . . for Demas hath forsaken me
2 Timothy 4:9, 10

Tuesday

What a tragic choice Demas made. Paul says that it was because of his "having loved this present world." The seeds for this choice had been sown, no doubt, at the time of Paul's first imprisonment, when Demas realized that the way of the Christian was the way of the Cross and that this was not quite so attractive. The way of the present world, by comparison, seemed easier. Did he want to go back to the material security, or the social acceptability, now that things were different? Although Paul had been on the march again, the devotion of Demas never was the same, until quietly one night when the second imprisonment came he packed his bags and went home.

The message went out to Timothy, "Come." What a revealing word that is. There is often something desperately lonely about spiritual greatness. In the hearts of those who are spiritual giants are human hearts craving for understanding. If Demas had learned much of Paul, Paul had learned much of Demas: the hurt of that empty place called for healing, healing that could only come when the empty place was filled.

Did Timothy answer the call? I am sure he did. Did Demas ever come back? I don't think so. And the older man was now to draw infinite comfort from the devotion of another and a younger man, until the day when the final summons came and that great saint went in to receive "the crown of righteousness." But Demas would not be there. His place was empty. The one who had been so close was now far, far, away. Demas had become a spiritual drop-out.

What Do You Want?

Jesus answered and said unto him, What wilt thou that I should do unto thee?

Wednesday

Mark 10:51

There are three things we can say about this man. He *knew what he wanted*. He was personally aware of his need, and his reply revealed that. "Lord, that I might receive my sight." He was passionately aware of it too. When many charged him to hold his peace, we are told that, "He cried the more a great deal." Are we as aware of our need when we find ourselves in Christ's presence?

He also *said what he wanted*. He was willing to respond to Christ when Christ asked him the question; when Christ gave the command for him to be called we are told, "He, casting away his garment, rose, and came to Jesus." He was willing to respond to Christ and he was willing to receive from Christ. He would have been foolish not to.

Finally this man *got what he wanted*. In Christ there was a power that changed his life and that power is still available. As a result of what that power wrought in his life, praise filled his heart. What a wonderful thing it is when Christ comes to us and says, "What do you want Me to do for you?" Do we know what we want? Do we say what we want? If we do, then we will get what we want.

Filled with the Spirit

Be filled with the Spirit

Thursday

Ephesians 5:18

What does it involve to be continually being filled with the Spirit? The command in Ephesians 5:18 is a command in the present tense. Surely it involves an assent to the activity of the Holy Spirit in our lives. I must be willing for the Holy Spirit to do in me what He wants to do and what He has been given to do. There will be no restriction imposed on His activity, there will be no restraining hand stretched out by me.

So many of us treat the Holy Spirit as we treat the dentist. Especially if the dentist is a new one and we are not sure if he knows how far he can go before we squeal, our hand is never far away from his hand so we can stop him doing what he wants to do whenever it begins to hurt.

In order to be filled and then to go on being filled continually there must be an utter willingness and a complete readiness for anything and for everything. My great task is to find out what the Holy Spirit has been given to do in me and through me, and then to allow Him to do it and to be it! "Being filled with the Spirit" means more than receiving Him; it means releasing Him, setting Him free to do what He wants in our lives. Such an experience involves an assent to the authority of the Holy Spirit so that scripture is fulfilled, that where the Spirit of the Lord is there is liberty.

The Start of It All

Friday

In the year that king Uzziah died I saw also the Lord
Isaiah 6:1-8

Here we have the beginning of Isaiah's spiritual life of usefulness. It was only when king Uzziah died that Isaiah saw the Lord. Perhaps God was concealed from him by a person; or he may have been preoccupied with the splendor of the royal house. God was revealed to him when that presence and that splendor were removed.

Sometimes God has to take people away from our lives before we too can see the Lord. When Isaiah saw the Lord a problem was created immediately in his mind, because Isaiah realized what a sinful man he was! But that problem was resolved when God spoke to him of a divine provision that would solve it. One of the seraphim took a coal, with the tongs, from off the altar and touched his lips with the cleansing fire.

God has made a provision for our cleansing from another altar, the only altar that the Christian knows—the cross itself!

Fighting Against God

There wrestled a man with him until the breaking of the day

Saturday

Genesis 32:24

When God came into Jacob's life, Jacob wrestled with Him, just as we so often do. There is no doubt that Jacob had gone aside to meet with God for he was a frightened man. Word had reached him that Esau was on the road ahead waiting for him, so Jacob wanted to meet God to ask Him to deal with Esau. He found to his dismay that God wanted to deal with *him.* So Jacob wrestled with God. The struggle lasted the whole night through, but it ended at last.

In our lives we sometimes want God to deal with someone else while all the time God wants to deal with us! We don't like this and so we struggle with God and fight against Him. Our struggles can last much longer than Jacob's. He struggled for a whole night; we can sometimes struggle not for hours, but for days or months or years. Are we fighting against God?

Mary's Part

And in the sixth month the angel Gabriel was sent from God . . . to a virgin . . . and the virgin's name was Mary

Sunday

Luke 1:26, 27

Some of us are a little bit afraid of Mary, but we forget that if there had been no Mary there would have been no Christ born in Bethlehem. The part that Mary played is, in a sense, a very beautiful picture of the part that God wants us to play in His redemptive purposes. Think of the *purpose of God revealed to Mary.* How personal was the relationship God wanted to establish. She was to be the mother of the Lord, bearing in her own body the unborn Christ. We are called into a similar personal relationship in which our bodies become the temple of the Holy Spirit. How fearful was Mary's response. So often we are afraid too. "What will others think, what will others say?"

Then note the *problem for God raised by Mary.* She raises an objection: "Then said Mary unto the angel, How shall this be, seeing I know not a man?" And sometimes we face God's purpose for us by raising problems and difficulties. "How can this possibly be? How could I possibly keep it up?" But the objection raised was met by the operation that was promised, a work of the Holy Spirit (verse 35). "The Holy Ghost shall come upon thee, and the power of the Highest shall overshadow thee." And the same promise holds good for us. The purpose of God can be wrought out by the Holy Spirit.

Finally we come to the *prayer to God recorded of Mary*, and what a wonderful prayer it was. "Mary said, Behold the handmaid of the Lord; be it unto me according to thy word" (verse 38). What a total and willing submission that was. We can see the salvation achieved through that prayer, for if there had been no obedience by Mary there would have been no Savior for the world. Perhaps there is a plan of salvation to touch many lives which can only be achieved when God finds in us the submission He found in Mary. "Be it unto me according to thy word."

Bethlehem

Let us now go even unto Bethlehem

Monday

Luke 2:15

What associations with childhood the word "Bethlehem" has. And what a time for memories of childhood Christmas is, when the name of that little town is once again sounding in our ears. This invitation the shepherds gave one another is one to which we can respond. Think of the children we once were! And think of the love that was lavished on us, perhaps in a Christian home by Christian parents who prayed for us, who taught us the Word of God and how to pray.

Perhaps that life was very different from the life we are living now. I wonder how many years have passed since our childhood days when life was marked by comparative innocence, and if there were sins, they were in a sense little sins! But as we remember that, we are compelled to remember the choices we have since made. As we look back over the years, we think of the pressures we have had to face. It was so easy in a Christian home. But the time came when we left home, or our parents left us and we had to face the hard, hard world alone. How powerful the pressures were. And as a result of those pressures, sometimes the priorities we formed have been unworthy. There was a time when indeed we did "seek first the kingdom," but other priorities have usurped the place of Christ.

Perhaps the very mention of Bethlehem gives us a kind of "homesickness of the soul" as we long for a return to the faith we once held and the life we once lived. But Christmas has come again and Bethlehem speaks of the chances that we still have. The offer of the love of God still holds and the answer to the love of God is still possible. We can respond as the shepherds responded, and come with haste to find the Christ again at Bethlehem.

Right and Wrong

Every creature of God is good, and nothing to be refused, if it be received with thanksgiving

Tuesday

1 Timothy 4:4

There is one question the Christian will want to ask as he thinks out the basic principles of Christian conduct, and it is this: "What praise does this evoke?" We could put today's verse this way: the question of right and wrong for the Christian is not just a matter of thinking, but of thanking! Notice the condition Paul says we are to fulfill, "If it be received with thanksgiving."

In effect what Paul says is that if you are not quite sure whether some course of action is right or wrong, then consider if you can bring it before the Lord and thank Him for it. If you cannot, then be careful, for it may be wrong for you as a Christian.

Let your thanksgiving, too, be intelligent and inclusive. Can you thank Him for the thing itself, for what is involved in it for others and for what it does to your own life? Thanking as well as thinking will help us solve many of the problems of conduct.

Everything in The Name

Whatsoever ye do in word or deed, do all in the name of the Lord Jesus

Wednesday

Colossians 3:17

The name of Jesus Christ is *given to us* when we are converted, born again of the Spirit, receive Christ into our lives, and thus become Christians. Just as a girl united in marriage to the man she loves bears his name, so the sinner united to the Savior at conversion henceforth bears His name.

We are told in Acts that "the disciples were called Christians." This is the name given to us but it must become the name *guarded by us*. Paul has just been speaking about "putting on the new man," and scripture speaks about putting on Christ as if the Christian is to wear Christ. Christ would then be what the world sees.

We are all familiar with uniforms which serve the purpose of making a person instantly identifiable and recognizable. But wearing a uniform (whether it be school, regiment, or profession) involves not only wearing it but bearing its honor. The name of Jesus Christ has been given to us, and we must make sure that nothing we do or say brings shame upon it.

The Longing of Love

Let him kiss me with the kisses of his mouth
Song of Solomon 1:2

Thursday

These words express a longing for the beloved in a relationship of love, affection and acceptance. She was not longing for a kiss on the feet which would speak of homage, nor a kiss on the hand or the cheek which might be the kiss of friendship. She was longing for the kisses of his mouth, the kiss of love. She longed for the assurance of his love, and for the sense of his presence. She wanted acceptance by the beloved.

We might do well to pause just a moment to ask what the Person of our Lord and Savior means to us. Paul speaks of wanting to "know Him," to "win Him." John writes in his Epistle of "loving Him." So often it is not the Lord that really matters in our lives, it is the church! We enjoy the meetings, we want the status. We love the work and we are blessed by the friends we meet and the fellowship we enjoy. But where does *He* come into it all? He mattered so much to Paul that He meant everything, and Paul could say, "To me to live *is* Christ." Christ was everything to Paul—what is He to us?

Believing is not Enough

Thou believest that there is one God; thou doest well:
the devils also believe, and tremble
James 2:19

Friday

James is warning Christians that mere belief in a fact is not the same as faith in a person. The implication is that the devils believe the true facts about God, but this believing is not saving faith. Saving faith in Christ is more than just believing the facts about Him. The devils, no doubt, believe that Christ died for the sins of the world. They know He did, but this is very different from putting one's faith in the Christ who died that death. This is saving faith.

The word faith when used in relation to Jesus Christ is always active, suggesting movement towards, commitment to, dependence on. This is brought out by the use of the same word translated differently. In John 3:16 we have the word used, "God so loved the world, that He gave His only begotten Son, that whosoever *believeth* in Him should not perish, but have everlasting life." Exactly the same word is used in the previous chapter. "Jesus did not *commit* Himself unto them" (John 2:24). The word is the same; it is the word believe, trust. Saving faith then is more than just believing the truth.

Lovely Living

. . . let him shew out of a good conversation his works
with meekness of wisdom

Saturday

James 3:13

The RSV translates this, "By his good life let him show his works in the meekness of wisdom," and one of our modern scholars translates the phrase, "good life," with the much more suggestive phrase, "by the loveliness of his behavior." This is the reverse of arrogance and ambition, which James rebuked earlier in his letter.

Here we have a humility that is attractive, something that is much more in keeping with the character of our Lord who, when He invited the people to learn of Him said, "Learn of Me; for I am meek and lowly in heart." Humility has been defined as the silence of the soul before God. But there is also a silence that humility displays before others, indeed before life. There is an attraction about the person who is not bent on superimposing his opinions and wishes upon others, but whose mind is open and ready to listen. We feel we can talk to a person like that. He will not only be ready to listen but ready to consider that we may be right.

A truly wise man is not so much concerned with, or conscious of what he knows, but is more concerned with what there is still to learn. Similarly in the true teacher, the person of true spiritual influence, there is a humility that makes him attractive and a loveliness about his behavior.